THE
SAS
IN WORLD WAR II

OSPREY
PUBLISHING

THE
SAS
IN WORLD WAR II

Gavin Mortimer

First published in Great Britain in 2011
by Osprey Publishing, Midland House,
West Way, Botley, Oxford, OX2 0PH, UK
44-02 23rd Street, Suite 219, Long Island City,
NY 11101, USA
E-mail: info@ospreypublishing.com

OSPREY PUBLISHING IS PART OF THE OSPREY
GROUP

Gavin Mortimer has asserted his right under
the Copyright, Designs and Patents Act, 1988,
to be identified as the author of this work.
A CIP catalogue record for this book is
available from the British Library

ISBN: 978 1 84908 646 2

Page layout by: Ken Vail Graphic Design
Index by Auriol Griffith-Jones
Typeset in Bembo and Garamond Pro
Originated by PDQ Media, UK
Printed in China through Worldprint Ltd

11 12 13 14 15   10 9 8 7 6 5 4 3 2 1

Osprey Publishing is supporting the Woodland
Trust, the UK's leading woodland conservation
charity, by funding the dedication of trees.

www.ospreypublishing.com

Imperial War Museum Collections

Many of the photos in this book come from
the Imperial War Museum's huge collections
which cover all aspects of conflict involving
Britain and the Commonwealth since the start
of the 20th century. These rich resources are
available online to search, browse and buy at
www.iwmcollections.org.uk. In addition to
Collections Online, you can visit the Visitor
Rooms where you can explore over 8 million
photographs, thousands of hours of moving
images, the largest sound archive of its kind in
the world, thousands of diaries and letters
written by people in wartime, and a huge
reference library.
www.iwm.org.uk

FRONT COVER: The SAS in North Africa.
(IWM E 21337)
PAGE 2: Members of L Detachment board a
Bristol Bombay transport aircraft prior to a
practice jump. (IWM E 6406)
IMPRINT AND CONTENTS PAGE: The backbone
of L Detachment were the NCOs such as
Seekings (front), Riley (passenger seat), Badger
(driver's seat), Tait (arm in sling) and Cooper
(right). (Courtesy of the SAS Regimental
Archive)

CONTENTS

Dedication   6

Acknowledgements   7

Introduction   9

CHAPTER 1   Stirling's leap of faith   13

CHAPTER 2   L Detachment takes wings   33

CHAPTER 3   Stirling's capture   61

CHAPTER 4   The SRS in Sicily and Italy   81

CHAPTER 5   Bill Stirling and the boys of 2SAS   111

CHAPTER 6   Roy Farran: from Taranto to Termoli   121

CHAPTER 7   Back to Blighty   129

CHAPTER 8   D-Day for 1SAS   143

CHAPTER 9   2SAS earn their wings   175

CHAPTER 10   2SAS return to Italy   191

CHAPTER 11   Operation *Archway*: The drive into Germany   203

CHAPTER 12   Operation *Howard*: Paddy Mayne's last hurrah   221

CHAPTER 13   Delighted then demobbed   237

Glossary   244

Endnotes   245

Index   251

DEDICATION

Most of the interviews with SAS veterans were conducted nearly ten years ago and unfortunately many have since passed on. But at the time of writing Abert Youngman and Bob Lowson are still going strong so I dedicate this book to them, two courageous, compassionate but above all modest men.

ACKNOWLEDGEMENTS

Thanks first to the ever helpful staff of the Imperial War Museum reading room and the National Archives in Kew, who assisted me in my research. A particular debt of gratitude to the SAS Regimental Association who not only granted permission to reproduce some of the photographs in their collection but also provided answers to any wartime questions I had.

Thank you to John Kane in Northern Ireland and John Robertson in Scotland, the latter being the creator of www.specialforcesroh.com, an excellant website that is well worth a visit. John allowed me to reproduce some photos from his site.

Several publishers were good enough to grant me permission to quote from their works and so I thank Sutton (*Paddy Mayne* by Hamish Ross); Greenhill (*SAS and the Maquis* by Ian Wellsted); Cassell (*Winged Dagger* by Roy Farran); Pen and Sword (*The Drums of Memory* by Stephen Hastings) and Strong Oak (*Parachute Padre* by Fraser McLuskey).

Kate Moore and Emily Holmes at Osprey provided excellant support in the writing and editing of the book, and were tolerant of any missed deadline.

Thank you to Peta-Jane, daughter of Des Peter Middleton, Yvonne Greig, daughter of Jeff Du Vivier and Nicky Mellonie, daughter of Bob Sharpe. They went to great lengths to provide me with an array of wonderful photos, documents and other memorabilia and I am so very grateful. Thank you also to Mrs Joan Sharpe, widow of Bob, who unearthed some photos of her daring husband, and to Joe and Chris Bonington for providing valuable information on Charles.

INTRODUCTION

I n June 1941 a young Guards officer lay recovering from a parachute accident in Cairo's Scottish General Hospital. Normally a spell in bed would have been just the ticket for the 25-year-old lieutenant who had been nicknamed 'the Giant Sloth' by friends on account of his disdain for unnecessary physical exertion; but on this occasion he was desperate to throw off the bedclothes and get to work. Unfortunately for David Stirling he was going nowhere for a while, not until he had recovered from severe spinal shock and heavy concussion, a consequence of hitting the ground at a frightening speed after a section of his parachute ripped on the tailplane as he exited an aircraft at 1,000ft.

It took a week for the feeling to return to Stirling's toes and in that time he received a steady stream of visitors to his bedside among whom were Evelyn Waugh and Jock Lewes. Both were fellow officers in Layforce, a composite commando unit commanded by Colonel Robert Laycock that had sailed to the Middle East in February 1941 with the intention of launching a string of lightning assaults on Italian positions on the North African coast and Mediterranean islands. Only it hadn't quite worked out that way, and instead of inflicting heavy casualties on the enemy, Layforce had lost many good men on ill-conceived and poorly planned missions. It was Waugh, recently returned from a botched Layforce operation to Crete, who informed Stirling that Layforce had been disbanded and its surviving members were to be returned to their original units.

The news was disappointing for Stirling, but hardly surprising, it was confirmation of something he had already discussed with Lewes: namely, that the thinking behind Layforce wasn't flawed, just its deployment. The enemy was indeed vulnerable to attack along the lines of its coastal communications and various aerodromes and supply dumps, but not with a seaborne force of 200 men as Layforce had attempted. A commando raid would work best if executed by small units of men attacking not just one target but a series of objectives having first been inserted by parachute.

9

That was why Stirling – along with Lewes and four other men – had been jumping out of a plane in the first place, to master a military art that was still in its infancy. His injury was but a minor hiccup and had done nothing to deflect Stirling from his belief he was on to something. Now the news of Layforce's demise made him more determined than ever to develop his idea. Lying in his hospital bed in the sweltering heat of the North African summer, Stirling drafted a memo entitled *Case for the retention of a limited number of special service troops, for employment as parachutists.* In a summarisation of the memo shortly after the war Stirling wrote:

> I argued the advantages of establishing a unit based on the principle of the fullest exploitation of surprise and of making the minimum demands on manpower and equipment. I argued that the application of this principle would mean in effect the employment of a sub-unit of five men to cover a target previously requiring four troops of a Commando, i.e. about 200 men. I sought to prove that, if an aerodrome or transport park was the objective of an operation, then the destruction of 50 aircraft or units of transport was more easily accomplished by a sub-unit of five men than by a force of 200 men. I further concluded that 200 properly selected, trained and equipped men, organised into sub-units of five, should be able to attack at least thirty different objectives at the same time on the same night.[1]

Drafting the memo was the easy part, delivering it into the hands of General Claude Auchinleck, Commander-in-Chief, Middle East Forces, was a different matter altogether. The 'Auk', as Auchinleck was known, liked to tell his troops 'Always be bold', so that's exactly what Stirling did the moment he was well enough to leave hospital.

According to Stirling, when he hobbled up to the entrance of General Headquarters (GHQ) his way was barred by the sentries when he failed to produce a pass. So he walked round the perimeter fence until he saw a loose flap of wiring under which he slipped. Once inside headquarters Stirling headed straight for General Neil Ritchie's office, the Deputy Chief of Staff with whom his father used to shoot grouse.

Stirling saluted, handed Ritchie the memo and briefly explained its contents. Ritchie looked mildly interested and promised to discuss it with Auchinleck. Three days later Stirling received a summons from Ritchie and arrived to find himself standing before Auchinleck and Major General Arthur Smith, Chief of the General Staff. Stirling impressed his audience during the discussion of the idea. Not only was it well conceived but he had already envisioned how it could be implemented. 'In order to help sell the proposition,' Stirling said later, 'I put forward a detailed plan for the employment of the unit in the approaching offensive (November 1941), the preparation for which was no secret.'[2]

In addition, Stirling's idea had been conceived at an opportune moment, coming just weeks after Laycock had written to General Smith advising him that there were several hundred highly trained commandos sitting on their backsides under the North African sun. 'Unless we are actively employed soon I anticipate a serious falling off in morale which was at one time second to none,' warned Laycock. 'The effect on the troops may be summed up by an inscription found written up on a partition in the mess deck of one of the Glen ships (the culprit was never apprehended) which read: "Never in the history of human endeavour have so few been b———d about by so many." Frivolous as this may seem I cannot but sympathise with the sentiment expressed.'[3]

Smith had no doubt passed Laycock's concerns on to Auchinleck, who was already sold on Stirling's scheme and, promoting Stirling to captain, authorised him to recruit six officers and 60 other ranks. The unit would be called 'L' Detachment of the Special Air Service Brigade

Who Dares Wees: the SAS help Brussel's Manneken Pis celebrate the end of the war. (Courtesy of the SAS Regimental Archive)

so that if one of the myriad enemy spies lurking in Cairo got wind of the nascent force he would report back that the British had an airborne brigade at its disposal.

Stirling was delighted that his idea had been given the go-ahead but nonetheless he had one further demand to make of Auchinleck. Stirling had a visceral dislike of staff officers, a species he termed 'fossilised shit' on account of their outdated ideas as to how a war should be run. Stirling therefore 'insisted with the C-in-C that the unit must be responsible for its own training and operational planning and that, therefore, the commander of the unit must come directly under the C-in-C. I emphasized how fatal it would be for the proposed unit to be put under any existing Branch or formation for administration.'[4]

Auchinleck agreed and Stirling went off to raise his new unit. The SAS had been born.

CHAPTER 1

STIRLING'S LEAP OF FAITH

The 'fossilised shits' were soon making life hard for Stirling as he sought to recruit soldiers for his new unit. 'It was essential for me to get the right officers and I had a great struggle to get them,' he recalled, labelling the middle and lower levels of Middle East Headquarters (MEHQ) as 'unfailingly obstructive and uncooperative … astonishingly tiresome.'[1] The officers he wanted were all members of the recently disbanded Layforce – bored and frustrated and desperate for some action – but MEHQ didn't want to see them join what they considered a renegade unit, despite the fact it had Auchinleck's seal of approval. One by one, however, Stirling got his men: lieutenants Peter Thomas and Eoin McGonigal, Bill Fraser, a Scot, Jock Lewes, a Welshman, and Charles Bonington. In his late 20s, Bonington was the oldest of the officers, an Englishman with a taste for adventure who had abandoned his wife and nine-month old son six years earlier and gone to Australia where he worked as a newspaper correspondent. (The son, Charles, would grow up to become one of Britain's most famous mountaineers.) Bonington was actually half-German, his father being a German merchant seaman who had taken British citizenship as a young man, changed his name from Bonig to Bonington, and then married a Scot. The one officer whose superiors were only too pleased to see join Stirling's mob was Blair Mayne. Though the 6ft 4in Irishman had distinguished himself with Layforce during the battle for Litani River, a

RIGHT AND OPPOSITE
The recruits at Kabrit practised their landing technique from steel gantries designed by Jim Almonds. However, it was Jock Lewes's idea to have the men leap from the back of a speeding truck, which resulted in a slew of injuries, including a broken wrist for Jeff Du Vivier and a damaged shoulder for Bill Fraser. (Right IWM E 6390, Opposite Courtesy of the SAS Regimental Archive)

seaborne assault on Vichy French positions in Syria, Mayne had a reputation for hot-headedness away from the battlefield. While in Cyprus in the summer of 1941 he had threatened the owner of a nightclub with his revolver over a dispute about the bar bill, and a month later he had squared up to his commanding officer, Geoffrey Keyes, son of Sir Roger Keyes, Director of Combined Operations, and the sort of upper-class Englishman Mayne despised.

Legend has it that Mayne was in the glasshouse when Stirling – on the recommendation of Colonel Laycock – interviewed him for L Detachment, but in fact the Irishman was idling away his days at the Middle East Commando base while he waited to see if his request for a transfer to the Far East had been accepted. Mayne hoped he would soon be teaching guerrilla warfare to the Chinese Nationalist Army in their fight against Japan, but within minutes of Stirling's appearance he had pledged his allegiance to an incipient band of desert guerrilla fighters.

With his officers recruited Stirling now set about selecting the 60 men he wanted. Though he picked a handful from his old regiment, the Scots Guard, Stirling plucked most from the disenchanted ranks of Layforce. 'We were just hanging around in the desert getting fed up,' recalled Jeff Du Vivier, a Londoner who had worked in the hotel trade before joining the commandos in 1940. 'Then along came Stirling asking for volunteers. I was hooked on the idea from the beginning, it meant we were going to see some action.'[2]

Another volunteer was Reg Seekings, a hard, obdurate 21-year-old from the Fens who had been a boxer before the war. 'When I enlisted they wanted me to go in the school of physical training and I said "not bloody likely", I didn't join the army just to box, I want to fight with a gun, not my fists.' Seekings had got his wish with Layforce, though the raid on the Libyan port of Bardia had been shambolic. Nonetheless it had given Seekings a taste for adventure. 'Stirling wanted airborne

The menacing Paddy Mayne was a born guerrilla fighter who surpassed David Stirling when it came to sabotage. (Author's Collection)

troops and I'd always wanted to be a paratrooper,' he reflected on the reasons why he volunteered. 'At the interview a chap went in in front of me and Stirling said to him "why do you want to join?" and he said "Oh, I'll try anything once, sir." Stirling went mad "Try anything once! It bloody matters if we don't like you. Bugger off, get out of here." So I thought I'm not making that bloody mistake. When it was my turn he asked why I wanted to be in airborne and I said I'd seen film of these German paratroopers and always wondered why we didn't have this in the British Army. Then I told him that I'd put my name for a paratrooper originally but been told I was too heavy. He asked if I played any sport and I told him I was an amateur champion boxer and did a lot of cycling and running. That was it, I was in.'[3]

The youngest recruit was Scots Guardsman Johnny Cooper, who had turned 19 the month before L Detachment came into existence. He stood in awe of Stirling when it was his turn to be interviewed. 'Because of his height and his quiet self-confidence he could appear quite intimidating but he wasn't the bawling sort [of] leader,' said Cooper. 'He talked to you, not at you, and usually in a very polite fashion. His charisma was overpowering.'[4]

Having selected his men, Stirling revealed to them their new home. Kabrit lay 90 miles east of Cairo on the edge of the Great Bitter Lake. It was an ideal place in which to locate a training camp for a new unit because there was little else to do other than train. There were no bars and brothels, just sand and flies, and a wind that blew in from the lake and invaded every nook and cranny of their new camp. 'It was a desolate bloody place,' recalled Reg Seekings. 'Gerry Ward had a pile of hessian tents and told us to put them up.'

Ward was the Company Quarter Master Sergeant, one of 26 administration staff attached to L Detachment, and it was he who suggested to Seekings and his comrades that if they wanted anything more luxurious in the way of living quarters they might want to visit the neighbouring encampment. 'This camp was put up for New Zealanders,' explained Seekings, 'but instead of coming to the desert they were shoved in at Crete [against the invading Germans] and got wiped out. So all we had to do was drive in and take what we wanted.'

Something else they purloined, according to Seekings, was a large pile of bricks from an Royal Air Force (RAF) base with which they built a canteen, furnished

PARACHUTE TRAINING IN THE DESERT

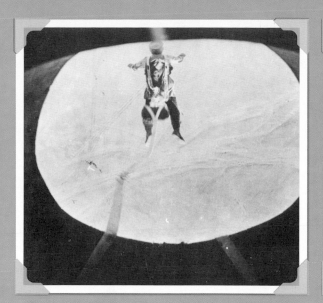 

No one in L Detachment relished their parachute training at Kabrit, particularly after the deaths of troopers Joe Duffy and Ken Warburton due to faulty static lines in October 1941. (Courtesy of the SAS Regimental Archive)

with chairs, tables and a selection of beer and snacks by Kauffman, an artful London who was a better scrounger than he was a soldier. Kauffman was soon RTU'd (returned to his unit) but his canteen lasted longer and was the envy of the officers who had to make do with a tent. Not that there was much time for the men of L Detachment to spend in their canteen in the late summer of 1941, despite the 'Stirling's Rest Camp' sign some wag had planted at the camp's entrance. They had arrived at Kabrit in the first week of August and had just three months to prepare for their first operation, one which would involve parachuting, a skill most of the men had yet to master.

'In our training programme the principle on which we worked was entirely different from that of the Commandos,' remembered Stirling. 'A Commando unit, having once selected from a batch of volunteers, were committed to those men and had to nurse them up to the required standard. L Detachment, on the other hand, had set a minimum standard to which all ranks had to attain and we had to be most firm in returning to their units those were unable to reach that standard.'[5]

Stirling divided the unit into One and Two Troops, with Lewes in charge of the former and Mayne the latter. 'The comradeship was marvellous because you all had to depend on one another,' said Storie, who was in Lewes's Troop.[6]

Lewes oversaw most of the unit's early training, teaching them first and foremost that the desert should be respected and not feared. They learned how to navigate using the barest of maps, how to move noiselessly at night, how to survive on minimal amounts of water, and how to use the desert as camouflage. The men came to respect the earnest and ascetic Lewes above all other officers. 'Jock liked things right, he was a perfectionist,' recalled Storie. 'He thought more about things in-depth while Stirling was more carefree... Stirling was the backbone but Lewes was the brains, he got the ideas such as the Lewes Bomb.'

The eponymous Lewes bomb had finally been created after many hours of frustrating and solitary endeavour by the Welshman. What Lewes sought was a bomb light enough to carry on operations but powerful enough to destroy an enemy aircraft on an airfield. Eventually he came up with a 1lb device that Du Vivier described in the diary he kept during the training at Kabrit.

It was plastic explosive and thermite – which is used in incendiary bombs – and we rolled the whole lot together with motor car oil. It was a stodgy lump and then you had a No.27 detonator, an instantaneous fuse and a time pencil. The time pencil looked a bit like a 'biro' pen. It was a glass tube with a spring-loaded striker held in place by a strip of copper wire. At the top was a glass phial containing acid which you squeezed gently to break. The acid would then eat through the wire

Members of
L Detachment board
a Bristol Bombay
transport aircraft prior
to a practice jump as
part of their parachute
training at Kabrit.
Those who successful
completed their jumps
were permitted to
wear the SAS wings
on the shoulder.
(IWM E 6406)

and release the striker. Obviously the thicker the wire the longer the delay before the striker was triggered [the pencils were colour coded according to the length of fuse]. It was all put into a small cotton bag and it proved to be crude, but very effective. The thermite caused a flash that ignited the petrol, not just blowing the wing off but sending the whole plane up.

Lewes also earned the respect of the men because he never asked them to do something that he was not prepared to do himself. 'Jock Lewes called us a lot of yellow-bellies and threw out challenges,' said Seekings. 'We met the challenges and Jock, whatever he wanted done, showed us first, and once he'd shown us we had to do it. He set the standard for the unit, there's no two ways about that … he used to say that it's the confident man with a little bit of lady luck sitting on his shoulders that always comes through.'

During the initial training Lewes tested the men's self-confidence to its limits. They trained for nine or ten hours a day and often, just as the men thought they could crawl into their beds, Lewes would order them out on one of his 'night schemes' – forced marches across the desert with the soldiers required to navigate their way successfully from point to point. Any soldier Lewes considered not up to scratch, either physically or emotionally, was RTU'd, leading some recruits to perform extraordinary acts of endurance. On one 60-mile march the boots of Private Doug Keith disintegrated after 20 miles so he completed the remaining distance in stockinged feet with a 75lb pack on his back.

What the men hated above all else, however, was parachute training. Without an aircraft Lewes initially improvised by drawing on the practicality of one of the recruits, Jim Almonds, to construct a wooden jumping platform and trolley system from which the men leapt to simulate hitting the ground at speed. Lewes decided this was too tame and resorted to another method, as recalled by Mick D'Arcy who said 'there were a great number of injuries during ground training jumping off trucks at 30–35 mph'.[7] Du Vivier broke his wrist leaping from the tailgate of a truck, and

Johnny Cooper (second left) and Reg Seekings (far right) were two of the original members of the SAS who served from 1941–45. Here they feed bullets into the drums of twin Vickers. (Author's Collection)

he wasn't the only recruit to end up in hospital as a consequence of Lewes's ingenuity; nevertheless hurling oneself from a moving vehicle was preferable to jumping out of an aircraft at 800ft.

The day DuVivier completed his first parachute jump proper was 16 October, a Thursday, and like the other nine men in the Bristol Bombay aircraft he ran the gamut of emotions. 'My knees began to beat a tattoo on one another as I stretched up to adjust my static line,' he wrote in his diary. 'We moved towards the door and I glanced down. Mother Earth looked miles away and I wished I'd never been born … what happened next I can only faintly remember. The earth seemed to be above me and the sky below, then suddenly a big white cloud burst over me and I began to recognise it as being my 'chute. Everything steadied itself and I found myself sitting comfortably in my harness. My brain cleared and I felt an overwhelming feeling of exhilaration.'

Stanley Bolland (far right, in trunks) bathing with some commando pals in Egypt's Great Bitter Lake in 1940. Bolland was one of the original members of L Detachment and was killed during the first fateful raid in November 1941. (Courtesy of John Robertson)

But two of the men weren't so fortunate. Ken Warburton and Joe Duffy were in the next stick of ten aspiring parachutists. First out was Warburton, then Duffy, who seemed to hesitate for a moment before he leapt, as if he sensed something wasn't quite right. He jumped nonetheless and it was only then that the dispatcher, Ted Pacey, saw that the snap-links on the men's static line had buckled. He pulled back Bill Morris, the third in line, but it was too late for Warburton and Duffy. 'When we got to Duffy his parachute was half out, he had tried to pull it out but couldn't twist round and get it out,' recalled Jimmy Storie, who had seen the tragedy from the ground. 'After that we all used to give the static line a good tug first before jumping.'

The problem with the static line was quickly solved and the next day Stirling jumped first to inspire his men. Outwardly he remained his usual insouciant self but inside he was livid with the British Army parachute training school at Ringway, Manchester, who had ignored his numerous appeals for assistance. 'I sent a final appeal to Ringway,' he reflected after the death of Duffy and Warburton, 'and they sent some training notes and general information, which arrived at the end of October … included in this information we discovered that Ringway had had a fatal accident caused by exactly the same defect as in our case.'[8]

Perhaps in acknowledgement of their role in the deaths of Duffy and Warburton, Ringway sent one of their best instructors to North Africa. Captain Peter Warr arrived at Kabrit on 15 November, the day Stirling celebrated his 26th birthday and the eve of L Detachment's first operation.

As Stirling had informed Auchinleck in July it was common knowledge that an Eighth Army offensive would be launched against Axis forces in November. It was codenamed 'Crusader' and its aims were to retake the eastern coastal regions of Libya (a region known as Cyrenaica) and seize the Libyan airfields from the enemy, thereby enabling the RAF to increase their supplies to Malta, the Mediterranean island that was of such strategic importance to the British. But General Erwin Rommel also prized Malta and was busy finalising his own plans for an offensive; he intended his Afrika Korps to drive the British eastwards, take possession of the airfields and prevent the RAF reaching Malta with their precious cargoes. In addition, the fewer British planes there were to attack German shipping in the Mediterranean, the more vessels would reach North African ports with the supplies he needed to win the Desert War.

Stirling's plan was to drop his men between these two vast opposing armies and attack the Axis airfields at Gazala and Timimi in eastern Libya at midnight on 17 November. On the day of his birthday Stirling wrote to his mother, telling her that: 'It is the best possible type of operation and will be far more exciting than dangerous.'[9]

That same day, wrote Du Vivier in his diary, Stirling revealed the nature of their operation for the first time. 'The plans and maps were unsealed, explained and studied until each man knew his job by heart. There was a lot of work to be done such as preparing explosives, weapons and rations.'

Stirling hadn't a full complement of men for the operation. Several soldiers, including Lieutenant Bill Fraser and Private Jock Byrne, were recovering from injuries sustained during parachute training. In total Stirling had at his disposal 54 men, whom he divided into four sections under his overall command. Lewes was to lead numbers one and two sections and Blair Mayne would be in charge sections three and four.

Mayne, by this stage, was known to one and all as 'Paddy'. If Lewes was the brains of L Detachment during its formative days, then Mayne was the brawn, a fearsomely strong man, both mentally and physically, who like Lewes set himself exacting standards. The difference between the pair was that Mayne had a wild side that he set free with alcohol when the occasion arose. Jimmy Storie had known Mayne since the summer of 1940 when they both enlisted in No.11 Scottish Commando. 'Paddy was a rough Irishman who was at his happiest fighting,' Storie recalls. 'He didn't like sitting around doing nothing. In Arran [where the commandos trained in the winter of 1940] he was known to sit on his bed and shoot the glass panes out of the window with his revolver.'

Just about the only members of L Detachment unafraid of Mayne were Reg Seekings and Pat Riley. Riley had been born in Wisconsin in 1915 before moving to Cumbria with his family where he went to work in a granite quarry aged 14. Three years later he joined the Coldstream Guards and he was reputed to be the physical match of the 6ft 4in Mayne. Seekings was smaller, but he could work his fists better than the Irishman. 'Mayne's appearance was a bit over-awing and he had a very powerful presence,' recalled Seekings. 'But I never had any trouble with him when drinking, nor Pat Riley, because we weren't worried about his size and we both had the confidence we could deal with him. And Paddy respected us for that so there was no problem... Paddy said once "Of course, Reg, I'd be too big for you" and I said "the bigger they are the harder they fall." He laughed and said "sure, we'll have to try it sometime". It became a standing joke but we had too much respect

(L–R) Charlie Cattell, Jock Byrne, Arthur Phillips, Jimmy Storie and Arthur Warburton, photographed in Cairo in 1941 sporting the short-lived white beret. With the exception of Cattell all of these men would be captured during the war in North Africa. (Author's Collection)

OPPOSITE
Jeff Du Vivier sits
atop a captured Axis
tank that the SAS
used for target
practice during their
training in Kabrit.
(Author's Collection)

for each other … the problem with Paddy was that people were frightened of him and that used to annoy him to such an extent that sparks would fly, particularly if he'd had a drink.'

One of Mayne's fellow officers in Layforce was Lieutenant Gerald Bryan, a recipient of the Military Cross for his gallantry at Litani River. He recalled of the Irishman: 'When sober, a gentler, more mild-mannered man you could not wish to meet, but when drunk, or in battle, he was frightening. I'm not saying he was a drunk, but he could drink a bottle of whisky in an evening before he got a glow on… One night, when he had been on the bottle, he literally picked me up by the lapels of my uniform, clear of the ground, with one hand while punching me with the other hand, sent me flying. Next day he didn't remember a thing about it. "Just tell me who did that to you Gerald," he said. I told him I'd walked into a door. He was a very brave man and I liked him very much.'[10]

Mayne's two sections comprised 21 men in total and his second-in-command was Lieutenant Charles Bonington. Their objective was the airfield at Timimi, a coastal strip west of Tobruk which was flat and rocky and pitted with shallow wadis. It was hot during the day and cool at night and apart from esparto grass and acacia scrub there was scant vegetation. The plan was simple: once the two sections had rendezvoused in the desert following the night-time parachute drop on 16 November, they would march to within five miles of the target before lying up during the daylight hours of 17 November. The attack would commence at one minute to midnight on the 17th with Bonington leading three section on to the airfield from the east. Mayne and four section would come in from the south and west, and for 15 minutes they were to plant their bombs on the aircraft without alerting the enemy to their presence. At quarter past midnight the raiders could use their weapons and instantaneous fuses at their discretion.

At dawn on 16 November Stirling and his 54 men left Kabrit for their forward landing ground of Bagoush, approximately 300 miles to the west. Once there they found the RAF had been thoughtful in their welcome. 'The officers' mess was put at our disposal and we kicked off with a first-rate meal after which there were books, games, wireless and a bottle of beer each, all to keep our minds off the coming event,' wrote Du Vivier in his diary.

He was in Jock Lewes's 11-man section, along with Jimmy Storie, Johnny Cooper and Pat Riley, and it wasn't long before they sensed something wasn't quite right. Stirling and the other officers were unusually tense and all was revealed a little while before the operation was due to commence when they were addressed by their commanding officer. Stirling informed his men that weather reports indicated a fierce storm was brewing over the target area, one that would include winds of 30 knots.

'Then along came Stirling asking for volunteers. I was hooked on the idea from the beginning, it meant we were going to see some action.'

Jeff Du Vivier

The Brigadier General Staff coordinator, Sandy Galloway, was of the opinion that the mission should be aborted. Dropping by parachute in those wind speeds, and on a moonless night, would be hazardous in the extreme. Stirling was loathe to scrub the mission; after all, when might they get another chance to prove their worth? He asked his men what they thought and unanimously they agreed to press ahead.

At 1830 hours a fleet of trucks arrived at the officers' mess to transport the men to the five Bristol Bombay aircraft that would fly them to the target area. Du Vivier 'muttered a silent prayer and put myself in God's hands' as he climbed aboard.

Du Vivier's was the third aircraft to take off, behind Stirling's and Lieutenant Eoin McGonigal's. Bonington and his nine men were on the fourth plane and Mayne's section was on the fifth. Each aircraft carried five (or in some cases, six) canisters inside which were two packs containing weapons, spare ammunition, fuses, explosives, blankets and rations.

The men would jump wearing standard issue desert shirts and shorts with skeleton web equipment on their backs containing an entrenching tool. A small haversack was carried by each man inside which was grenades, food (consisting of dates, raisins, cheese, biscuits, sweets and chocolate), a revolver, maps and a compass. Mechanics' overalls were worn over all of this to ensure none of the equipment was caught in the parachute rigging lines during the drop.

Mayne's aircraft took-off 40 minutes behind schedule, at 2020 hours instead of 1940 hours, though unlike the other planes they reached the drop zone (DZ) without attracting the unwanted attention of enemy anti-aircraft (AA) batteries. At 2230 hours they jumped with Mayne describing subsequent events in his operational report:

> As the section was descending there were flashes on the ground and reports which I then thought was small-arms fire. But on reaching the ground no enemy was found so I concluded that the report had been caused by detonators exploding in packs whose parachutes had failed to open.
>
> The landing was unpleasant. I estimated the wind speed at 20–25 miles per hour, and the ground was studded with thorny bushes.
>
> Two men were injured here. Pct [parachutist] Arnold sprained both ankles and Pct Kendall bruised or damaged his leg.
>
> An extensive search was made for the containers, lasting until 0130 hours 17/11/41, but only four packs and two TSMGs [Thompson sub-machine guns] were located.
>
> I left the two injured men there, instructed them to remain there that night, and in the morning find and bury any containers in the area, and then to make to the RV [rendezvous point] which I estimated at 15 miles away.

It was too late to carry out my original plan of lying west of Timimi as I had only five hours of darkness left, so I decided to lie up on the southern side. I then had eight men, 16 bombs, 14 water bottles and food as originally laid for four men, and four blankets.[11]

Mayne and his men marched for three-and-a-half miles before laying up in a wadi. He estimated they'd covered six miles and were approximately five miles from the target. When daylight broke on the 17th, a dawn reconnaissance revealed they were six miles from the airfield, on which were 17 aircraft.

Back in the wadi, Mayne informed his men of the plan: they would move forward to attack the target at 2050 hours with each man carrying two bombs. He and Sergeant Edward McDonald would carry the Thompson sub-machine guns. Until then they would lie up in the wadi. But as Mayne noted later in his report the weather intervened:

At 1730 hours it commenced to rain heavily. After about half an hour the wadi became a river, and as the men were lying concealed in the middle of bushes it took them some time getting to higher ground. It kept on raining and we were unable to find shelter. An hour later I tried two of the time pencils and they did not work. Even if we had been able to keep them dry, it would not, in my opinion, have been practicable to have used them, as during the half-hour delay on the plane the rain would have rendered them useless. I tried the instantaneous fuses and they did not work either.

Mayne postponed the attack and he and his men endured a miserable night in the wadi. The rain eased the next morning, 18 November, but the sky was grey and the temperature cool; realising that the fuses wouldn't dry, Mayne aborted the mission and headed south. Though bitterly disappointed that he hadn't been able to attack the enemy, the Irishman was nonetheless pleased with the way his men had conducted themselves in arduous circumstances: 'The whole section,' he wrote, 'behaved extremely well and although lacerated and bruised in varying degrees by their landing, and wet and numb with cold, remained cheerful.'

Mayne led his men to the RV, a point near the Rotondo Segnali on a desert track called the Trig-al-Abd 34 miles inland from both Gazala and Timimi airfields, at dawn on 20 November. Waiting for them were members of the Long Range Desert Group (LRDG), who a few hours earlier had taken custody of Jock Lewes's stick. They welcomed members of Mayne's section with bully beef and mugs of tea and the men swapped horror stories. 'It was extraordinary really that our entire stick landed without

Left: Du Vivier at Kabrit. This was the uniform the men wore underneath their flying overalls during their first raid, and which proved wholly inadequate in the face of the fierce storm they encountered. (Author's Collection)

Above: Fred Senior (left) and Stanley Bolland on a tour of the pyramids in 1941. The pair were Scots Guardsmen who joined the commandos and then the SAS. Neither survived the war. (Courtesy of John Robertson)

injury because the wind when you jumped was ferocious and of course you couldn't see the ground coming up,' recalled Johnny Cooper. 'I hit the desert with quite a bump and was then dragged along by the wind at quite a speed. When I came to rest I staggered rather groggily to my feet, feeling sure I would find a few broken bones but to my astonishment I seemed to [have] nothing worse than the wind momentarily knocked out of me. There was a sudden rush of relief but then of course, I looked around me and realised I was all alone and, well, God knows where.'

Lewes and his men had jumped in a well-organised stick, the Welshman dropping first with each successive man instructed to bury his parachute upon landing and wait where he was. Lewes intended to move back along the compass bearing of the aircraft, collecting No.2 jumper, then No.3 and so on, what he called 'rolling up the stick'. But the wind had dragged Jeff DuVivier for 150 yards until finally he snagged on a thorn bush, allowing him a chance to take stock of the situation. 'When I finally freed myself, I was bruised and bleeding and there was a sharp pain in my right leg,' he wrote in his diary. 'When I saw the rocky ground I'd travelled over, I thanked my lucky stars that I was alive.'

Eventually Du Vivier found the rest of the stick and joined his comrades in searching for the containers. 'We couldn't find most of the containers with our equipment so Jock Lewes gathered us round and said that we'd still try and carry out the attack if we can find the target,' said Cooper.

They marched through the night and laid up at 0930 hours the next morning. Sergeant Pat Riley was sent forward to reconnoitre the area and returned to tell Lewes that there was no sign of the Gazala airfield and in his opinion they had been dropped much further south than planned. Nonetheless Lewes decided to continue and at 1400 hours they departed the wadi and headed north for eight miles. But in the late afternoon the weather turned against them once more and the heavens opened, soaking the men and their explosives. 'The lightning was terrific,' recalled Du Vivier. 'And how it rained! The compass was going round in circles. We were getting nowhere. And we were wallowing up to our knees in water. I remember seeing tortoises swimming about.'

Lewes, with the same grim reluctance as Mayne, informed the men that the operation was aborted and they would head south towards the RV. The hours that followed tested the resolve of all the men, even Lewes who, cold, hungry and exhausted like the rest of his section, temporarily handed command to Riley, the one man who seemed oblivious to the tempest. Du Vivier acknowledged Riley's strength in his diary: 'I must mention here Pat Riley, an ex-Guardsman and policeman... I shall always be indebted to him for what he did. I'm sure he was for the most part responsible for our return.'

Riley had the men march for 40 minutes, rest for 20 minutes if there was any dry ground to be found, march for 40 minutes and so on. On through the night they stumbled, often wading through water that was up to their knees. Inadequately dressed against the driving rain and freezing wind, Du Vivier had never experienced such cold. 'I was shivering, not shaking. All the bones in my body were numbed. I couldn't speak, every time I opened my mouth my teeth just cracked against one another.'

The rain eased and the wind dropped the next morning (18 November) but it was another 36 hours before Lewes and his section made contact with the LRDG. The return of Mayne's stick took the number of survivors to 19. A few hours later the figure increased by two when David Stirling and Sergeant Bob Tait were brought in by a LRDG patrol. In Tait's operational report he described how their aircraft was delayed in its approach to Gazala by strong winds and heavy AA fire. When they did eventually jump they 'all made very bad landings which resulted in various minor injuries. They had considerable difficulty in assembling, and sergt Cheyne was not seen again.'★

★ In some wartime histories of the SAS L Detachment veterans recall Sergeant John Cheyne as having broken his back jumping with Lewes's section, but one must assume Tait's report to be the more reliable as it was contemporary.

Everyone from David Stirling to the Italian engineers were impressed by the bomb invented by Jock Lewes. Here Du Vivier rolls a block of plastic explosive prior to assembling a Lewes bomb. (Author's Collection)

Unable to find most of their containers, and with many of his men barely able to walk, Stirling decided that he and Tait (the only man of the stick to land unscathed) would attack the airfield while the rest, under the command of Sergeant-Major George Yates, would head to the RV. But Stirling met with the same fate at Mayne and Lewes, abandoning the mission in the face of what the noted war correspondent Alexander Clifford called 'the most spectacular thunderstorm within local memory'.[12]

For a further eight hours Stirling and his men waited at the RV in the hope of welcoming more stragglers, but none showed and finally they agreed to depart with the LRDG. The next day, 21 November, the LRDG searched an eight-mile front in the hope of picking up more of L detachment, but none were seen.

Stirling later discovered that the aircraft carrying Charles Bonington's section had been shot down by a German Messerschmitt. The pilot, Charles West, was badly wounded, his co-pilot killed and the ten SAS men suffered varying degrees of injury. Doug Keith, the man who had marched for 40 miles in his stockinged feet during training, succumbed to his injuries and his comrades were caught by German troops. Yates and the rest of Stirling's section were also taken prisoner but of McGonigal's section there was no word; their fate remained a mystery until October 1944 when two of the stick, Jim Blakeney and Roy Davies, arrived in Britain having escaped from their prisoner-of-war (POW) camp. Blakeney's account of the night of 16 November 1941 was explained in an SAS report: 'After landing he lay up until dawn and found himself alone with other members of his party, including Lt McGonigal, who was badly injured and died later [as did Sidney Hildreth]… This party, which endeavoured to make for the LRDG RV got lost and made their way to the coast, and were picked up by an Italian guard at Timimi airport.'[13]

Mayne was deeply affected by McGonigal's failure to reach the RV and while at a later stage of the Desert War, when Gazala was in Allied hands, he would go there to search for the grave of his friend, but for the moment he brooded on his disappearance, vowing to have his revenge on the enemy.

Stirling was also brooding on the way to the Eighth Army's forward landing ground at Jaghbub Oasis. Thirty-four of his men were missing, either captured or dead, and yet no one from L Detachment had even fired a shot in anger at the enemy. But despite the abject failure of the operation Stirling wasn't totally despondent; already he had decided that in future the SAS would reach the target area not by parachute but by in trucks driven by the LRDG. In this way, as Stirling later commented, the LRDG would be 'able to drop us more comfortably and more accurately within striking distance of the target area'.[14]

The remnants of L Detachment reached Jaghbub Oasis on the afternoon of 25 November. As well as housing the Eighth Army's forward landing ground there was also, set among the ruins of a well-known Islamic school, a first-aid post. Before despatching the wounded into the care of the medics, Stirling assembled his men to tell them that L Detachment was far from finished despite the obvious disappointment of its inaugural operation. He promised there would be 'a next time' to which Jeff Du Vivier replied in his diary: 'I don't fancy a next time if this is what it's going to be like.'★

★ One upshot of the failed raid was the shelving of a plan to raise a Middle East airborne battalion. Shortly before the operation, Stirling had been asked to submit his thoughts on the idea and he had written an enthusiastic appraisal, stating that 'such an establishment should amply allow for the weeding out of unsuitable and the physically unfit; it could broadly consist of 4 Coys. of 100 men each, a small operative HQ group and a non-operative Administrative Coy. of 100 men.'

CHAPTER 2

L DETACHMENT TAKES WINGS

The day after the L Detachment survivors arrived at Jaghbub Oasis Stirling had an audience with General Alan Cunningham, commander of the Eighth Army. The first week of Operation *Crusader* had not gone well; in fact, it was a disaster and all the months of meticulous planning had come to naught when Rommel seized the initiative with a bold counter-thrust that pushed the British back into Egypt.

The whereabouts of 34 parachutists didn't therefore create undue alarm for Cunningham, whose only interest was if Stirling had seen any German tanks on his travels. Stirling hadn't, and he was dismissed with an instruction to return to Bagoush and await further orders.

Hours later, however, Cunningham was relieved of his command, replaced by Neil Ritchie, the general to whom Stirling had first gone with his idea for a unit of highly trained parachutists. Ritchie wasn't bothered by the failure of L Detachment either, although he did have orders that piqued the interest of Stirling. Auchinleck was disappointed by Operation *Crusader*'s lack of success but by no means downhearted. He saw a chance to derail Rommel's offensive by striking at his over-extended supply lines along the Libyan coast.

Ritchie's orders, therefore, were to send two flying columns under the command of brigadiers Denys Reid and John Marriott to attack the Axis forces hundreds of

OPPOSITE
An SAS patrol somewhere in the North African deserts c.1941. (© Topfoto)

miles behind the frontline. In the meantime, the Eighth Army would launch a secondary offensive against the Afrika Korps.

To the LRDG fell the task of attacking Axis aerodromes at Sirte, Agheila and Agedabia, timed to coincide with the attacks of the two flying columns, but their commanding officer wasn't altogether happy with the idea. On 28 November Lieutenant Colonel Guy Prendagast sent a signal from his base at Siwa Oasis: 'As LRDG not trained for demolitions, suggest pct [parachutists] used for blowing dromes.'[1] Prendagast's suggestion was accepted and Stirling received permission to launch an overland assault on the aerodromes the following month.

Stirling moved his men to Jalo Oasis, recently seized from the Italians and a caricature of a desert haven: an old fort set among palm trees and pools of water, though there were also thousands of flies and a wind that never rested. The 21 survivors from the first operation were augmented by the handful of L Detachment men who had been held back for varying reasons, among them Bill Fraser, whose broken arm had healed.

Roger Boutinot (second left) and a group of French SAS soldiers watch a bear dancing in Damascus in 1941. Of the five Frenchmen in the photo only Boutinot survived the war. (Author's Collection)

On 8 December, two days after their arrival at Jalo, Stirling, Mayne and nine other men from L Detachment set out to raid the aerodromes at Sirte, 350 miles to the north-west. They were travelling in seven Chevrolet trucks driven by the LRDG and painted pink and green for camouflage, but three days out from Jalo and 20 miles from Sirte the convoy was spotted by an Italian Ghibli reconnaissance aircraft. There was an exchange of fire and then the Ghibli dropped its two bombs, neither of which found a target, before departing. Stirling ordered his men under cover and they barely had time to conceal themselves among some camel scrub before two more Italian aircraft appeared on the horizon on what turned out to be a fruitless search.

The two Frenchmen on the left were among those who lived and fought alongside the British SAS in 1942 before forming their own regiments later in the war. (Courtesy of John Robertson)

The raiders had survived one contact with the enemy but Stirling knew the operation had been compromised and that the Italians would tighten security at Sirte. Facing the prospect of another failure Stirling improvised, instructing Mayne to attack Tamet aerodome, 30 miles to the west of Sirte, while he and Sergeant Jimmy Brough proceeded to Sirte in the hope of slipping unnoticed on the airfield.

As it turned out, Stirling and Brough were thwarted when the 30 Italian bombers they had under surveillance took off just before dusk. Stirling couldn't believe it. He and Brough returned to the RV ruing their misfortune and overwhelmed by despondency. Suddenly away to their west, there was a clap of thunder and the sky lit up. The pair paused and then Brough shouted: 'What lovely work!'[2]

Mayne's report on the Tamet operation was characteristically laconic:

Execution
Party left Jalo Oasis to reach Wadi Tamet, being lightly and inefficiently strafed by Italian air force on the way. Left LRDG trucks at 1830 hours, returned at 0300 hours. Party was then conveyed to Jalo.
Results
(a) Bombs were placed on 14 aircraft.
(b) 10 aircraft were destroyed by having instruments destroyed.
(c) Bomb dump and petrol dump were blown up.
(d) Reconnaissance was made down to the seafront but only empty huts were found.
(e) Several telegraph poles were blown up.

JEFF DuVivier's log book

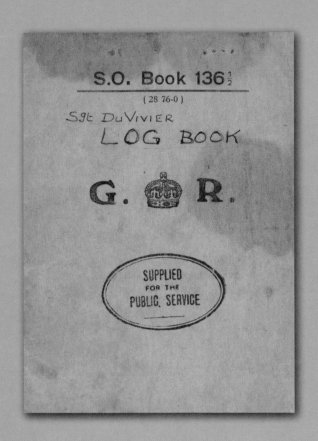

The log book kept by Jeff Du Vivier inside which he meticulously recorded distances travelled by SAS patrols during operations in the desert in autumn 1942. (Author's Collection)

TIME	SPDO	CSE	DIST	REMARKS
1400	900.4	220	10.1	contd from overleaf
	10.6	220	10.2	
	14	220	3.4	VISTOPONE
	24.1	220	10.1	
	29.4	217	5.3	TRACKS
	43.1	220	13.7	
	54.5	220	11.4	+10% 642.59

DAY'S RUN 141.6" TOTAL 690.5"

31.10.42 (SATURDAY)

6.30	954.5	220		
	967.5	220	13.0	
	96.4	244	28.9	MAKING FOR BLACK HILL
	1006.2	244	9.8	BLACK HILL
	14.3	237	8.1	STOP STUCK
13.15	18.4	237	1.1	TIFFIN
14.30	28.4	VARN	13	CORRN
	43.2	261	14.8	By passed Beacon Hill
	47.5	261	4.3	Soft going
	54.7	261	7.2	

DAY'S RUN 100.2" TOTAL 790.7"

E	SPDO	CSE	DIST	REMARKS
1115	2142	250		Start
	62	250 apr	20	
	74	225 =	12	Changeable bearing
	86	200	12	
	97	245	11	FORT - CUFRA
.002204			7	CAMP

DAY'S RUN 62 TOTAL 418-38=380

Returned to Cufra by taking route further North of the Oasis

(f)   Some Italians were followed and the house they came out of was attacked by machine gun and pistol fire, bombs being placed on and around it. The inhabitants there appeared to be roughly thirty. Damage inflicted unknown.

Remarks

The guards were slack and when alarmed wasted many rounds in misdirected fire.[3]

On point (f) of his report, Mayne had been economical with the truth, recognising in hindsight that he had been imprudent. Having crept on to the aerodrome, the nine raiders were unable to find any aircraft in the inky blackness. What they did see, however, was a thin strip of light that on closer inspection was the bottom of a door to a house. From within came the hubbub of convivial conversation. Later, in a more colourful account of the raid on Tamet, Mayne described what happened next:

> I kicked open the door and stood there with my Colt 45, the others at my side with a Tommy Gun and another automatic. The Germans stared at us. We were a peculiar and frightening sight, bearded and unkempt hair. For what seemed an age we just stood there looking at each other in complete silence. I said: 'Good evening.' At that a young German arose and moved slowly backwards. I shot him… I turned and fired at another some six feet away. He was standing beside the wall as he sagged … the room was by now in pandemonium.[4]

The occupants of the house were in fact a mix of German and Italian air crew, none of whom had ever imagined they were vulnerable to such an attack hundreds of miles behind their own lines. After the initial shock, however, some recovered and dived for cover, drawing their sidearms and exchanging fire with their attackers. Mayne left four men to continue the firefight while he and four others took care of the aircraft.

Mayne ordered his men to plant the bombs on the left wing of each aircraft with 30-minute fuses. When they ran out of bombs, they jumped up on to the wings of ten aircraft and destroyed the instrument panels with gunfire.

When all 24 planes had been destroyed or adorned with Lewes bombs, the five men withdrew from the airfield to join their four comrades who had ended the resistance of the pilots with grenades and machine-gun fire and were already on their way to the RV. 'We had not gone fifty yards,' recalled Reg Seekings, 'when the first plane went up. We stopped to look but the second one went up near us and we began to run. After a while we felt safe and stopped to take another glance. What a sight! Planes exploding all over, and the terrific roar of petrol and bombs going up.'[5]

Mayne's party had destroyed 24 planes as well as killing several enemy pilots, all of whom would be harder to replace than the aircraft. It was a wonderful coup, one with enormous propaganda potential. Those back in Britain on the Home Front would be encouraged by the daring raid, and so too the Americans who, a few days earlier had declared war on Japan and Germany. One newspaper carried a report of the attack on Sirte with details supplied by Stirling:

> In the officers' mess on an Axis aerodrome just beyond Sirte, 30 German and Italian pilots sat one night drinking, laughing and talking. The campaign was not going well for them. Rommel was retreating. But they were still a long way from the fighting line. The mess snugly blacked out, a bright fire was burning, some of them were playing cards.
>
> Suddenly the door flew open. A burst from a Tommy gun swept the card players and drinkers at the bar. Drinking songs turned to shouts of fear, and those who were not killed or wounded desperately trying to make for the doors and windows were mown down. They were 500 miles behind the front line, but a British patrol was in their midst.[6]

Mayne and Stirling returned to Jalo without incident. Three days after their arrival at the desert oasis, Jock Lewes arrived from Agheila (60 miles east of Sirte). Though they'd found the aerodrome bereft of aircraft, it wasn't a total waste of a trip. Lewes knew from intelligence reports that an Italian transport depot was nearby so that's where they headed. 'It was used by Italians as a parking area for trucks,' recalled Jimmy Storie, who waited in their Italian Lancia truck while Lewes and Jim Almonds planted more than 30 bombs on vehicles.[7]

On 23 December, a week after Stirling and Mayne had reached Jalo Oasis, Lieutenant Bill Fraser and his party returned from their mission to bomb the aerodrome at Agedabia (also spelt Jebabya), 150 miles north-west of the oasis. They had left four days earlier in the company of a LRDG patrol, reaching a point 16 miles from the target at 0100 hours on 21 December. Fraser had with him Jeff Du Vivier, Jock Byrne, Arthur Philips and Bob Tait. Du Vivier and Tait had participated in the first luckless operation but for the other three this was their first time in action with L Detachment. Phillips was a cantankerous Englishman who spoke warmly of communism; Byrne and Fraser knew each other from days in the Gordon Highlanders when the pair had been lifted from the Dunkirk beach.

Fraser was – and always would be – something of an enigma to the rest of L Detachment. He was a loner by nature, happiest in the company of his dachshund dog, Withers, than with his fellow officers. 'Paddy Mayne used to give him a hell of

These two reconnaissance photographs of an Axis airfield in the desert were taken by Pat Riley prior to a raid. (Courtesy of the SAS Regimental Archive)

a time because he thought he was that [way] inclined,' recalled Storie. 'Paddy could be cruel especially after a few.'

The men nicknamed the fresh-faced Fraser 'Skin' because they suspected he was homosexual, yet no one gave a hoot what his sexual preferences were. He had proved himself a courageous and competent officer with Layforce during the battle for Litani River and that was all that mattered as far as they were concerned. 'He was very quiet, a deep thinker and yet he was a very good soldier,' remembered Storie.

The raiding party was travelling light. Each of the five men carried a revolver, eight Lewes bombs, a water bottle, a tin of emergency chocolate, a ration bag containing a mixture of raisins, lumps of cheese and broken biscuits, a length of rubber tubing and six feet of string. Byrne was in possession of the section's one Thompson sub-machine gun and between them they carried eight spare magazines. 'The Lewes bombs,' recalled Byrne, 'were fitted with two-hour time pencils plus a quick action pull switch to enable us to explode the bombs in 14 seconds if it was necessary.'[8]

After parting company with the LRDG patrol they continued on foot with the intention of reaching a point of observation three miles from the aerodrome. But there was too much enemy traffic and too little cover so the five men concealed themselves among some rocks eight miles from the aerodrome. Dawn on the 21st revealed to Fraser 150 Germans digging defences half a mile to the north, while enemy soldiers could also be seen to the east and west. Also visible through the binoculars was Agedabia. 'We took note of where every aircraft was positioned on each side of the runway,' said Du Vivier. 'And we were able to plan our escape route to reach the LRDG rendezvous.'[9]

There was the odd rain shower during the day and a young man tending a herd of goats passed close by and noticed the five men concealed among the rocks. 'He just looked at us and walked on,' recalled Du Vivier, 'We told ourselves he wouldn't spill the beans.'

At 1830 hours they left their position and moved towards the aerodrome. It was dark and as the men moved slowly and noiselessly in Indian file through the German positions they could hear the low murmur of conversation among the defenders. Suddenly they were caught in the beam of an enemy vehicle. 'We held our breath, to lie flat or to run would have caused suspicion,' said Du Vivier. 'So we carried on, the vehicle passed on, too, and we breathed again.'

There were two further moments of anxiety as they edged ever closer to the target. 'Two tripwires were tripped over without results!' wrote Fraser in his official report of the operation.[10] At 2115 hours they had breached the outer defences of Agedabia aerodrome but as Fraser recorded in his report there now ensued several fraught and frustrating hours:

> Some difficulty was experienced in finding the planes, detours being necessary to avoid AA guns and strolling sentries. The first plane was located at 0005 hrs (on the 22nd December). At first the aircraft were fairly well dispersed, but nearer the hangars they were closer together, one batch of C.R 42s [Italian fighters] standing wing to wing … charges were laid in thirty seven aircraft and in one dump of Breda ammunition. The first charge exploded at 0042 hrs and the aerodrome was evacuated at 0055 hrs, by which time four aircraft were blazing.

Du Vivier described how they counted more than 40 explosions as they withdrew from the chaos which they had created. Then they heard a 'blood-curdling deafening roar' and guessed the flames had spread to a bomb dump. 'Though we must have been at least half a mile away by this time,' wrote Du Vivier, 'we felt the concussion press on our lungs.'

They were helped in their escape from the aerodrome by the arrival of three British bombers, attracted by the fires like moths to a flame, and amid the confusion

Chris O'Dowd from southern Ireland joined the regiment in 1942 and established a reputation as a brilliant special forces soldier. He was later killed at Termoli. (Author's Collection)

no one took any notice of five men striding confidently away from the carnage. At 0425 hours they made contact with the LRDG and soon Fraser and his men were en route to the Wadi el Faregh where Brigadier Denys Reid's flying column was leaguered. Byrne later described the meeting between Reid and Fraser.

'How many aircraft did you get?'

'All of them.'

'How many is that?'

'37, sir.'

Whereupon the brigadier gave Bill a whacking great thump on the back and said:

'There's nothing to stop us now.'

Fraser and his party arrived at Jalo late on the afternoon of 23 December. Stirling celebrated their return, and the news they brought with them, by throwing a premature Christmas party. Amid the singing of songs and the toasting of success, Stirling debriefed the five men on the raid. Bob Tait had some interesting observations to make that would form the basis of his report on the attack. There were no individual sentries on aircraft but they did find men asleep under the heavy bombers. Asked what they had done with the sleeping men, Tait replied 'We did not wake them!'[11]

Where the planes were close together, continued Tait, they had placed bombs on alternate machines, and though they each had carried eight Lewes bombs they would have been able to hold ten in their haversacks. Finally, and most importantly, it was noted that the night in question was warm and as a result the 30 minute time pencils had ignited after an average of just 18 minutes.

Fraser's men had scant time to rest on their laurels. On 25 December, barely 36 hours after their return from Agedabia, they were off again, this time to attack the aerodrome at Arae Philaenorum, known to the British as 'Marble Arch' on account of the preposterous arch that Mussolini had erected nearby as a monument to his conceit. Stirling and Mayne had departed from Jalo on Christmas Eve to attack Sirte and Tamet, while Lewes travelled in the same convoy as Fraser's section bound for Nofilia, a coastal airfield that lay 60 miles to the west of Arae Philaenorum.

Mayne once more struck gold, destroying 27 aircraft that had only arrived the previous day to replace the squadron he'd wiped out ten days earlier. He and his five men encountered a similar problem with the fuses to that of Fraser's section at Agedabia. The first bomb exploded after 22 minutes instead of 30, illuminating the raiders as they made a hasty withdrawal. Mayne threw a grenade at an Italian guard who challenged them but in the confusion the raiders left behind four haversacks, which were passed for examination to the Italian engineers.

There were 19 charges inside the haversacks, as well as two unexploded charges that were removed from the wing roots of two aircraft, and in the opinion of the engineers they had failed to explode because of 'faulty manufacture in the part joining the detonating fuse of the charge to the slow match fuse of the igniter'.[12]

With schoolboy enthusiasm the engineers repaired the fuses before finding a couple of old aircraft on which to place the charges. They laid them in exactly the same spot as the British raiders and stood back and watched, reporting the effects in their subsequent report:

David Stirling in his 'Blitz Buggy', a stripped down Ford V8 staff car. (Courtesy of the SAS Regimental Archive)

> In every case, the firing of the charge, besides causing other considerable damage due to the explosion, set the fuel alight, both in the aircraft and in the vehicle, thus causing complete destruction of the material. The fires, however, do not seem to have been due to any particular qualities of the explosive but to the accurate placing of the charges in proximity to the fuel tanks and, in the case of the aircraft, to the specific facility of combustion owing to greater inflammability of the fuel.[13]

In short, the Italian engineers were mightily impressed by Jock Lewes's creation.

When Mayne and his men reached the RV to find Stirling had again drawn a blank at Sirte he couldn't resist a gloat. Fifty-one planes to Stirling's nil. 'It's obvious I'll have to pull up my socks,' reportedly replied a rueful Stirling, whose frustration at finding their target too heavily guarded was offset by Mayne's latest success.[14]

The two officers saw in the New Year of 1942 at Jalo Oasis, waiting anxiously for the return of Lewes and Fraser. Late in the evening of 1 January a truck arrived carrying four LRDG troopers and three members of Lewes's section: Bob Lilley, Jim Almonds and Jimmy Storie. They had no news of the other nine LRDG soldiers or their L Detachment comrade Corporal Geordie White. Unfortunately they were able to inform Stirling that Jock Lewes was dead.

The trio described to Stirling how they had breached the aerodrome all right, only to discover there were just two aircraft. The next morning as they headed to the RV to collect Fraser's party they were bounced by a Messerchmitt 110. Storie recalled later how the German fighter came in very low 'at about 30 feet and from behind us with his cannons firing'. A shard of shrapnel tore a strip from Storie's shorts, but Lewes wasn't so fortunate. 'He got a burst in the back and the two offside wheels were blown off. I don't know how I got away with it because Jock was alongside me.' Later, after the Messerchmitt had expended its ammunition they laid Lewes to rest in the desert. 'We just buried him, said a prayer, stuck a rifle in the ground with a steel helmet where his head was and scratched his name on the helmet hoping someone would go that way again,' said Storie.

The convoy had been split up during the attack* and it was only the ingenuity of a LRDG trooper who succeeded in coaxing the truck into life that they were able to make it back to Jalo. Nonetheless, recalled Storie, 'Stirling kicked up hell because we didn't bring back Lewes's body.'

Lewes's death was a bitter blow, not just to Stirling but to every man in L Detachment. 'He was more austere than Stirling and didn't suffer fools gladly,' remembered Cooper, 'but his intelligence was phenomenal and his innovative ideas were invaluable in the early days of the regiment.'[15]

For nearly another fortnight there was no news of Fraser and his four men (Du Vivier, Byrne, Phillips and Tait), and Stirling began to fear the worse. Then on 12 January Stirling received word from Eighth Army HQ that Fraser and his section had been picked up after an epic nine-day trek across the desert following their aborted raid on Arae Philaenorum. In Fraser's report he described how on the sixth night they had almost been captured as they rested in a wadi: 'A party of twelve men advanced in line towards the position from 200 yards. The section withdrew successfully. I returned later and found that a telephone line had laid over the position.' Fraser concluded his report with words of high praise for his men who 'behaved admirably … and made the task much easier by their cheerfulness and ready obedience to orders'.

---

* The LRDG troopers arrived at Jalo a week later having walked 200 miles in eight days. Corporal White had dropped out with raw feet and was taken prisoner.

Tait also wrote a report on their unsuccessful mission in which he highlighted the positives, particularly the training instilled in them by Lewes: 'We always had the advantage over the enemy, who were obviously not accustomed to night movement.'[16]

Jeff Du Vivier confined his thoughts in a letter to his mother, reassuring her that he was indestructible despite all the danger he faced, and the fact they had survived by eating lizards, berries and snails: 'I must have more lives than a cat. Although I have seen quite a bit of action I always seem to get away with it, and something tells me I always will.'[17] For Mrs Du Vivier back in south London, these were the words she wanted to hear from one of the four sons she had serving in the military.

Fraser and his men rejoined L Detachment at Kabrit in the second week of January to learn that Stirling had been promoted to major, Mayne to captain and both had been recommended for the Distinguished Service Order (DSO). There were other medals in the offing, too, among them a Military Cross for Fraser and Military Medals for Du Vivier and Tait.

Stirling was altogether more pleased with life now that he had come to terms with Lewes's death. He had been to Cairo to see General Auchinleck, who himself wore the look of a satisfied man. The initial sluggishness of Operation *Crusader* had been transformed into a successive offensive with Rommel driven back across Libya. The port of Tobruk had been relieved, the port of Benghazi captured and more than 300 Axis aircraft had been destroyed. The SAS had accounted for 90 of that number, and Auchinleck was quick to congratulate Stirling for his contribution. He also acceded to Stirling's request to recruit a further 40 officers and men, and authorised him to begin planning a raid on Bouerat, a port in western Libya, a few miles beyond Tamet airfield.

Paddy Mayne (far right) with David Stirling on his right. The pair had contrasting personalities but together they complemented one another to devastating effect. (Courtesy of John Robertson)

The raid on Bouerat was not a resounding success. Stirling had hoped to destroy enemy shipping moored in the harbour but there was none to be found. Instead they planted bombs on wireless stations and petrol carriers before withdrawing across the desert. As the raiding party approached Jalo on 30 January they picked up a BBC news bulletin on their wireless set that left them stunned, and also accounted for the empty harbour: Rommel had counter-attacked, retaking Benghazi and pushing the Eighth Army east across Libya as far as Gazala. Alerted to what had happened, Stirling pulled in briefly at Jalo and then pressed on east to Siwa with the advancing Axis army not far behind.

Stirling arrived at Kabrit in early February to discover all was not well with L Detachment. Before leaving on the Bouerat raid, Stirling had appointed Paddy Mayne the unit's training officer with instructions to whip the new recruits into shape. It was the role Lewes had accomplished with aplomb a few months earlier but it was a role for which Mayne was ill-suited; he was a fighting soldier, the most successful one in L Detachment, and he bitterly resented being made to stay in camp while Stirling went off to have another crack at the enemy.

Instead of drilling the new recruits – among which was a contingent of 52 Free French paratroopers under the command of Captain George Berges – Mayne had spent most of his time either in his tent reading one of the Penguin paperbacks that his mother sent him or boozing in the sergeants' mess. One of the men who had volunteered for L Detachment in January was Arthur Thomson, a Londoner who been in No.7 Commando, part of Layforce. 'We soon came to realise that Paddy was a quiet man but a very hard man,' recalled Thomson, 'and that there were two things he loved above all else: a booze up and a punch up. At Kabrit we would be in the sergeants' mess having a beer about 10 at night, and then Paddy would walk in at 11, and it was an unwritten rule that nobody left till he did, and that was usually 2 in the morning.'[18]

Stirling quickly remedied his error by reassigning Mayne to operational duties and appointing Sergeant-Major Pat Riley the new training officer, with Jeff Du Vivier

According to George Jellicoe it was Paddy Mayne's idea in June 1942 that the SAS should use jeeps to attack Axis targets, a move that soon produced spectacular results. (Courtesy of the SAS Regimental Archive)

his second-in-command. Du Vivier's expertise lay in night navigation and one recruit, Les Ward, recalled later that 'we would sit propped up beside our jeep while Jeff explained all the stars and constellations in the sky'.[19]

In addition to the French paratroopers there was a new face in Captain Bill Cumper, like Du Vivier a Londoner, and a man who had risen through the ranks of the Royal Engineers to become an officer and an expert in explosives. 'Bill taught us how to make the Lewes bomb, which gave you a bit of a headache because of the ammonal,' recalled Albert Youngman, a Norwich-born commando who joined L Detachment in 1942. 'He'd make us sit there and make them over and over until he was satisfied. He also taught us in the use of gelignite, primer cord, gun cotton, which was used mainly for cutting railway lines.'[20]

The new recruits saw little of Stirling when he returned from Bouerat. He was already planning L Detachment's next raids, scheduled to take place in March, so much of his time was spent in Cairo, in discussion with MEHQ or organising the operation from his brother's well-appointed flat (Peter Stirling was a secretary at the British Embassy). 'Stirling was hard to get to know,' remembered Thomson. 'When he looked at you it wasn't with a blank stare but with very little expression on his face. But once you knew him then you knew what he was doing; he was sussing you out, observing your body language, the way you conducted yourself, what you said and so forth. He could judge you. He was a quiet, methodical man.' Meanwhile at Kabrit the new recruits were undergoing the same rigorous training that the original members of L Detachment had experienced the previous summer. For the French recruits, however, desperate to strike at the enemy following the capitulation of France 18 months earlier, there was no question of failure no matter how punishing the instruction. 'The training was very hard,' recalled Roger Boutinot, an assistant in a St Mâlo patisserie before rowing across the English Channel in May 1940 to escape the invading Germans. 'We did a lot of marching across the desert and a lot of explosives training and sabotage work. And every morning Sergeant Major [Gus] Glaze took us for P.T. [physical training]. Everybody went, British and French. We played basketball against the English, and football. The camaraderie was excellent, lose or win, it was just a laugh, and we were always well received by the British. There was never any feeling that we had to prove ourselves to the British as Frenchmen.'[21] For the L Detachment veterans, the handful of men who had come through the early operations unscathed, February and early March offered them the chance to grab some well-earned leave in Cairo.

By now the unit had their own beret and insignia. The cap badge to be worn on the snow white beret had been designed by Bob Tait, victor of a competition held by Stirling the previous October. His winning entry was the flaming sword of

OVERLEAF
In addition to the single Vickers next to the driver's seat and the twin Vickers in the rear, SAS jeeps also carried a Browning machine gun such as the one in this photograph. (Courtesy of the SAS Regimental Archive)

Excalibur above the motto 'Strike and Destroy'.★ Stirling was less impressed with the motto, however, and plumped for one of his own – 'Who Dares Wins'. Tait's cap badge was manufactured by John Jones in Cairo, as were the unit's operational wings that were the work of Jock Lewes. Designed with a straight edge on top to distinguish them from other airborne units, the wings represented a scarab beetle with a parachute replacing the scarab. The background colours were light blue, the colour of Cambridge University, where Stirling had been an undergraduate, and dark blue for Oxford University, Lewes's alma mater.

Every member of L Detachment who successfully undertook parachute training was entitled to wear the wings on the shoulder, and those soldiers who completed three missions were allowed to sport them above their left breast pocket.

But on their first leave in Cairo L Detachment veterans soon encountered a problem with their new attire, one that ran counter to the creed imposed by Stirling, who warned: 'There had grown up in the commandos a tradition that to be a tough regiment it was necessary to act tough in barracks and on leave and they were liable to be badly dressed, ill-disciplined and noisy in the streets and restaurants of Cairo. We insisted with L Detachment that toughness should be reserved entirely for the benefit of the enemy.'[22]

Yet the moment L Detachment veterans strolled through Cairo proudly wearing their snow white berets there was trouble. Some had their sexuality questioned by mocking Australians while Jimmy Storie remembered: 'When we wore the white berets we were mistaken for Russians and got called names. It was causing so much trouble that [they] were changed to sand-coloured berets.'

Nonetheless, wherever possible the men heeded Stirling's warning about behaving themselves in Cairo. No one wanted to run the risk of incurring their CO's wrath and being returned to their unit. 'Arthur Phillips and I were in a bar when these Australian and English soldiers squared up to each other,' remembered Storie. 'Then the bottles began flying and we were stuck in the middle wearing our white berets. We thought the best thing to do was stay absolutely still and hope for the best … after that we kept away from the so-called popular bars and went into the not so popular bars where there was less likely to be trouble.'

Johnny Cooper and Reg Seekings, by now the best of pals, went everywhere together in Cairo with the taciturn Fenman acting as chaperone to the younger and more exuberant Cooper: 'I did have a habit of singing once I'd had a few beers, I couldn't help it,' remembered Cooper. 'Poor old Reg was very tolerant, although

---

★ The cap badge is now more commonly referred to as a 'winged dagger', a misnomer attributed to Roy Farran, a flamboyant wartime SAS officer who published his memoirs in 1948 as *Winged Dagger* because it sounded more gung-ho than 'Flaming Sword'.

before we'd go out he'd often ask me not to start singing. But I think perhaps he secretly liked hearing me sing!'

After the fluidity of the winter months, the Desert War had become a stalemate by March 1942. Auchinleck was consolidating his defensive positions at Gazala and Rommel was augmenting his thinly stretched supply lines while planning his next move. The British wouldn't be in a position to launch a fresh offensive for several more months but Auchinleck nonetheless was keen to strike a blow at Rommel. It was decided therefore that L Detachment would attack a string of Axis aerodromes in the Benghazi area, while Stirling would lead a raid against the port itself.

With Jalo in the hands of the enemy, L Detachment made their base at Siwa Oasis, a far more salubrious alternative. There were palm trees full of dates and a sparkling expanse of water known as 'Cleopatra's Pool' where the men could bathe under the hot sun.

On 15 March the raiding party left Siwa for the 400-mile trip to Benghazi, among their number a 48-year-old Belgian called Bob Melot on his first operation with L Detachment. A veteran of World War I, Melot was a fluent Arab speaker working for Belgian Steel in Cairo when the next world war erupted. He offered his services to the British general staff and was now putting his vast knowledge of North Africa to good use under Stirling's command.

An SAS patrol prepares to head 'up the Blue' – British Army slang for the desert. Note the steel sand channels on the bonnet to help in the event of the vehicle becoming stuck in soft ground. (Courtesy of the SAS Regimental Archive)

Just south of Benghazi, Mayne split from the main party and headed off to attack Berka satellite airfield in the company of Bob Bennett, Graham Rose and Jock Byrne. The others continued on their way before Fraser left to tackle Barce, a new officer called Lieutenant Roy Dodd went off to Slonta and Gordon Alston headed to the main airfield at Berka.★

Fraser blew up the solitary aircraft he found on Barce, along with eight repair wagons, but neither Alston or Dodd had any success. Nor did Stirling, who found plenty of shipping in Benghazi but was unable to launch his folding boat. Fortunately Mayne saved the day, again, destroying 15 aircraft on the Berka satellite airfield. In a letter to his brother, Douglas, Mayne described what happened after they fled the scene of devastation:

> The day and night after the raid we couldn't find our rendezvous. The maps are awful, we had been walking from 1.30am to 7 o'clock the next night and couldn't find the damn place anywhere. We must have covered about fifty miles, first of all getting to the drome and then coming away. It was dark and we were due here [the RV] at dusk. It was no good walking around in circles in the dark and I had more or less resigned myself to a 250-mile walk to Tobruk, and so we (three of us, two corporals [Rose and Bennett, Jock Byrne was captured by the Germans] and myself) went to the nearest Senussi camp for some water and, if possible, a blanket.
>
> The Senussi were very suspicious at first, but once they were sure that we were 'Inglesi' everything changed and we were ushered into one of their tents, our equipment brought in, blankets put down for a bed. There was a fire just outside and everyone crowded in. First of all they boiled us some eggs, which were damned good, then platters of dates and bowls of water and a huge gourd of goats' milk was brought in … and now listen to this and never believe in luck again or coincidence, or whatever you like to call it. The men who were waiting for us at the rendezvous – and they would have left the next morning – had got a chicken which they had bartered for some sugar. They wanted it cooked and had an English-speaking Arab with them, so they sent him to get it cooked. In that area must have been thirty or forty different encampments spread over the three-odd miles we were from each other and he picked the one that we were lying in to come to![23]

Throughout the spring of 1942 General Auchinleck came under increasing pressure from Winston Churchill to break the stalemate in the Western Desert. He and

---

★ Dodd was RTU'd shortly after and joined the Parachute Regiment where he was killed during the drop into Arnhem in 1944.

Rommel were biding their time, like two grand chess masters waiting for one to make the first move, and it infuriated the British Prime Minister. He believed Malta was in danger of falling into German hands, which, in a wire he sent to Auchinleck at the end of April, he emphasised would be 'a disaster of the first magnitude for the British Empire'. Auchinleck retorted that he must have more time to build up his reserves but when Churchill was told a large convoy would sail for Malta during a moonless period in June he issued Auchinleck with an ultimatum: either launch an offensive against the Axis forces before the middle of June or be relieved of your command. While the pair squabbled, Rommel acted, launching an offensive of his own on 26 May.

The British defences held firm initially and repulsed the German attack, and on 2 June Churchill cabled Auchinleck to inform him that the supply convoy would soon be headed towards Malta. 'There is no need for me to stress the vital importance of the safe arrival of our convoys … and I am sure you will take all steps to enable the air escorts, and particularly the Beaufighters, to be operated from landing-grounds as far west as possible.'[24]

'I kicked open the door and stood there with my Colt 45, the others at my side with a Tommy Gun and another automatic.'

Paddy Mayne

Stirling was summoned to Cairo and instructed to formulate a plan to aid the passage of the two-pronged convoy (from Gibraltar and Alexandria) to Malta. Stirling ensconced himself in his brother's flat, along with Johnny Cooper and Reg Seekings, and came up with his most audacious plan to date. On the night of 13 June they would launch simultaneous attacks against a string of enemy aerodromes in the Benghazi sector. It wasn't the first time that Seekings and Cooper had helped Stirling in the planning of a raid; he trusted their judgement and valued their opinion. 'We used to plan out beforehand what we were going to do according to the aerial photographs,' recalled Seekings. 'We didn't just go in. And we also had an emergency plan. You never go in without one so you're not caught napping. But unless the situation has changed and there's been a big influx of men or weapons [on the airfield], the plan you made back in base sitting down and concentrating, that's going to be just as good as the day you arrive on the scene. If you start talking about it when you arrive you're going to cock it up because indecision will creep in. Once you've made up your mind to do something, do it.'

The subsequent report on these raids stated that:

The results of these operations in June were as follows:

Aircraft	destroyed	27 at least (others damaged)
Aero engines	"	20 to 30
Truck	"	5
Fuel dumps	"	numerous

A good many casualties were inflicted on the enemy[25]

For the first time on an operation Paddy Mayne returned empty-handed, thwarted from blowing up aircraft on Berka satellite by the premature attack against Berka Main by a party of French SAS troops. 'They went in an hour before their time and we were caught on the damned 'drome putting bombs on various things,' remembered Jimmy Storie. The French blew up 14 aircraft on Berka Main but their British comrades had time to plant bombs on just one plane before all hell broke loose. Nervous German and Italian troops fired at each other from opposite ends of the airfield as the four raiders melted into the darkness.

'Then we split up with Warburton and Lilley going one way and me and Paddy going another,' said Storie. They walked for a while, then rested, then continued on their way at first light. 'We got to top of one escarpment and just over the side I spotted an armoured car,' said Storie. 'We were on its blind side so we just slid back down and waited an hour until away it went.' There was also a detachment of German soldiers nearby combing the area for the raiders but they didn't climb the escapement. Later the pair took refuge in a Senussi encampment where they found Lilley already enjoying the hospitality on offer. Over dates and goats' milk, Lilley described how he strangled an Italian soldier who had blocked his path, but of Warburton he had no news, he had simply vanished. 'We believe Warburton fell down a well in the dark,' explained Storie. 'Some of the airfields had wells nearby and they were 20 feet deep. If you fell into one there was no way of getting out by yourself.'

When Mayne arrived at the RV he found Stirling waiting with a triumphant smile. Finally, he had broken his duck! Mayne listened as he heard how Stirling, Cooper and Seekings had caused havoc at Benina, the Germans' chief repair base for their aircraft, planting bombs in hangars and workshops on vital pieces of equipment. It had required all their stealth to avoid the numerous guards as they crept from building to building, further testament to the training instilled in them by Lewes. In one hangar Stirling and Cooper had deposited bombs on more than 30 crates containing spare engines while Seekings acted as lookout. With their supply of bombs exhausted, Stirling turned his attention to the guardroom on the edge of the base, perhaps mindful of Mayne's daring attack on the pilots' mess at Tamet six months earlier.

Seekings later described how he and Cooper covered their commanding officer as he kicked in the guardhouse door and threw in a grenade. 'The twenty Germans who had just come off guard were inside. Their officer was sitting at a desk no doubt making his report. "Here catch," said the CO. The Jerry at the desk did in fact catch it, and in a voice of horror cried "nein, nein". "Ja, Ja", said the CO and closed the door. A moment later there was a big explosion. We then ran like hell as the bombs in the hangars had also started to go off.'

Still coursing with adrenaline at the rendezvous, Stirling accepted Mayne's challenge of driving into Benina and on to Benghazi to attack anything that took their fancy. Plus, as Mayne reportedly teased Stirling: 'I want to make sure you're not exaggerating.'

Stirling sweet-talked the LRDG into lending them a truck and jumped into the front passenger seat alongside Mayne who was driving. Into the back clambered Seekings, Cooper, Jimmy Storie, Bob Lilley and an Austrian Jew attached to L Detachment by the name of Karl Kahane. 'It was a bloody silly thing to do, but

'We were a wild-looking lot,' remembered one SAS officer during the summer of 1942 when they operated from their remote base at Bir el Quseir. One of the 'wild' men in this photo is the SAS medical officer, Malcolm Pleydell, standing second from the right in the middle row (in shirt sleeves). (Courtesy of the SAS Regimental Archive)

funny at the time!' remembered Cooper. 'David, in his usual self-confident way, reassured us that there wouldn't be any roadblocks along the way. We didn't waste time taking back routes, just went straight along the main road towards Benina all unconcerned at the potential danger we were driving into.'

After six miles they encountered their first roadblock, manned by what appeared

to be a solitary Italian holding a red lamp. No one in the truck expected the Italian to be anything other than cooperative, but as he peered at the strange truck and the bearded occupants who said they were German he barked a command. Suddenly a dozen Germans rushed from the guardhouse, their weapons levelled at the truck as they fanned out in a semi-circle. The sergeant-major in charge demanded the password. Kahane cursed him and said they had no idea of the password, that they had been fighting the Tommies for the past three days and were tired and hungry and in no mood for this nonsense. The sergeant-major took a couple of steps towards the truck to get a better look at the men inside. Mayne described subsequent events in a letter home:

An SAS patrol sets off up the Blue. Note the Arab headdress worn by the driver of the lead vehicle and the water coolant-condenser fitted to the front. The radiator grill has also been removed to increase air flow and allow quicker repair in the case of bullet holes. (Courtesy of the SAS Regimental Archive)

Graham Rose (left) and Jimmy Storie up the Blue in the summer of 1942. Not long after this photo was taken, Storie was captured and spent nearly three years in a POW camp. (Courtesy of the SAS Regimental Archive)

Fritz isn't satisfied so he walks to about three feet from the car on my side. I'm sitting there with my Colt on my lap and suddenly I remember that it isn't cocked, so I pull it back and the Jerry has one look and then orders the gates to be opened. Which they did in a chorus of 'Guden Nachtens' and we drove on. We thought later that he came to the conclusion, the same one that I had come to, that if anyone was going to be hurt he was going to be a very sick man very early on.[26]

They drove on towards Benghazi aware that the alarm would have been raised by the sergeant-major. Soon they encountered a hastily erected roadblock. Mayne accelerated through it, scattering the Italian soldiers, while Seekings opened up with the Lewis machine gun. Mayne and Stirling agreed to postpone the visit to Benghazi and instead just shoot up whatever came their way in the next couple of miles. They came to a transport filling station complete with petrol storage tank, which was unmanned and easy to festoon with bombs. A mile or so further on, at the village of Lete approximately five miles east of Benghazi, a most appealing sight hove into view. 'It was a roadside café and sitting out on the verandah having a drink were a lot of Germans and Italians,' remembered Storie. 'We knew we would have to do something about this so we drew up alongside the cafe and opened fire. They didn't have time to defend themselves, we blew everything to bits.'

Stirling decided it would now be prudent to retire. They left the road and headed into the Wadi el Gattara that ran parallel; it was the only alternative route to the one just taken and which was now crawling with the enemy. It was dark and bumpy, but Stirling confidently navigated Mayne towards the track that would lead them down the escarpment to safety. Suddenly they saw the lights of another vehicle tearing across the desert in their direction in the hope of cutting them off. Mayne put on his lights and went hell for leather for the escarpment. In the back, Seekings attempted to fire at their pursuer's lights as the truck jolted from side to side. Mayne got to the track that cut across the wadi and accelerated down it, leaving the enemy vehicle helpless on the wrong side of the escarpment. The evening's excitement wasn't quite finished, however, despite the fact that the men began to drift off to sleep as Mayne headed for the RV across flatter, smoother ground. Suddenly there was a shout of 'Burning fuse!' from Bob Lilley, and in a second all seven men had leapt from the truck. Moments later there was a terrific explosion as a time pencil blew the vehicle sky high.

The dash up the wadi had jolted a fuse to life but fortunately Lilley had heard its climatic fizz in the nick of time. 'What was left of [the truck],' reminisced Storie, 'could have been put in a haversack.'[27]

They surveyed the wreckage in silence and then began to giggle. Soon they were laughing out loud, marching across the desert towards a Senussi camp without a care in the world. 'It wasn't very wise in hindsight,' reflected Storie, 'but it did you good sometimes to treat the war as a joke.'

UP THE BLUE
DECEMBER 1942.
(NOTE THE BEAR/S)

CHAPTER 3

STIRLING'S CAPTURE

There was little amusement to be found when Stirling's party returned to Siwa on 21 June and heard the news. The Germans were galloping east across the desert and British forces had fallen back 150 miles; Tobruk was in Rommel's hands and now his troops were pushing into Egypt. The Royal Navy was pulling out of Alexandria and in Cairo British staff officers burned papers in anticipation of the German arrival, though their anxiety turned out to be premature: the Eighth Army withdrew to a small railway station called El Alamein and would stem the Axis advance across a 35-mile wide front. The LRDG were in the process of breaking camp before the Oasis was overrun, so Stirling ordered his men back to Kabrit while he headed to Cairo to see how he could be of help.

In Cairo Stirling discovered that most of the convoy sent to Malta had ended up at the bottom of the sea but two ships had reached the island providing invaluable supplies to the beleaguered inhabitants. Stirling in turn was able to report to MEHQ on L Detachment's latest successes. They had now destroyed 143 enemy aircraft in the last six months, although this was a conservative estimate. It might well have been more, but as Seekings later recalled: 'Stirling reduced all tallies by ten per cent, he wouldn't let anyone claim higher. At first they [MEHQ] couldn't believe we were destroying so many. Impossible. We were destroying more than the best fighter squadrons.'[1] In addition they'd laid waste to numerous petrol bowsers, repair bases and

OPPOSITE
Two beards and one broad smile from these three SAS soldiers somewhere in western Libya. (Courtesy of the SAS Regimental Archive)

Bill Fraser, Jim Chambers and Captain R. P. Schott in the summer of 1942. Chambers was a popular and outgoing officer who died of diphtheritic infection of desert sores in early 1943. (Author's Collection)

bomb dumps. It was even rumoured that the Germans had a name for Stirling – 'the Phantom Major', such was his ability to ghost onto airfields, wreak havoc and then vanish without a trace. Not surprisingly, as Stirling himself noted, the enemy was taking measures to put an end to the menace of the Phantom Major. 'By the end of June L Detachment had raided all the more important German and Italian aerodromes within 300 miles of the forward area at least once or twice,' Stirling wrote later. 'Methods of defence were beginning to improve and although the advantage still lay with L Detachment, the time had come to alter our own methods.'[2]

According to a contemporary L Detachment report written by Captain Lord George Jellicoe, 'Capt. Mayne suggested to Major Stirling that jeeps should be provided' to the unit to transport them to their targets in future.[3] The idea was enthusiastically embraced by Stirling and in Cairo he took possession of 15 American jeeps, known as Willie Bantams, and fitted them with a dozen Vickers K machine guns from the obsolete Gloster Gladiator biplane. Capable of firing 1,200 rounds per minute, the Vickers were mounted fore and aft in the jeeps by some Royal Electrical and Mechanical Engineers, charmed by Stirling into performing a favour for his unit.

On 3 July Stirling led a raiding party from Kabrit bound for Qaret Tartura on the north-western edge of the Qattara Depression, once a huge salt bog 150 miles long and 75 miles wide. Having assembled at this remote spot on 6 July, they headed north for 60 miles before splitting into their raiding parties. The objectives were a series of aerodromes on the Egyptian coast, about 50 miles behind the German frontline at El Alamein, timed to coincide with attacks by the 9th Australian Division and 1st South African Division. A French party under Andre Zirnheld and Jellicoe would strafe the coastal road, while Bill Fraser and a French officer called Augustin Jordan targeted two airfields at Fuka. Stirling and Mayne were destined for Bagoush, the airfield from which L Detachment had set out on that first fateful raid the previous November.

The raiders had mixed success. Fraser found his airfield too well guarded and prudently withdrew; Jordan also encountered strong enemy defences but used his fluent German to convince an Italian sentry he was a friend; the Frenchman had planted bombs on eight Messerchmitt 109s before the Italians realised they had been duped. In the ensuing firefight, one of the Frenchmen was wounded but he and his comrades withdrew safely. Jellicoe carried out a useful reconnaissance on the road between Fuka and Galal and also captured a few frightened Italians, one of whom revealed that the main fighter base of the Axis Air Force was at El Daba. Mayne and Stirling, meanwhile, were having an eventful time at Bagoush, as Jellicoe later described in his operation report:

> Capt. Mayne went on with a small party to make his attack. Normal equipment was carried, each man having one Tommy gun or Colt automatic, two hand grenades, and special [Lewes] bombs. The bombs were placed on the wings of the aircraft and Capt. Mayne came back to report to Major Stirling. He then did the same thing again. Major Stirling had meanwhile been examining the road to see if there was any chance of establishing a road block, but had not made one as he did not think it worthwhile to disclose his position for the sake of an odd truck. When Capt. Mayne had returned for the second time, Major Stirling and he drove on to the aerodrome and destroyed by machine gun fire from their vehicles, a further ten or fourteen aircraft. Subsequently a reconnaissance showed that in all thirty-seven aircraft had been destroyed, mostly C.R. 42s and Me.109s. Major Stirling was by this time encountering considerable opposition from MGs [machine guns] and 20mm guns distributed round the landing ground. He therefore withdrew but was unable to resist the temptation to return, to Capt. Mayne's disgust, in order to despatch a few more aircraft![4]

What Jellicoe's report omitted was an explanation as to why Stirling had driven on to the airfield after Mayne's initial foray. The Irishman had destroyed 22 aircraft but

OVERLEAF
The backbone of L Detachment as it expanded during 1942 were the NCOs such as Reg Seekings (front), Dave Kershaw (crouching by the rear wheel), Gerry Ward (far left, back row), Pat Riley (passenger seat), Ted Badger (driver's seat), Bob Tait (arm in sling) and Johnny Cooper (right). (Courtesy of the SAS Regimental Archive)

Mike Sadler (far left) was a brilliant desert navigator who later became intelligence officer for 1SAS. Here he poses alongside Bob Tait, Graham Rose and Oswald Rooney. (Courtesy of John Robertson)

the bombs on a further dozen or so had failed to ignite – it turned out the primer was damp. 'It's enough to break your heart,' Mayne reportedly said, forlorn at the thought of so many enemy aircraft sitting close by just waiting to be blown up.[5] It was at this point that Stirling suggested they finish the job with machine-gun fire. With Stirling driving the 'Blitz Buggy', a stripped down Ford V8 staff car, and Mayne at the wheel of the jeep, the raiders set off. There was no roar of engines or screech of tyres, rather the vehicles approached at a steady pace with the gunners mindful of Stirling's advice to shoot low and at the petrol tanks. Jonny Cooper was manning the forward gun on the Blitz Buggy. 'We drove on to the airfield and started firing,' he recalled. 'He [Stirling] kept to a nice steady pace of about 15mph and I opened fire at a line of CR 42s that were soon in flames. Unfortunately after three magazines the Vickers had a seizure from overheating … but the damage done to the gun was more than compensated by the devastation caused to the enemy.'[6]

Another series of raids were launched on the night of 11/12 July and Mayne once again led the way, destroying between 15 and 20 aircraft at Landing Ground 18 while Jordan accounted for eight planes at Fuka. By now L Detachment had been behind the lines for nearly a fortnight, moving their base 25 miles west from Qaret Tartura to Bir el Quseir after fearing they'd been compromised by an Italian spotter aircraft. Stirling considered it time they had a resupply so he set off for Cairo on 13 July, taking the bulk of the unit with him but leaving a party of 23 men behind including Lieutenant Steven Hastings and the unit's medical officer Malcolm Pleydell. Hastings later described the ten days they spent waiting for the return of Stirling.

There we lived … like rabbits in a bank, our six or seven vehicles driven into the crevices made by dried water courses in the side of the little cliff and heavily camouflaged with nets and scrubs … all of us had been out in the 'Blue' [the army slang for the desert] for about a month and most were burnt black except for the unfortunates who stayed bright red. Most wore a pair of shorts, sandals or boots with rubber soles and either bush hats or big khaki handkerchiefs over their heads like the Bedouin. We all had beards. We were a wild-looking lot … it was blazing hot in the daytime and cold at night. The best moments were at dawn and dusk.

There were no flies then and the desert was transformed from minute to minute, drawing pictures in itself with long purple and brown shadows of castles, cliffs and ravines … every evening we watched the sun crawl down, a great orange ball, its progress eventually perceptible to the human eye as it dropped below the far escarpment, now turned black, the outline of every rock standing sharp against a livid sky. Slowly the hated thing disappeared, leaving the whole desert bathed in colours so rich, hard and brilliant as to defy the painter's brush.[7]

In Cairo, meanwhile, Stirling was busy appropriating more trucks and jeeps (20 of the latter in total), as well as rations, rum, equipment and men, one of whom was Mike Sadler.

Sadler was a 22-year-old Englishman with a benign face and a keen brain. Having emigrated to what was then Rhodesia in the late 1930s to farm, Sadler had wound up in the LRDG in 1941, navigating L Detachment to several airfields during their early raids. 'Stirling got the jeeps first but hadn't the means to navigate them, that's when he talent spotted me, if that's the word,' recalled Sadler, who though not over-awed by the 'Phantom Major' was nonetheless impressed. 'Stirling had a very good social manner and he also had a compelling personality. He was a terribly quiet chap and didn't raise his voice [and] could talk you into anything, but he didn't have

Des Peter Middleton took this photograph of an RAF pilot who dropped in on an SAS patrol in the desert to ask for directions. (Author's Collection)

to do much talking. He managed to make one feel you were the only person who could possibly do it … but I also slightly felt he was thinking of something else at the same time … always thinking of improvements to make.'[8]

In Cairo in mid-July Stirling addressed the problem of the strengthened airfield defences. The spur-of-the-moment raid at Bagoush had revealed the potential of driving straight on to the dromes but the method needed refining. As Stirling put his mind to the problem, he received from MEHQ 'Operation Instruction No.99', which stated: 'The order of priorities is Tank Workshops, tanks, aircraft, water, petrol. You will use your own judgement in assessing the value and reliability of information, importance of target assessed in terms of numbers of tanks, aircraft, etc. and possibilities of successful attack.'[9]

Stirling replied to the Instruction with a memo entitled 'New tactics', in which he outlined how L Detachment intended to surmount the improved enemy airfield defences:

> A 'mass [jeep] attack' would nullify the value of sentries on individual aircraft (the enemy's normal custom) and would necessitate perimeter defence, which past experience has shown to be comparatively easy to penetrate by 'stealth'. Thus the alternative employment of two methods of attack – either by a small party on foot reaching its objective without being observed, or by a 'mass' attack in vehicles – should leave the enemy hesitating between the two methods of defence. A combination of perimeter defence with sentries on individual aircraft would be most uneconomical in men … the psychological effect of successful attacks should increase the enemy's nervousness about the defence of his extended lines of communication.[10]

Stirling wasted no time in putting his new tactics to the test. Having returned to the desert hideout on 23 July (much to the relief of Steven Hastings and the others who had begun to think they'd been abandoned), Stirling briefed his men on an impending attack against Sidi Hanesih, an airfield approximately 30 miles east-south-east of Mersa Matruh. Describing how they would drive on to the airfield in two columns with a distance of ten yards between vehicles and an interval of ten yards between columns, Stirling explained that he would direct the attack from his jeep positioned between the heads of the two columns. Once the men had grasped the plan, Stirling ordered a dress rehearsal on the evening of 25 July. 'The rehearsal was one of the more bizarre moments of the war for me,' recalled Johnny Cooper, 'firing thousands of rounds deep behind enemy lines in preparation for a raid the following night.'

The next day the men counted down the hours before the departure for the 70-mile journey north to Sidi Haneish. 'I think everyone felt a little bit of fear, but it was more eager anticipation,' remembered Cooper. 'No one liked hanging around and we had a desire to get on with it. We checked and rechecked our guns, the jeeps, and loaded the drums in the right order: one tracer, one armour-piercing and one incendiary.'

Mike Sadler wouldn't be participating in the raid itself; his job was to navigate the raiders to the airfield and then wait at its south-east corner as a RV point in case any jeep was disabled and its occupants forced to flee on foot. 'When you went on an operation, it wasn't the raid itself you worried about it was how the hell we were going to get away afterwards because the Germans were like bees in chasing us,' he reflected.

Sadler navigated them the 70 miles north in only four hours. It was a moonlit night and except for six punctures and a LRDG truck hitting a mine, the approach to the target was uneventful. A mile from the airfield, Stirling halted the column and issued a last set of instructions. 'Gun discipline was vital,' Storie remembered as the gist of Stirling's final briefing. 'We had to keep in a strict formation, two abreast, firing outwards the whole time.'

The force then moved cautiously forward at four to five miles an hour, one or two jeeps dipping in and out of unoccupied rifle pits, before they formed into two columns. On a green Verey light fired from Stirling, the attack began.

Middleton joined the SAS in June 1942 and proved one of the regiment's most effective operators, though he also had the dubious distinction of being shot in the backside on three separate occasions! (Author's Collection)

Some subsequent accounts state that the jeeps roared through the thin perimeter defences and moved down the airfield at around 20mph, but Jellicoe's operational report is contradictory. He wrote: 'The firing of Verey lights and of tracer and incendiary ammunition having disclosed the approximate positions of the aircraft, the column was directed to the centre of the dispersal area and shot the planes up one by one, the pace, while shooting was going on, being reduced to one or two miles an hour. In this way about thirty were destroyed, though only eighteen actually burst into flames. Fire was also directed at the guards as they ran for cover.'[11]

Watching from his vantage point on the south-eastern corner of the airfield was Mike Sadler. 'I had a ringside view of the tracer hitting and the aircraft going up,' he recalled. 'The whole thing was very impressive.'

It took a few minutes for the airfield's defenders to gather their wits but as the two columns doubled back they came under attack from a 20mm gun and small-arms fire. Stirling's jeep was damaged but not disabled, but a bullet killed John Robson, a 21-year-old rear gunner in Sandy Scratchley's jeep. They departed the airfield and split up, some vehicles heading south and others south-west, all in a hurry to find cover before dawn broke in an hour and a half. Most did but a detachment of French jeeps were caught in the open by a patrol of German Junker 87s and the much admired officer Andre Zirnheld was killed.

Nonetheless, the raid had been every bit as successful as Stirling envisaged, a satisfying way with which to bring July to a close. In the month that they'd been operating self-sufficiently from their remote desert base, L Detachment destroyed a minimum of 86 enemy aircraft and between 36 and 45 motorised vehicles. It was a surprise to some of the men that the Germans didn't form a similar unit to try and counter L Detachment's achievements. 'The Afrika Korps had been trained in a different type of warfare,' reflected Jimmy Storie. 'They had been trained in European warfare … they lacked the skill but also the transport so we went places they never went.'[12] In Mike Sadler's estimation the answers could be found in the soldiers' blood. 'It's in the national character,' he said. 'If you look down the ages Britain has had these type of soldiers so to some extent it might be a cultural thing.'

Despite their success, however, at the beginning of August L Detachment was ordered to return to Cairo. MEHQ was concerned their desert base was in danger of being discovered by Italians who had recently occupied Siwa Oasis and were believed to be actively searching for L Detachment following the devastating raid on Sidi Haneish. In addition, as Stirling suspected the moment he received the order to return, MEHQ had something in mind for L Detachment. Stirling arrived in Cairo to discover that Churchill had sacked Claude Auchinleck and replaced him with General Harold Alexander. There was also a new commander of the

A group of officers from B Squadron plan an operation during the late autumn of 1942. The officer sitting on the ammunition box is believed to be Wilfred Thesiger, who served with the regiment briefly, and the officer to his right is Major Peter Oldfield, captured by the Germans not long after this photo was taken. (Author's Collection)

Eighth Army, the acerbic General Bernard Montgomery. He was planning a big offensive for the end of October to start from the Alamein front and he had a job for Stirling which would be of some assistance. Montgomery's concern was that Rommel's Afrika Korps were being greatly strengthened by regular supply convoys arriving in the ports of Tobruk and Benghazi. Therefore he wanted L Detachment together with elements of Middle East Commando and the Special Boat Section (SBS) to raid the latter while a combined force of commandoes and infantry launched a simultaneous seaborne strike against Tobruk.

Stirling was horrified at the plan, considering it anathema to L Detachment's modus operandi. They were suited to small-scale raids, lightning guerrilla warfare, yet the Benghazi raid – codenamed Operation *Bigamy* – was large and cumbersome consisting of 200 men and a couple of Honey tanks. It reminded him of the Layforce approach and the disastrous results of similar misguided plans. But Stirling was helpless in the face of MEHQ support for the attack and reluctantly began to plan for the operation scheduled for the night of 13/14 September. The Benghazi operation unfolded exactly as Stirling had feared. 'The whole raid was a nonsense,' recalled Sadler, who said the details of the attack were being openly discussed in Cairo long before they set out to attack the port. 'In the lead up to Benghazi rumours had been buzzing around Cairo that something was up.'

The large column was ambushed on the approach to the city and forced to withdraw in haste towards the shelter of a faraway escarpment before first light. Those vehicles that failed to reach cover in time were machine gunned by enemy aircraft. From the escarpment it was another 25 miles to the RV in the Jebel Mountains and there they regrouped, tending their wounded and taking stock of the situation. 'I saw David and Paddy at sundown that day,' recalled Malcolm Pleydell, the unit's medical officer. 'David was his normal calm self and apologised for keeping me so busy with the wounded. But then he appeared unsettled for the first time I could remember and informed me that we were moving off shortly but because we had lost so many vehicles to Italian planes there weren't enough places for the wounded.'[13]

To Pleydell fell the task of deciding which of the wounded men were fit enough to travel and which must be left to the Italians. All but four soldiers were loaded onto the truck for the 800-mile trek back to Cairo. It was a melancholic moment for Pleydell as the convoy drove away from the quartet of wounded men in the company of a medical orderly who had volunteered to remain with them. 'Someone began to play a mouth organ. The sobbing notes rose and fell, seemed to draw close and then recede,' Pleydell wrote later. 'The grumbles stopped and the men listened … it became one of those moments that remain intimately in the memory.'

The Tobruk raid was similarly disastrous leaving Stirling infuriated with himself and in particular the staff officers to whom he still referred to as 'fossilised shit'. Writing later of the Benghazi debacle Stirling commented: 'It was a sharp lesson which confirmed my previous views on the error of attacking strategical targets on a tactical scale.'[14]

Perhaps in part to placate Stirling, MEHQ promoted him to Lieutenant-Colonel and authorised the expansion of L Detachment to regimental status, 1 Special Air Service, comprising 29 officers and 572 other ranks in four squadrons: A, under the command of Major Paddy Mayne; B under Stirling; C, a French squadron; and D, a Special Boat Section.★

Stirling commissioned Mike Sadler and invited him to join B Squadron. Mayne, meanwhile, cherry-picked L Detachment's most seasoned veterans, among them Bill Fraser, Bob Lilley, Jimmy Storic and Chris O'Dowd. Sadler by now had had the chance to compare Stirling and Mayne in action, and the contrast he found fascinating: 'David was tall and slim, a much different build from Paddy,' he recalled.

I always thought of David as a stag hunter out on the moors but I felt that the great difference between him and Paddy on an operation was that Paddy was focused on the operation and knew everything that everybody was doing and where they were. David tended to be thinking ahead, 'Next time we'll need some other equipment and we could do it differently.' He was the strategic fellow, he had the ideas and was always thinking of improvements to make.

Paddy felt his true vocation in war; he was well suited to war and he enjoyed it. But he wasn't totally fearless. There's this slight impression that he wasn't at all

---

★ The SBS was renamed in January 1943 as the Special Boat Squadron, a separate entity from the SAS, and under the command of George Jellicoe.

Fred Senior (left) during his commando training on the Isle of Arran in 1940. Senior joined the SAS in 1942 and was killed in Tunisia in early 1943 while serving with B Squadron. (Author's Collection)

scared. He was well aware of the risks around at any particular moment – and I don't think he fancied the idea of being shot more than anyone else – but he had a very good control of himself.

As well as the old hands, Mayne welcomed several new officers to the SAS: the dapper Harry Poat, a tomato grower on Guernsey before the war, who was in Sadler's opinion a 'professional Englishman'; Tony Marsh, whose bonhomie and boyish good humour concealed a hard core, and Johnny Wiseman, a short, stocky bustling Yeomanry officer who amused and irritated Mayne in equal measure. 'He was an exceptional man, you don't meet many Paddys,' recalled Wiseman, who shared Mayne's love of rugby. 'But he was a very odd type, the kind of chap that gets thrown up in wars … in action you couldn't have a better man. Out of action he was a menace. I didn't provoke him purposely but I must have; I always talked too much.'[15]

In October Mayne led A Squadron 'up the Blue' where they operated out of a remote base in the Grand Sand Sea. For three weeks they harassed Axis forces between Tobruk and Matruh, cutting railways lines and attacking vehicle convoys prior to the commencement of the Eighth Army offensive at El Alamein. 'It was very nice living in the desert, very clean and agreeable,' recalled Wiseman. 'There were no inhabitants where we were. It was all a great adventure, I was young and glad to see some action.'

Mayne appeared to be enjoying himself, too, especially as the weather was cooler than it had been at the height of summer. In a letter to his brother he portrayed their life: 'We are in the Sand Sea about 200 miles from the nearest oasis and just going out and acting the fool from here.' He went on to describe how they had recently ambushed an enemy convoy, first disabling the trucks and then dispossessing the Italians of their valuables. 'I got another camera, a very nice little one, £15–£20 worth. I'll send you some photographs, not snaps. Funniest thing were the prisoners – we can never afford to take many, as they eat too much of our rations, so I intended only to take one. I put him on the truck and told the others to beat it, but he started to cry and the others looked so pitiable at being left that I took a couple more – they are useful at washing dishes and keeping my equipment clean.'[16]

With the start of the British Eighth Army's offensive at El Alamein, and the invasion of French North Africa by Anglo-American forces, the war in the desert was drawing to a climax with defeat inevitable for Rommel and his Italian allies. In mid November A Squadron established a new base at Bir Zelten, further west, and at the end of the month Stirling's B Squadron joined them. After a raucous reunion party, the two squadrons went their separate ways with Mayne's men shooting up retreating enemy transport between Sirte and Agheila, and B Squadron motoring west to attack targets close to the Libyan capital of Tripoli.

By January 1943 the Axis armies were trapped in a pincer by the Eighth Army advancing from the east and the First Army approaching through Tunisia. Stirling, despite B Squadron suffering several casualties during December's raids, secured permission from MEHQ for one final scheme before the end of the war in North Africa. It was typically audacious, but also impressively ambitious, particularly as Stirling was a physical wreck. Exhausted, plagued by desert sores and suffering frequent migraines, Stirling was motivated as much by securing a role for the SAS in the next phase of the war as by striking another blow at Rommel. There was also his tacit rivalry with Paddy Mayne, whose A Squadron had caused mayhem among the Germans in the run up to Christmas while incurring minimal losses. The biggest

This German transport column on the Agheila–Agedabia road, south of Benghazi, is under attack by an RAF Bristol Blenheim, but this route was also a favourite hunting ground for the SAS towards the end of 1942. (IWM CM 1439)

Five SAS veterans enjoy a cigarette on New Year's Eve 1942 prior to departing El Agheila to Kabrit. (L–R): Trooper Jeffs, Charlie Cattell, Bob Lilley, Malcolm Pleydell and Johnny Wiseman. (Author's Collection)

setback for A Squadron was arguably the capture of L Detachment original Jim Storie during a three-jeep patrol led by Lieutenant Bill MacDermot. The patrol was spotted by a Germany 88mm battery, which sent a salvo of armour-piercing shells towards the jeeps. Two of them escaped unscathed but Storie's vehicle was hit and the crew baled out expecting to be rescued by their comrades. 'The other jeeps were full of new lads and what they should have done is come right round and picked us up,' recalled Storie. 'But they didn't.'

For two days Stories and his men headed towards the coast in search of water and a vehicle with which to reach British lines. Using a compass disguised as a button on his trousers, Storie found the main coastal road but the first vehicle they encountered was a truck full of Luftwaffe personnel. At first the Germans assumed the ragtag bunch were Italians, but when they stopped to offer them a lift they realised they were British. 'We had nothing to identify us, no badges or anything and being in that part of the world they presumed we were shot down RAF men,' said Storie, who recalled that the Germans thankfully 'treated us like gentlemen.'

Stirling proposed to continue attacking the Germans as they retreated into Tunisia while also reconnoitring to see if Rommel was preparing to make a stand on the Mareth Line, a defensive wall from an earlier era of warfare. There was also the enticing prospect of being the first unit from the Eighth Army to link up with the First Army.

On 21 January, Stirling's patrol rendezvoused with Augustin Jordan and his 21 Frenchmen at Bir Soltane in central Tunisia. Word had just reached Stirling that Tripoli and Gafsa had fallen to the Allies and it was imperative they attack the Axis lines of communication between Sfax and Gabes forthwith. Jordan left at 1600 hours on the 21st for the Gabes Gap, a geographical bottleneck between the Tunisian salt-flats and the Mediterranean Sea. Stirling followed 12 hours later, his 14 men travelling in five jeeps.

They passed through the Gabes Gap at dusk on 23 January and early the next day were on the road to Gafsa. 'It was a lovely morning,' remembered Sadler, who was

Geoff Caton (left) and James McDiarmid on patrol in 1942. Caton was the only fatality during the landings at Cape Murro di Porco, shot as he moved forward to accept an Italian white flag. (Courtesy of the SAS Regimental Archive)

ABOVE
Jeff Du Vivier reads a letter from home in early 1943. (Author's Collection)

OPPOSITE TOP
Mayne took over command of the SAS following Stirling's capture, and though he lacked his predecessor's social tact in dealing with HQ staff, the Irishman led the regiment by example for the rest of the war. (Courtesy of the SAS Regimental Archive)

in the lead jeep alongside Johnny Cooper and the French interpreter called Freddie Taxis. 'We were driving in bright sunshine across farmers' dust fields until we got up into hilly terrain. There were some wadis running through the hills and we got into one of these.'

Once they'd dusted away their tracks and camouflaged the jeeps the men lay down to sleep. Cooper and Sadler were parked furthest up the wadi, their vehicle out of view from the rest of the patrol. 'They were down the wadi, 200 yards maybe,' said Sadler. 'There was a bend in the wadi so we weren't in their sights.' Cooper, Sadler and Taxis climbed into their sleeping bags and were soon fast asleep in the lee of their jeep. Sadler was woken some time later by the sound of heavy boots crunching up the wadi floor. He opened his eyes and 'got a nasty start looking up at two fellows … they motioned for us to lie down.'

The two Germans disappeared up the wadi in search of other prisoners and the moment they were out of sight Cooper, Sadler and Taxis leaped out of their sleeping bags and scrambled up and over the side of the wadi. 'It was a hard run up a hillside but luckily we managed to get into a little narrow gulley among some camel scrub,' remembered Sadler. 'We were absolutely knackered and just lay there.'

The Germans belonged to a company of Luftwaffe troops assigned to hunt down marauding Allied troops following a skirmish the previous day between Jordan's patrol, who escaped but was captured a few days later by Italian troops. Unlike Cooper, Sadler and Taxis, immediate escape was impossible for Stirling, though he did manage to bolt that evening, only to be recaptured the following day. Field Marshal Rommel was delighted when he heard the 'Phantom Major' had been caught. In a little over a year, Stirling's unit had destroyed 327 Axis aircraft, innumerable motorized vehicles and petrol dumps, and seriously disrupted his lines of communication. Writing to his wife at the start of February, Rommel explained that with Stirling's capture 'the British lost the very able and adaptable commander of the desert group which had caused us more damage than any other British unit of equal size'.

CHAPTER 4

THE SRS IN SICILY AND ITALY

In the same month that Rommel wrote to his wife crowing over the demise of Stirling, Malcolm Pleydell, the SAS medical officer, sent a letter to his girlfriend back in England: 'I arrived back yesterday to hear that David Stirling is missing, believed Prisoner of War. I suppose that doesn't convey much to you, but he is our commanding officer and there is no one with his flair and gift for projecting schemes. He ran the unit … so now the ship is without a rudder. There are only now three old operatives who remain from the time when I joined the unit, and it isn't the same by a long way. No longer the free and very easy camaraderie, but majors galore, sirs, salutes and parading for the men.'[1]

With Stirling gone the SAS was plunged into crisis but now Paddy Mayne rose to the challenge of leading the regiment in place of Stirling, overcoming his abhorrence of administration and controlling his contempt for staff officers. 1SAS was reorganised into the Special Raiding Squadron (SRS) and the Special Boat Squadron (SBS) under the overall command of HQ Raiding Forces. Jellicoe took the latter off to Athlit while on 21 March Mayne led his squadron to their new base at Azzib in Palestine.

Mayne divided his force of approximately 280 men into three troops. One troop was under the command of Bill Fraser, along with Mayne the only surviving officer of the seven who had joined L Detachment in the summer of 1941; Major Harry Poat was

OPPOSITE
When the SAS was restructured in the wake of Stirling's capture, George Jellicoe took the Special Boat Squadron (SBS) to this camp at Athlit in Palestine. (Courtesy of the SAS Regimental Archive)

Alex Muirhead (standing) and Peter Davis at the finish of the 45-mile march in Palestine, a test of endurance that was agony on most men's feet. (Author's Collection)

OC of Two Troop and Captain David Barnby was in charge of Three Troop (he was later replaced by Captain Ted Lepine). There were some notable absentees, however, including Mike Sadler who had been invalided back to Britain with severe stomach ulcers; Johnny Cooper, at Officer Cadet Training Units (OCTU) learning how to be an officer, and Jeff Du Vivier, who was in north-eastern Algeria helping to train recruits in the recently established 2SAS. It wasn't a task Du Vivier much enjoyed – particularly as the camp was fested with mosquitoes – but 2SAS required experienced instructors to whip the men into shape before they began operations in the Mediterranean.

As was his norm, Mayne divided opinion among the men under him. Lieutenant Peter Davis, a debonair young officer in Two Troop who had joined the SAS at the end of 1942, thought Mayne 'remarkable'; Alex Griffiths, a private in Three Troop, considered him a 'right sod who would RTU someone if their beret wasn't on properly'.[2]

Griffiths' resentment might have been fuelled in part by the training programme that Mayne devised in Palestine in the spring of 1943. 'For the first month every man in the regiment had to go through a second recruits' training,' remembered Peter Davis, 'and pass a test in all elementary subjects based on the standard T.O.E tests [Table of Organization and Equipment] before carrying on with the more advanced and more interesting training.'[3]

For men fresh from guerrilla warfare it was a pointless task but compared to what awaited them it was an unexacting chore. Mayne, recalled Davis, was determined to 'test the fitness of the men by making them march under conditions approximating to those of war, from the shores of Lake Tiberias, which was 600ft below sea-level, over the coastal hills and back to our camp by the sea.'

It was 45 miles in total, and Three Troop set off first under the glare of the midday sun. An error in navigation among the squadron's greenest recruits resulted in a costly detour and only eight of the 60 troops completed the course. Next up was One Troop and last to go was Two Troop, among whom was Private Sid Payne from Birmingham. 'We had 24 hours to do this march but it was across desert and over hills and back down again,' he recalled. 'I'd just had a pair of boots repaired and they were perfect, well broken in and comfortable, so I wore them. By the time I finished they'd completely split and the bottom was all away from the top. I think my Troop did the march in 23 hours but it was terrible.'[4]

As well as the physical training there was more specialised training. Each of the three troops was divided into two equal sub-sections, each under a corporal or lance-sergeant. These sub-sections were then further sub-divided into three-man squads of specialists: Bren gunners, riflemen and rifle bombers. In addition, each troop was assigned a mortar section, an engineers' section and a signallers' section.

Peter Davis was impressed with Mayne's organisation. 'Each sub-section was, on paper at least, a highly efficient little fighting unit, capable of providing its own support in many of the usual situations which one expects to meet in battle.'

By the end of June 1943 the SRS was preparing vigorously for an operation though they knew not where. This didn't prevent them rehearsing the attack in which One and Two Troops landed by assault craft on the south coast of a small foot-shaped peninsula about 400 yards from the gun battery situated almost on the toe. This was the squadron's objective, four powerful guns sited on the eastern side of a cluster of buildings. One Troop would launch a frontal attack on the battery with Two Troop swinging west and striking from the northern side. Three Troop, meanwhile, having landed half a mile to the west from One and Two Troops, would push inland and capture two farms on the road that led from the gun battery and which were believed to be an army barracks.

On 28 June the squadron was assembled on the deck of the *Ulster Monarch*, an erstwhile passenger ferry converted into a troopship, for an inspection by General Bernard Montgomery. Sid Payne remembered an incident that showed Mayne still had some way to go in emulating Stirling's social savoir-faire. 'Paddy introduced Montgomery to Graham Rose, our RSM [Regimental Sergeant-Major] and Monty ignored him. So Paddy grabbed hold of Monty and said "And this is my RSM!"'

After the inspection Montgomery addressed the SRS, informing them that they were in the vanguard of the operation and exhorting them to kill the enemy. It had been agreed beforehand that the squadron would desist from giving the general the customary cheer until he had reboarded his launch prior to visiting the next troopship. This caused some confusion on Montgomery's part with the general unsure if he should depart despite having heard no hurrah. Peter Davis looked on as Monty took his leave of the *Ulster Monarch* muttering to himself, 'Wonderful discipline, wonderful discipline! Very smart. I like their hats.'

Six days after Montgomery's inspection, on 4 July, the SRS sailed aboard the *Ulster Monarch* bound for Sicily. They now knew that the gun battery they must eliminate was located on Cape Murro di Porco (Cape of the Pig's Snout) on the south-east tip of the island. It was imperative it was destroyed without delay for a few hours sailing time behind the SRS came the main British invasion fleet, sitting ducks if the guns remained intact. 'Each man was left to his own thoughts and his own fears,' recalled Peter Davis as they neared the target. 'As we waited for the landing which was now so imminent, it was too easy to look at the group of faces we had come to know so well and to let the thought possess us that almost certainly there would be many we would never see again after the next few days had passed.'

Just after 0100 hours on 10 July, the three troops transferred from the *Ulster Monarch* to the Landing Craft Assault (known as LCAs, they were 40ft vessels capable of holding 35 soldiers). It was a hazardous procedure; the sea was running

Jeff Du Vivier (left) and Alex Muirhead (centre) in Nahariva, Palestine in May 1943. (Author's Collection)

high and the men were carrying up to 80lbs on their back with their Mae West life preservers further restricting their movement. Once inside the LCAs the soaked men lined up in three columns, two against the sides of the craft and one down the middle. Many of them were sea sick as they headed inland. 'Shivering, ill, and making full use of the cardboard buckets provided, we sat huddled in the sides of the boat,' remembered Davis, 'longing to have our feet again on firm land, no matter what lay then before us.'

As they neared the shore, the storm abated and shouts of desperate men drifted on the wind through the darkness. They were British airborne troops bound for the Ponte Grande bridge, south of Syracuse, whose gliders had fallen well short of their target and were now all about invisible in the water save for the small red lights that shone on their flimsy life preservers.

Some LCA pilots refused to stop for the stranded paratroopers, insisting that they had to adhere to the timetable. 'It was terrible to hear their cries as we went past,' remembered Alex Griffiths. 'And we could hear too what some of them were calling us.' The pilot of Sid Payne's LCA stopped to rescue half a dozen airborne troops clinging to the broken wing of a glider, and Johnny Wiseman ordered his pilot to collect whatever men they saw, one of whom turned out to be Brigadier Philip Hicks, the commander of the airborne force. 'I said to him "look, old boy, I can take you into the beach but you'll have to keep out of my line because I've got a job to do".'[5]

Wiseman, in Bill Fraser's One Troop, was tasked with leading the frontal assault on the gun battery. Once ashore he and his men moved towards the battery as Captain Alex Muirhead's mortar section rained bombs on the Italian gunners. They snipped through the barbed wire undetected and waited for the mortar fire to cease. The moment it did Wiseman struck, attacking the Italian positions with stunning ferocity. Within minutes the SRS had captured or killed 40 of the enemy without sustaining any losses themselves. Wiseman was subsequently awarded a Military Cross for his courage and leadership. 'We landed, got up the cliff and the area where the gun had barbed wire round it and I got there first and we cut the wire,' recalled Wiseman. 'I thought it might be mined but it wasn't so we went through a gap I'd cut in the wire and my troop took the first gun without any bother … they were Italians, which made life a bit easier and they gave in very easily.'

As dawn broke Sergeant Bill Deakins and his engineers section began preparing the charges to blow the four guns. Meanwhile One and Two Troops started to 'mop up', searching buildings and dugouts for stray Italians. They were dismayed by what they found: 'Some of our lads were busy round the entrance to a deep air-raid shelter from which certain signs of life had been detected,' recalled Peter Davis.

THE SRS AND THE ULSTER MONARCH

ABOVE
The *Ulster Monarch*, a former passenger ferry between Belfast and Liverpool, transported the SRS throughout their operations in Sicily and Italy. (Courtesy of the SAS Regimental Archive)

RIGHT
General Montgomery addresses the SRS aboard the *Ulster Monarch*. The men were ambivalent towards 'Monty' while in turn, he admired their hats! (Courtesy of the SAS Regimental Archive)

After repeated threats and exhortations, accompanied by some forceful persuasions with small-arms fire and grenades, they succeeded in extracting the occupants. They were a sorry sight. The men came out grinning sheepishly, and obviously glad that they had been left alive. Many were considerably shaken, and some wounded. But what really surprised us was the fact that down in that dugout were also women and children. They were a poor lot: dirty, shabby and ill-equipped, ingratiating and fawning, they formed a startling contrast to the mental picture we had formed of the tough, experienced and fanatically patriotic defenders we had expected to meet.

Engineers from the SRS inspect one of the captured coastal guns at Cape Murro di Porco shortly before its demolition. (Author's Collection)

At 0520 hours Bill Deakins reported to Paddy Mayne that the guns had been blown and the Irishman fired a green star rocket into the grey sky to signal to the invasion fleet that the coast was clear. 'Shortly afterwards the great fleet, just visible on the horizon, began to steam towards the shore,' recalled Davis. 'We watched them with pride, for we realised that it was only by our achievements that they were now able to approach so close to the land.'

The raiders slumped down in the lee of the rocks to watch the fleet arrive, enjoying the warmth of the early morning sun on their tired bodies. Suddenly, recounted Davis, 'we were roused by a sharp explosion from inland, which interrupted our peaceful reverie in the rudest way'. Several more thumping detonations followed and out to sea, a short distance in front of the approaching

The SRS captured over 500 Italians during their successful seizure of the guns at Cape Murro di Porco, among whom were this sorry but relieved-looking bunch. (IWM A 17966)

invasion fleet, the SRS saw fountains of foam erupt. 'At once we realised that another coastal battery, a mile or two inland, had started to engage our shipping,' said Davis.

Mayne reacted with his customary alacrity, instructing One and Two Troops to march their 200 prisoners towards the farm seized by Three Troop, in which the squadron's HQ was established. One and Two Troops then advanced inland at 0600 hours towards the battery approximately 2½ miles north-west, encountering sporadic pockets of resistance along the way. Reg Seekings's section happened upon a group of Italian soldiers waving a white flag but as they approached the men fell flat and a machine gun opened fire from a nearby pillbox. Geoff Caton, a 22-year-old who had been with Mayne in the commandos, was mortally wounded. Enraged, Seekings charged the pillbox and killed all within, an act for which he was awarded the Military Medal to go with the Distinguished Conduct Medal (DCM) he'd already won in the desert. 'Battle and fighting more or less face to face can be a bloody terrifying prospect for some people,' recalled Seekings. 'I was good at it and I suppose to a certain extent I enjoyed it, but it's not everyone's cup of tea… I enjoyed the killing, I used to fret if a job was cancelled and I enjoyed the adrenaline rush. I was scared but I would have gone into action every day if I could.'[6]

Once the second battery was located, Muirhead's mortars subjected it to a heavy pounding and then Two Troop attacked. Peter Davis remembered it as a very 'light-hearted affair' with the men soon realising they were up against a poorly trained and ill-disciplined enemy who had trouble shooting straight. 'After a time the lads began to take this situation for granted,' he described, 'and would deliberately expose themselves in order to draw the fire of the panic-stricken Italians, and thereby to learn their exact position. Nonchalantly chewing pieces of grass, or sucking at the small orange tomatoes growing in profusion all around, our sections pressed forward.'

When Two Troop stormed the battery they found the Italians waiting for them, arms in the air, grinning from ear to ear. 'Such was our first morning on Sicily and for many of us the first taste of action,' said Davis, 'and a very pleasant form of fighting it was!'

Geoff Caton was the only fatality of the SRS operation to eliminate the batteries. In return they had killed approximately 150 Italians and captured 500, including the commandant. The squadron spent the day in repose; some slept, others gorged on tomatoes and nuts, one or two fraternised with the local women.

On the morning of 12 July the squadron moved down into Syracuse harbour and some local boats ferried them out to the *Ulster Monarch*. While the men showered and ate, the officers were briefed on their next job, a landing at Augusta.

Augusta was an important naval port 11 miles north of Syracuse that the Eighth Army wanted as a platform from which to push north. Built on a spit of land attached to the mainland by bridge, the centrepiece of Augusta was its vast brick citadel that commanded imposing views of the port and surrounding countryside. Intelligence reports stated that a white flag had been seen from the citadel and it was the task of the SRS to go ashore and ensure that the port was safe for a large-scale landing.

'We watched them with pride, for we realised that it was only by our achievements that they were now able to approach so close to the land.'

Peter Davis

Mayne briefed his officers on the operation: the *Ulster Monarch* would land them in the port and Three Troop would disembark first, heading with all speed across the bridge and to the railway station. Once the station was secure they would push on to a crossroads a mile outside Augusta until joined by the vanguard of 17 Brigade. One and Two Troops would ensure that the citadel and town was indeed clear of enemy troops. As speed was of the essence, and bearing in mind the port was reportedly deserted, the operation would commence in daylight at 1930 hours.

As the *Ulster Monarch* approached Augusta, escorted by the Royal Navy destroyers, *Kanaris*, *Nubian* and *Tetcott*, it encountered the cruiser HMS *Mauritius*. Davis was later told that the conversation between the two captains ran along the following lines:

> For the attack on the Coastal Battery 183239 on
> Cape Murro di Porco on 10th July 1943, Lieut. John Wiseman
> D.C.L.I., had command of the leading section of the forward
> Troop.
>
> While the battery was under fire from our mortars,
> by clever use of ground, he led his section to the outskirts
> of the position without being detected and made his way
> through the wire.   Immedediately the mortar fire finished
> he went straight in, acheiving complete surprise, killing,
> capturing and wounding forty of the enemy.   By his good
> leadership and control he acheived this without sustaining
> a single casualty to his section.   Although the darkness
> of the night made control difficult, he maintained complete
> command, and the information which he sent back was invaluable
> to the proper conduct of the operation.
>
> For his determination, initative, leadership and
> personal bravery, he is reccommended for a Military Cross.
>
> 　　　　　　　　　　　　R.B. Mayne. Major.,
> 　　　　　　　　　Commanding Special Raiding Squadron,
> 　　　　　　　　　　　　　　　1st S.A.S. Regt.
>
> Field.
> 24/7/43.

Mauritius: '*Ulster Monarch*, what the hell are you doing here?'

Monarch: 'I am about to land troops in Augusta.'

Mauritius: 'Advise against carrying out operations. Enemy strength unknown.'

Monarch: 'I intend carrying out my orders and landing troops in Augusta as planned.'

Mauritius: 'In that case, is there anything we can do to help?'

Monarch: 'Yes. Follow along and support us if and when necessary.'

The skipper of the *Mauritius* also informed the *Monarch* that he had on board Rear
Admiral Thomas Troubridge, Flag Officer Commanding Overseas Assault Forces,
who had been heading to Augusta earlier in the day on HMS *Eskimo* when the ship
came under fire from batteries located in the hills overlooking Augusta. Nineteen
sailors were killed, 22 wounded and the *Eskimo* sustained severe structural damage.
After consultation with the captain of the *Ulster Monarch*, Paddy Mayne informed
his men that they would land in the LCAs in two waves – One and Three Troops
first and then Two Troop and Alex Muirhead's mortar section in the second wave.
Once ashore the objectives were the same.

Signaller David Danger remembered that before the landings at Augusta, the SRS were offered Benzedrine pills, what the men called 'stay awake pills'. 'We were told they would give us some verve,' he said. 'It was an entirely voluntary thing. Some boys took them but I didn't because I've never liked taking pills or any form of medication.'[7]

In the hills above Augusta the men of the Schmatz Battle Group of the Hermann Goering Division observed the first wave of SRS soldiers transferring from the *Monarch* to the LCAs. As the first shells began to fall into the sea the *Monarch* and the *Tetcott* both retaliated. The captain of the *Tetcott*, Lieutenant Commander Richard Rycroft, described his vessel's role in his official report on the landing:

At 19:25 *Ulster Monarch* lowered her assault craft and a light high velocity gun opened fire from the ridge overlooking Augusta. It gave its position away by the smoke and I opened fire with 4-inch which quickly silenced it. There was also some machine gun fire from some cement works near the shore and I proceeded to close as near as prudent – about three cables [a unit of length approximately 600ft] – and blasted the place with 4-inch, pom-pom and Oerlikon. The effect was terrific, especially as first HHMS *Kanaris* and later HMS *Nubian* joined in. One gun however went on firing for some minutes, shifting his fire from the assault craft to the ships, but he hit nothing. I also searched some vineyards with 4-inch to discourage any enemy who might still be lurking in them. A two-gun light howitzer battery also opened fire, apparently with no spotting or organised control. He did no damage but I was quite unable to spot where it was firing from.[8]

HMS *Tetcott*, with the *Ulster Monarch* alongside, engages shore batteries at Augusta as the SRS head towards the harbour in their landing craft. Despite the daylight operation casualties were mercifully light. (IWM A 18089)

'We could hear rounds thudding into the landing craft and the whoosh of shells exploding in the water all around,' said Albert Youngman of Three Troop as the LCAs neared Augusta.[9] The moment the doors opened, the men dashed forward, splashing through the water with their weapons held above their heads. They came under immediate small-arms fire. Stretcher bearer George Shaw was hit as he tended to a wounded man and Arthur Thomson's pal Dougie Eccles was shot in the leg. 'Blood everywhere,' remembered Thomson. 'You didn't want to leave your mates, but it was instilled into you: keep going and finish the job no matter what. So I told him help was coming and pressed on.'[10]

As Three Troop advanced over the bridge and towards the railway station, Two Troop and the mortar section began the hazardous voyage across the sea. '[Billy] Stalker, one of my riflemen, is lodged in the bows, firmly gripping a pair of Vickers light machine guns, ready to reply to any fire which might be directed at us from the area towards which we are heading,' remembered Davis. 'We hug the bottom of the boat as we distinguish the vicious whistle of small arms bullets flying overhead.'

But it was obvious to Davis and his men that the incoming fire was from the other side of the bay and not where they were headed. Nevertheless Billy Stalker fired a burst from the Vickers at the waterfront just in case. Just as Davis began to wonder when they would reach land, he felt a gentle bump and saw the doors open. 'We find ourselves leaping into about two feet of water. As we stumbled over the slippery rocks, bullets chip into the ground around us and someone from the previous wave yells at us to get into single file and out of the beach area which is under heavy fire from the machine guns across the bay. Bent low, we double through a small gap to find ourselves in a narrow street, sheltered temporarily at least, from the watching eyes across the water.'

Further inland Three Troop had secured the railway station and now sections were advancing down the line towards the crossroads on the outskirts of Augusta. Albert Youngman's section, led by Ted Lepine, passed a file of men in the dark on the other side of a dry-stone wall. For a moment they presumed they were a returning SRS patrol, then they realised they were Germans. A Bren gunner called 'Snowy' Kirk opened fire first and the rest of his section followed. After checking the Germans were all dead, Youngman helped himself to a Schmeisser sub-machine gun and a Luger pistol.

The firing alerted the German defenders dug in at the crossroads and soon machine-gun fire and 4in mortar bombs were being sent the way of Three Troop. 'They were good troops, those Germans,' reflected Youngman. 'A lot different from [the Italians at] Murro di Porco.'

Joe Goldsmith (right), better known as 'Buttercup', takes a break during the fighting for Augusta. (Author's Collection)

Mayne withdrew Three Troop under the covering fire of Alex Muirhead's mortar section and sent a messenger to summon Davis and Derrick Harrison, another Two Troop officer, to a briefing behind a smouldering house. Davis arrived to find Mayne and Harry Poat acting with their usual 'rock-like coolness'. Neither appeared fazed by the German resistance as they issued instructions for Two Troop to move up in support of Three Troop.

As Two Troop began to move across the bridge another order came through from Mayne – fall back and take up strong defensive positions around the citadel, it appeared the Germans might be massing for a counter-attack involving tanks. Davis positioned his 20-man section among the turrets and archways of the citadel, which to him resembled a cross between a fortress and a monastery (the castle was built in the 13th century and served as a prison for many years). For several hours the SRS strained their eyes and ears for the enemy but the darkness revealed nothing. 'Suddenly, at about four in the morning, we sat up with a jerk,' recalled Davis. 'Again we caught the faint sound – tanks moving along the road. The noise reached us in waves, sometimes loud and sometimes almost inaudible according to the vagaries of the mind.'

The party that followed the seizure of Augusta involved a pianola (seen here) and plenty of booze as the men from SRS celebrated in style. (Author's Collection)

The men braced themselves for an attack but no attack came, and then they realised the sounds were growing more distant. At dawn Harry Poat appeared and informed Davis that the Germans had withdrawn and advance elements of 17 Brigade were already ashore and pushing inland; the SRS's task was complete.

Mayne moved among his men praising them for their conduct during a difficult and uncertain operation in which two of their number had been killed and six wounded. Then he told them to go and enjoy themselves for a few hours. The men did as instructed, descending on the deserted town and drinking the place dry. 'We spent the remainder of that day until late in the afternoon wandering around the town, entering any building we chose, and making deep inroads into the town's alcoholic beverages,' recalled Davis.

When the infantrymen of 17 Brigade began marching through Augusta, the SRS had pushed a pianola into the town square and were staging an impromptu concert party. 'I went into one bar and there was one of our officers, [Major Richard] Lea, I think, holding a bottle of champagne,' recalled Sid Payne. 'He said "Come and have a drink", and knocked the top off the bottle on a table and we had a drink together.' Other members of the squadron carried crates of champagne to the quayside and did a roaring trade selling bottles to the sailors.

Officers of 17 Brigade weren't happy with what they saw unfolding but when they demanded to know the officer in command, merry members of the SRS pointed to the giant figure of Paddy Mayne 'pushing a pram along the street full of booze'. Even the squadron's padre, Ronnie Lunt, spirited away a few bottles of wine, though as he told the men with a smile, they were purely for the purposes of communion.

___

On 17 August General Alexander, the Allied Deputy Commander-in-Chief, cabled Winston Churchill to inform him that 'the last German soldier was flung out of Sicily'.[11] Next stop was the Italian mainland itself. By this time the SRS were encamped at Cannizzaro, south-east of Mount Etna. Mayne had his men march up and down the volcano to keep them in shape for their next operation. The average time taken by the men was two and a half hours; Mayne did it in two. On 1 September they broke camp.

Three days later, on 4 September, the squadron landed in the darkness at Bagnara in southern Italy, a coastal town at the foot of a steep terraced hillside on which were scores of vines. The main British landings were occurring at Reggio, 11 miles south, and the job of the SRS was to secure Bagnara and the road that led from the town up to the plateau far above.

Harry Poat (front row, third from right) with Derrick Harrison to his left pose with some of the boys from Two Troop after operations in Sicily. Sid Payne is second left in the back row. (Author's Collection)

As the squadron approached the long stretch of sandy beach there was no incoming fire from the town or hillside. It was ominously quiet. Some of the men reckoned the beach must be mined. 'When we hit the beach the first man off was Paddy Mayne,' remembered Alex Griffiths. 'We were all thinking about mines but he walked right up the sandy beach with the rest of us all trying to get behind him. He might not have been a particularly nice fellow, but as a soldier he was the greatest.' Mayne soon realised they had been landed on the wrong beach, the northern beach instead of the southern one, though it later emerged that this was an unintended stroke of good fortune as the southern beach had indeed been heavily mined by the Germans.

Once ashore, Two Troop advanced inland to secure a bridge and One Troop moved through the town to seal off the Northern approaches to Bagnara. Three Troop, meanwhile, headed south to seize the roads and railways. Albert Youngman remembered approaching with caution a railway tunnel cut into the hillside only to discover scores of frightened civilians cowering inside.

As dawn broke over Bagnara, Peter Davis led his section over the bridge and past Tony Marsh and his men who were taking up defensive positions. Bringing up the rear of Two Troop was Derrick Harrison's section, among whom was Sid Payne, the last man but one as they moved in Indian file through the town in their rubber-soled boots. 'The chappie behind me tapped me on the shoulder,' recalled Payne, 'and pointed to his ear, then down the road. I could hear marching. So I tapped the bloke in front of me and signalled to him, and we all spread out on the road and round this bend came the first ranks of this column of Germans, carrying their rifles at ease.'

The Germans were engineers, recently arrived with orders to blow Bagnara's bridge to hinder the British invasion force at Reggio. They had no idea the enemy had beaten them to their objective. 'They got quite a surprise,' remembered Payne. 'They weren't even looking in our direction and we began laying it down. It was like being at the funfair when we opened fire.'

The few Germans who weren't killed in the initial fusillade fled back into the town and gladly surrendered to Pat Riley and his section of One Troop; their comrades dug in on the hillside rushed to their positions and began firing on the enemy that had landed without their noticing.

A cluster of mortar bombs landed close to where Bill Fraser had established his Troop HQ, killing two of his signallers, Charlie Richards and William Howell. Further down the road a tracer bullet clipped Harry Poat's trouser leg and killed Thomas Parris coming up behind. The maps in Poat's pocket caught fire but he continued to issue orders as he calmly patted out the flames. 'Poat was a smashing bloke and completely unflappable,' recalled Sid Payne.

Poat instructed Davis to move further up the hillside and take up defensive positions on one of the many hairpin bends in case the Germans launched a counter-attack. Davis led his section up the winding road, a sheer rocky cliff-face to their right and on their left the terraced hillside. They rounded a bend and Davis cursed at the sight of the straight road that stretched ahead 300 yards. 'It was indeed an unpleasant position in which to be caught if they should open on us,' said Davis. 'Our only hope was to press on round the next bend in the hope that there the lay of the ground would be in our favour.'

They were midway along the road when a flurry of mortar bombs fell on the road, landing slap bang between Davis and his lead section and the section led by Corporal Bill Mitchell 30 yards to the rear. As the smoke cleared a German machine gun opened up. Mitchell withdrew his section back down the road; Davis screamed at his 12 men to advance.

'We doubled like mad things down that road in a vain search for cover from those murderous eyes on the hillside above,' he said. 'We rounded a slight right-hand bend as the bullets started to chip into the asphalt beside us, our pleading eyes frantically searching for some trace of cover. And there, barely fifty yards ahead, was the most

Sandy Wilson (front row, centre) and some of his troop enjoy a spot of rest in between operations in Sicily and Italy. Wilson was one of 21 SRS men killed during the fierce fighting for Termoli. (Author's Collection)

The winding road at the top of this aerial reconnaissance photo of Bagnara is where Peter Davis's section was ambushed. (Courtesy of the SAS Regimental Archive)

wonderful sight we could wish for. It was a small one-roomed peasant cottage on the left side of the road.'

Once inside the cottage Davis realised that they were temporarily out of harm's way, but still horribly exposed to the well-camouflaged Germans positions visible from the window. They were dug in 200 yards ahead, at a point where the road crossed a deep gully and doubled back to the left at a sharp angle, affording them views of the town and the hillside road. Davis was sure the cottage would come under mortar attack but none fell, leading him to suppose they were either out of sight of the mortar observation post or they were too close to permit accurate fire. Knowing they had the men trapped in the cottage, the Germans turned their attention back to Bagnara, mortaring it at regular intervals and sending the occasional burst of machine-gun fire on to the road to deter Bill Mitchell's section from trying to reach their trapped comrades. On one occasion, Mitchell's section set out for the cottage but were forced back by a shower of mortar bombs that wounded several of their number.

Meanwhile Davis and his men made themselves comfortable in the cottage. 'We sat up in the brilliant sunshine of that cloudless Autumn morning and commenced eating our breakfast from the tiny ration packs we had brought with us,' said Davis. 'It is true to say that we were lulled into a sense of security by the gentle rustle of the vine leaves in the morning breeze, and by the rich, clean smell of the grapes.'

As the morning passed and the Germans sent no more fire the way of the cottage Davis formulated an escape plan. Accompanied by Sergeant Andy Storey and Private Charlie Tobin, he would dash for a culvert 15 yards away. Once safely inside they would crawl back down the road until they were out of sight of the German machine guns. The remaining men would follow in pairs at regular intervals.

As the three men prepared to rush from the door, Davis turned to Lance Sergeant Bill McNinch and issued some last-minute instructions. Storey and Tobin stepped out of the cottage and into a burst of fire from a German machine gun. Tobin was killed instantly, Storey ducked back inside unharmed. Another machine gun opened up, and another, and for several minutes the men huddled against the wall in the face of the firestorm. Then the firing stopped and the enemy reverted once more to attacking the town below.

Reg Seekings (second left) and men of One Troop shelter behind a wall on the road out of Bagnara. (Author's Collection)

Most of the shells fired by the Germans dropped harmlessly on Bagnara. The rest of Two Troop was dug in among the vine terraces, while Three Troop were still checking the tunnels for any Germans. Alex Griffiths rounded up a couple of engineers from the earlier ambush and marched them to the SRS HQ. 'These Germans were starving, poor sods, asking me the whole time for food,' he said. 'I didn't have any to give them but one of our lads gave them some biscuits and that made them happy. We didn't really need to guard them, they had no intention of escaping.'

Davis and his section remained in the cottage until dark. Then, slowly and silently, they crawled out one by one, Davis stopping to examine Tobin's body and remove his rifle and personal belongings. Back in Bagnara they were greeted warmly by comrades who had given them up for dead. After some food and a debrief, Davis wrapped himself in an old blanket and tried to rest. 'But it was a long time before sleep eventually came,' he remembered. 'Again and again I would hear dinning through my ears that murderous burst of fire which had sent Tobin to his death.' Early the next morning the British 15 Brigade began pouring into Bagnara; then a cruiser appeared and shelled the Germans on the hillside. By dusk on 5 September the Germans had fled and the SRS could move through the town without fear of molestation. Peter Davis sought out one of the men in Bill Mitchell's sub-section, Bob Lowson, and together they walked up the hillside to bury Charlie Tobin. 'Charlie was my best pal,' recalled Lowson. 'We'd been in the Middle East Commando together and joined the SAS at the same time. A great Irishman who loved his cards.'[12] Lowson and Davis buried Tobin behind the cottage in which he'd sought sanctuary. 'When I got back down the lads were all asleep on the railway station,' recalled Lowson. 'In the corner was an Italian local with a little squeeze box playing "Amapola". I could have bloody cried.'

The Special Raiding Squadron were resting in billets at Gallico, a short distance from Bagnara, when they learned of the Italian armistice on 8 September. A few days later Sergeant-Major Graham Rose sat down to write to the families of the five men killed during the recent operation. To John and Eve Howell, parents of William Kitchener, he wrote:

It is with great regret and my deepest sympathy that I have to inform you of the death in action of your son, William Kitchener. As his squadron sergeant major I feel it is my duty to write and tell you of the manner in which he met his death and of how much he will be missed by his comrades in this unit. 'Bill', as he was known to us all, came to the squadron some time in May as a troop signaller. At that time we were training hard for a big operation and your son worked well and hard, soon becoming a valuable addition to the squadron… It was during the

OPPOSITE
Charlie Tobin (left) and Bob Lowson (foreground) were best mates and founder members of the SAS card school. Lowson helped bury Tobin after his death at Bagnara. (Author's Collection)

invasion of Italy that he met his untimely end but I can assure you, in the hope that it will bring you some small comfort, that he passed away quietly and without pain. Your great loss is shared by the entire squadron. Bill was more than liked by the boys and many is the time that I have listened and laughed at his imitations of Maurice Chevalier. Always smiling, always ready to help anyone at any time, he leaves a gap in the ranks that can never be filled.

His personal effects will be forwarded to you at our earliest convenience together with the unit badge which is inscribed 'Who Dares Wins'. I pass on to you the condolences and sympathy of his commanding officer, officers and other ranks in this moment of your great bereavement. We pay homage to the memory of a brave soldier and a gentleman.

I beg to remain, yours sincerely, Graham Rose.[13]

There would be many more letters of condolences written by Sergeant-Major Rose the following month, after the SRS's landing at Termoli, an Adriatic Sea port 20 miles above the spur of Italy's boot. Of the 207 men who landed at Termoli early on the morning of 3 October, 21 were killed, 24 wounded and 23 taken prisoner.

Yet initially the operation – codenamed *Devon* – had started well with the SRS, along with 3 Commando and 40 Royal Marine Commando securing Termoli without incurring heavy casualties. The only setback had been the capture of Lieutenant John Tonkin's section as they pushed inland to seize one of two bridges over the Biferno River until relieved by the 78th Infantry Division. So quickly had they advanced that they found themselves overtaking the retreating Germans – elements of the 1st Parachute Division belonging to the Battle Group Rau. 'When daylight came I saw lots of Germans and I remember thinking "Cor, look at all those prisoners those blokes have got!"' recalled Alex Griffiths. 'Then all of a sudden they opened fire and we were taken prisoner. They disarmed us and we wandered along with them feeling pretty fed up.'

By sundown on 3 October, most of the SRS was billeted in Termoli having accomplished their task in securing the town for the 78th Division. With Termoli in Allied hands the road that led from the port to Campobasso, approximately 40 miles south, would expedite the Fifth Army's progress to Naples on the west of Italy despite the fact that two road bridges over the Biferno River had been blown by the enemy. For the cost of one dead, the SRS had killed or wounded 40 Germans and taken a further 39 prisoner.

The Germans had been taken completely by surprise and their High Command was stunned when, at 1030hrs on 3 October, a despatch rider arrived at Palata (12 miles south-west) bearing the bad news of the Allied landings. Recriminations

An olive grove provides some shelter for the SRS during Operation *Devon*. Though the coastal town was taken without problem, the Germans on the hills above offered stubborn resistance for 24 hours. (Courtesy of the SAS Regimental Archive)

quickly followed as more bedraggled survivors retreated from Termoli. It was suggested that the 1st Parachute Division were too drunk to counter the invasion, accusations vehemently denied by Ritter von Pohl, the most senior officer to escape. However, Von Pohl did concede that a detachment of engineers garrisoned in Termoli had been prone to excessive drinking and this might have been a contributory factor to the port's rapid seizure.

Von Pohl estimated that the enemy force comprised 'about 1,000 men' and were 'mainly paratroopers with no heavy weapons'.[14] Emboldened by Von Pohl's report, the Germans began to organise a counter-attack to regain Termoli.

The only SRS section to pass the first night outside the town was that of Peter Davis. They had pushed south-west after the initial landing before withdrawing to a barn three miles outside the town. A pleasing sight greeted Davis when the sun rose on the morning of 4 October. 'The coastal road was covered by a stream of transport pushing beyond us to the north west,' he recalled. 'The main forces [78th Division] had linked up with us and our part in the operation was now over.' One of Davis's men

Tommy Corps next to a German half-track and its former occupants, one of a number of vehicles ambushed by One Troop at Termoli. (Author's Collection)

commented that it was the easiest operation he'd ever experienced, to which another replied: 'If they were all like this one I wouldn't mind becoming a professional soldier!'

Davis's section arrived back in Termoli to much ribbing from their comrades, who described in detail how they'd spent the night in a monastery just off the main square with warm food and even a billiard table for entertainment. Davis had just made himself comfortable when Paddy Mayne appeared. 'Paddy came up to me to enquire whether I had heard anything of a powerful counter-attack which, according to rumour, the Germans had already started to set in motion.'

Davis mentioned the odd shell that had dropped their way during their return from the barn but he'd seen no sign of any Germans massing for a counter-attack. Mayne decided nonetheless to augment the town's defences – manned now by the 11th Infantry Brigade – with the sections belonging to Tony Marsh and Derrick Harrison. They were set to work digging defensive positions along an eastern ridge at Torrente Sinarca, along with a section from One Troop under Sandy Wilson, sent instead of Marsh's men, whom Mayne allowed to recuperate.

At dawn on 5 October the German counter-attack began. Tanks and hundreds of troops from the 16th Panzer Division (belonging to the Battle Group Stempel) advanced from the south, past the barn in which Davis's section had sheltered the previous night.

The 11th Infantry Bridge fell back in disarray, leaving the commandos and SRS to repel the onslaught. Tony Marsh's section of Two Troop engaged in a fierce firefight on their left flank and despite being heavily outnumbered the accuracy of their fire compelled the Germans to withdraw.

But elsewhere the Germans were pushing ever closer to Termoli. Shells began dropping into the town centre and at 1330 hours the Special Service Brigade HQ received a direct hit killing Captain Lincoln Leese. An hour later Mayne was instructed to send whatever men he had in reserve up to the front line to try and stem the German advance. Johnny Wiseman's One Troop began to pile into one of the five trucks parked in a side street between a building and a public garden. 'I put my fellows on a truck and said "right, we're going up the coast",' recalled Wiseman. 'Then at that moment I saw the colonel's [Mayne's] messenger coming to speak to me so I got out of the front of the truck to speak to him, and a shell dropped on the truck. He [the messenger] disappeared, my driver was dead and everyone on the truck was either wounded or dead. I'd lost my whole troop with that one shell. I was just talking to the messenger and he disappeared on the telegraph wires above my head. Crazy.'

The 105mm shell that destroyed Wiseman's troop was one of five that landed in the side street, directed by a German observation post in a nearby church tower. An Italian family that had come to wish the British luck were caught in the maelstrom, and the young son of the obliterated parents was left writhing in agony with his innards hanging out. Reg Seekings shot him, saying later: 'You couldn't let anyone suffer like that.'

Seekings had been fastening up the tailboard when the bomb dropped on the middle of the truck, killing 18 of his comrades. Miraculously all the damage he sustained was a split fingernail. As Seekings began to sift through the carnage he was joined by Peter Davis and his section, emerging through a thick cloud of dust having leapt into the public garden at the sound of the incoming shells. 'The truck had virtually disappeared, merely a twisted and shattered hulk remaining,' recalled Davis.

Around it and upon it lay ghastly morsels of burnt and shattered flesh, which was all what remained of twenty sound and living young bodies ... most of the casualties were mercifully dead, literally blown to pieces, while the wounded were a ghastly sight, such as to make hardened veterans turn pale and vomit feebly... I went out with four men to see if we could render any assistance but the sight I witnessed was too much for me, and with stomach writhing I perforce had to quit the scene. For here lay a man with half his head blown off, an arm lay there, and somewhere else an unrecognisable lump of flesh. In the back of the truck, over its

Tony Marsh (left) and Harry Poat (third from left) were two of the most popular and respected officers in the SAS, both proving their worth in Italy. (Courtesy of the SAS Regimental Archive)

sides and scattered over the street, lay the dead, blown into unrecognisable fragments, a horrible and bloody carnage.

Mayne took the news of the catastrophe without a word, merely attaching Wiseman and Seekings to HQ squadron and ordering Davis's section to reinforce the left flank. Over on the right (eastern) flank, Harry Poat was marshalling his troops along the ridge at Torrente Sinarca overlooking the railway line. During the afternoon the 78th Division had brought up a Bofors gun and six anti-tank guns but when 11 German tanks appeared in the early evening, the British gunners turned and ran. Poat was incensed and later, on seeing an officer of the 78th Division, asked what the divisional shoulder flash depicted. A battleaxe, he was told; 'It should be a knitting needle,' replied Poat with a cold smile.[15]

Not all of the 78th Division were running scared. A detachment of Kensingtons fought alongside the men of 3 Commando in an olive grove, beating back one German assault after another. Meanwhile Tony Marsh, the fun-loving captain who had once accidently burned down an officers' mess, was inspiring the men of Two Troop with his cool determination in the midst of a furious barrage of mortar bombs. The citation for the DSO Marsh subsequently won at Termoli praised 'his high standard of courage and complete disregard for personal safety … in saving a very dangerous situation.'[16] After each mortar bombardment, the German infantry attacked, only to be repelled, prompting another salvo of mortar bombs. Throughout the afternoon and early evening, Marsh and his men stood firm with the captain repeatedly exposing himself to enemy fire in order to help Alex Muirhead sight his mortars.

At one point in the afternoon two of the SRS signallers were despatched to the front line with food and ammunition for their comrades. 'We were on our way back when we came under fire,' recalled David Danger. 'So me and another chap took shelter in a ruined house as these shells screamed over. Suddenly a donkey put its head through a hole in the wall and brayed loudly. We jumped out of our skins. I felt sorry for the poor old thing, he was just looking for a bit of companionship.'

At dusk on 5 October Termoli was in grave danger of being retaken by the Germans, but instead of pressing the attack throughout the hours of darkness the enemy withdrew for the night. The SRS war diary later noted that: 'It seemed as if their troops were without the morale to advance far (again for fear of being cut off) and the attack was abandoned when the threat to the town was greatest.'[17]

Smoke pours from a German lorry, one of several vehicles ambushed by One Troop during the initial landing at Termoli on 3 October. (Author's Collection)

The Germans were indeed exhausted by sunset on the 5th. Despite bringing up a reconnaissance battalion to reinforce the Battle Group Stempel they had been unable to make any headway because – as a report later noted – of 'stiff resistance from enemy units dug into the clefts and ravines which lay between the Sinarca (valley) and Termoli'. That evening the 10th Army chief of staff telephoned the divisional operations officer of the 16 Panzer Division to ask if he thought they would prevail; the officer replied that though they were just 1.5km south-west of the port 'they were having a hard struggle as Termoli was built on high ground which gave the enemy observation of the approach routes'.[18]

By dawn the next day four Sherman tanks of the 38th Irish Brigade appeared through a cold sea mist and a squadron of Canadian tanks were also seen advancing from the south. The Germans launched one final attack on the eastern flank, mortaring a section of One Troop and killing Captain Sandy Wilson and his lance-corporal, before withdrawing in the face of an ferocious offensive from the London Irish Rifles, supported by RAF fighter aircraft.

The German casualties had been far greater, however, with the 16 Panzer Division alone suffering 56 killed, 73 missing and 246 wounded. Twelve of their tanks had also been destroyed and General Field Marshal Kesselring – 'Smiling Albert', as he was nicknamed – was reported to be 'very tetchy' when news reached him of the failed counter-attack. As overall commander of German forces in the

Eighteen men of Johnny Wiseman's troop were killed as a result of the shell that landed on this truck during the battle for Termoli. (Author's Collection)

Mediterranean it was his responsibility to inform Berlin of the setback, which he did 'by reference to the toughness of the enemy's defence, his skilful exploitation of the terrain and German problems in moving their armour and self-propelled equipments over the very arduous mountain roads'.[19]

Shortly before sundown on 6 October the men of the Special Raiding Squadron gathered in Termoli's public garden to bury their dead. 'Into the gathering dusk, the silent crowd of men emerged from their billets with heads bared and softened tread,' wrote Davis.

> The sight of that battered truck and of those crumbled, gaping walls vividly recalled those awful few minutes of the day before. The smell of death clung heavily to the surrounding masonry. The funeral was soon over. In a quiet voice the padre read the service and dismissed us. Somehow the occasion did not seem to warrant reminisces of that empty and futile kind often vented upon the dead … perhaps our regrets were sufficiently sincere and deep to make us realise how false and unavailing such sentiments are.

The Germans blew this bridge over the Biferno before it could be secured by One Troop during the landing at Termoli. The bronzed skin of some of the SRS soldiers in the foreground indicates the strength of the Mediterranean sun. (Author's Collection)

Later that evening the men washed and ate, and enjoyed the copious cartons of cigarettes lavished upon them by the Irish Brigade. There were few tales of derring-do exchanged among the squadron. Johnny Wiseman recalled that nearly everyone showed the strain of the past few days. Only Paddy Mayne seemed unaffected by the fighting. 'I think he rather enjoyed it actually,' recalled Wiseman. Reg Seekings talked to some of the German paratroopers taken prisoner during the battle, one of whom displayed his photographs from the Russian Front. Then he expressed his regret to Seekings that they were on opposing sides. 'He said it was a tragedy that men such as us should fight each other. "Good men don't kill good men."'

CHAPTER 5

BILL STIRLING AND THE BOYS OF 2SAS

The battle for Termoli was a notable occasion for the SAS, and not just because of the valour displayed and the casualties sustained. It was the first action in which 1SAS (albeit operating under the auspices of the Special Raiding Squadron) fought alongside 2SAS. On the afternoon of 3 October, a 20-man unit from D Squadron 2SAS under the command of Captain Roy Farran arrived at the port having driven up from the south in jeeps. Later, as the Germans threatened to retake Termoli, the 2SAS detachment was ordered to bolster Harry Poat on the eastern flank. Farran and his men collected a number of Bren guns discarded on the battlefield by the 78th Division and positioned themselves above the railway line. They remained there for a day, pouring fire upon the heads of any Germans seen advancing down the railway line. For a regiment looked down on by the SRS for their inexperience, the men of 2SAS proved themselves at Termoli fit to wear the sand-coloured beret. Not that it put an end to the disdain 1SAS liked to express for its sister regiment. Asked once by Roy Farran if it was true his men thought poorly of 2SAS, Paddy Mayne replied in the negative adding: 'We don't think about you at all.'[1]

Shortly before his capture David Stirling had won approval for the establishment of a second SAS regiment to be commanded by his older brother. Bill Stirling had a similar military background to his younger sibling: Scots Guards and commandos, and a shared frustration with the way the special forces unit had been deployed. By the end

OPPOSITE
2SAS would see extensive service in Italy during the war. Here three heavily armed members of the regiment are shown transporting the components of a Vickers heavy machine gun up a mountain pass near Castino, Northern Italy c.1945. (IWM NA 25407)

of 1942, when he started to raise 2SAS at their base in Philippeville in north-eastern Algeria (known now as Skikda), Bill Stirling was a lieutenant-colonel who had trenchant ideas about how his regiment should operate in conjunction with the First Army. What he envisaged was his men being deployed strategically, not tactically, in support of a larger army operation, just as his brother had when he first approached General Auchinleck in the summer of 1941. In a memo to the HQ 15th Army Group, Bill Stirling wrote that his regiment would best serve its purpose 'if a force of 300 men could work over hundreds of miles [in Italy] in up to 140 parties … so far rough landings by parachute have not been accepted. Second SAS Regiment is prepared to accept rough, unreconnoitred landings which can easily be undertaken with imperceptible increases in dropping casualties and advantages too obvious to mention.'[2]

Initially, Stirling's plea was ignored by 15th Army Group Special Operations Group and 2SAS endured the same early failures that had bedevilled L Detachment.

At the end of May 1943 a raiding party of 2SAS and George Jellicoe's SBS embarked upon Operation *Marigold*, the object of which was to land by boat on Sardinia and grab an enemy prisoner. Having approached in a submarine, the raiders then slipped into rubber dinghies and paddled inshore. 'Things went wrong from the start,' remembered Harry Challenor, known to his 2SAS pals as 'Tanky' on account of the Tank Corps beret he'd once worn.

There was a northwards set of about ½ knot, which lengthened our journey from the anticipated ½ hour to 1½ hours. When we landed it was decided that as we were so far behind schedule we would not deflate the dinghies. This decision probably saved

Termoli was the first time that 2SAS operated alongside 1SAS. Here some soldiers take cover during the German counter-attack. (Courtesy of the SAS Regimental Archive)

our lives. With great care we moved up to the bluff. Our feet were noisy on the loose shale and the going very difficult. Then it happened. Pte [private] Hughes dropped his gun. I can still hear the clatter now, it seemed to echo round the beach. In seconds a machine gun and riflemen opened up in our direction. Then the enemy lit a ground flare and suddenly, from pitch darkness, it was Piccadilly with the lights on.[3]

The men dispersed and withdrew back to the beach and their inflated dinghies. Challenor and three others launched one boat and began paddling furiously away from the shore only to discover they were circling back towards land. Challenor, at the front of the dinghy, glanced round and saw that one of their number, 'Butch', was paddling while facing the wrong way. 'He seemed to have gone numb with shock from the intensive fire,' recalled Challenor. 'So we all in turn got up and started to move round in our seats, and had just about succeeded when Butch did likewise. So we were back in the same position.'

'The thing about war is that you plan and plan, but the ones that win are the ones who are most able to overcome disasters, because nothing ever goes the way it's supposed to.'

Anthony Greville-Bell

Despite the danger, Challenor couldn't help laughing at the absurdity of it all. Eventually they all began paddling in the same direction and the firing petered out as they disappeared into the darkness. Then Challenor noticed that the dinghy seemed to be getting bigger: in the mad rush to launch the vessel one of them had inadvertently released the emergency air valve so the dinghy was inflating. Challenor adjusted the valve, whereupon it made a high-pitched wailing noise alerting the enemy to their whereabouts. More machine-gun fire came their way but finally they reached the submarine. Over a mug of rum, Challenor ruminated on an operation that had left one of their number missing and achieved nothing. On the bright side, however, it had provided him 'with the funniest slapstick comedy ever'.

Other early 2SAS missions fell victim to similar moments of black farce. Operation *Snapdragon* involved a group of men landing at Pantellaria, a Mediterranean island west of Sicily, to bring back a prisoner for interrogation. The raiders got ashore without being seen, scaled a cliff and came upon a solitary sentry. Unfortunately on their way back down the cliff they dropped the luckless Italian, who fell and broke his neck on the rocks below.

Like most of 1SAS Paddy Mayne (centre) looked down on Roy Farran (right) and everyone else in 2SAS, and he made sure they knew it! (Author's Collection)

Lieutenant Anthony Greville-Bell's task was to lead a sabotage party to Lampedusa and destroy a radar station. Greville-Bell was well-suited to 2SAS; not only was he the social equal of Bill Stirling, he was a former tank commander who had survived numerous close shaves during the Desert War. Above all, however, he had a well-developed sense of humour. 'It didn't occur to the planners,' he recalled, 'that the radar station would pick us up as we approached.'[4] The raiding party were in their canoes 300 yards from the beach when a green flare burst above their heads; machine-gun fire poured from the cliff top, chasing Greville-Bell and his men back to the waiting motor torpedo boats. 'You don't seethe against anyone, it's funny, you just laugh about it and say what a bloody balls-up,' reflected Greville-Bell of the earlier failures with 2SAS. 'You got so used to it in the British army, or in any army. The thing about war is that you plan and plan, but the ones that win are the ones who are most able to overcome disasters, because nothing ever goes the way it's supposed to.'

There were other disasters for Bill Stirling in the summer of 1943. Operation *Chestnut* was more what he had in mind when he'd memo-ed 15th Army Group Special Operations Group extolling the virtues of dropping small parties of men by parachute. On 12 July two sticks of ten men parachuted into Sicily to attack targets on the north-east coast of the island, but most of their equipment – including wireless sets – were damaged in the drop and they soon ran out of food. In addition, they were dropped too near towns and villages, and soon the Axis troops were hunting for them. Most managed to evade capture and link up with the advancing Allied forces but it was another lesson learned for Bill Stirling's 2SAS.

His next opportunity to establish 2SAS's reputation came in early September on the eve of the invasion of Italy. On 7 September 13 men of 2SAS gathered at Kairouan aerodrome in north Tunisia, among them Greville-Bell and Harry Challenor. Bill Stirling was there, too, to see them off as they embarked on Operation *Speedwell*. In the hours leading up to the start of the operation, the objective of which was to drop into northern Italy and blow railway lines in order to slow the flow of German traffic south to the landing beaches, Greville-Bell and Stirling played baccarat. 'I was very fond of Bill,' recalled Greville-Bell, who knew both brothers. 'He was a very deep, intelligent and well-read man. Bill Stirling was cleverer than David [Stirling]. David was more charismatic and more physical, the younger brother, and was outwardly very good at dealing with higher ups and getting what he wanted. Bill was much quieter and more intellectual. I don't think he ever went on an op with us and that was the right thing to do. But David on the other hand was absolutely right to do it because L Detachment was a fledging unit and it had to be well led from the front.'

At 1800 hours the 13 SAS men boarded two Albermarle aircraft. Into one climbed Greville-Bell and six other soldiers, including Captain Philip Pinckney, the officer in charge of Group One. In the second aircraft was Group Two, under the command of Captain Pat Dudgeon, and containing Harry Challenor. He remembered Dudgeon as a forceful character, always confident, always positive, 'something of a Captain Bligh' (of Mutiny on the *Bounty* fame). Yet Dudgeon's men adored him and, as Greville-Bell and Stirling played cards, he had produced a bottle of whisky and shared it with his men under the shade of an olive tree.

The men had been allowed to choose their own weapons for the operation. Most followed Greville-Bell in opting for the American Winchester Carbine. 'I had a US carbine, but I think the Schmeisser was the best machine pistol ever made,' he recalled. 'The Spandau had too high a rate of fire and was wasteful whereas the Bren was much more lethal because its rate of fire was only half [of the Spandau] and so it didn't waste so much ammunition. The Sten was bloody dangerous because it had a very bad safety catch and if the trigger guard – not the trigger itself – got caught in something it would fire the gun and no one quite knew why.'

Group Two dropped from 7,000ft over the Apennines and landed without difficulty. After rendezvousing, they slept for a few hours and at dawn on 8 September they collected the containers and laid up for the rest of the day. At dusk they dispersed in pairs: Challenor and Lieutenant Thomas 'Tojo' Wederburn going in the direction of the La Spezia-Bologna line; Sergeant Bill Foster and Corporal James Shortall heading for Genoa-La Spezia; and Dudgeon and Bernie Brunt, at 21 the youngest of the six, making for another section of the Genoa to La Spezia line. They arranged to meet in seven days' time by a stream between Pontremili and Villa Franca.

For two days and nights Challenor and Wedderburn traversed the Apennine mountains until they came to a railway tunnel long enough to lay charges at a good distance between the 'up' and 'down' lines. They observed the mouth of the tunnel for several hours and, finding it unguarded, descended from their vantage point at midnight. 'It was pitch black inside,' remembered Challenor.

We laid our first charge on the outside line of the down-line to La Spezia. We then walked for a considerable distance and planted another charge on the up-line. We were making our way back to the entrance when we heard a train coming. It was travelling on the down-line where we had placed the first set of charges. Running and falling we just cleared the tunnel mouth as the train thundered in. With a rumbling BOOM! the explosion echoed down the tunnel. There followed a crashing, smashing, banging, screeching sound of metal piling up. As we left the scene we both heard it – a train on the up-line! We listened in awe. BOOM! Again, more crashing noises and then an eerie, awful silence. We had claimed two trains and undoubtedly blocked the La Spezia to Bologna line as ordered. A very long hard climb into the mountains followed until Mr. Wedderburn called a halt and we rolled into our sleeping bags deep in the undergrowth.

The pair were the first to reach the pre-arranged rendezvous on 15 September. Wedderburn and Challenor waited three days, the time period specified by Dudgeon, and having seen no sign of their comrades they set off south. The days turned into weeks as the two men evaded German troops and those Italians still loyal to Mussolini. Sleeping rough, and relying on the kindness of peasants for food and water, Wedderburn and Challenor learned a few basic words of Italian from the phrase book they had been given prior to the operation. Already weak through hunger and exhaustion, Challenor then went down with a recurrence of malaria, a disease he picked up at 2SAS's mosquito-infested base at Philippeville. 'Soon I was aching in every limb and shaking like a leaf,' he recalled. He begged Wedderburn to leave him but the request was ignored, and instead the officer carried him to a village where a family gave them shelter until Challenor showed signs of improvement.

By the start of December they had travelled more than 250 miles south to the village of Coppito, just outside the city of L'Aquila, where they were taken in by Mama Domenica Eliseo, a remarkable woman whom Challenor called 'a Mother Earth figure'. She and her two children, 21-year-old Domenico, and 20-year-old Anita, owned a farm on which they were already harbouring three escaped British prisoners-of-war. At Christmas there was a noticeable increase in German activity around Coppito as they retreated north in the face of the advanced Allied armies. Wedderburn and Challenor decided to split up temporarily, the latter moving to a cave close to Mama Eliseo's farm and Weddeburn sheltering with a local woman called Philemena. On 27 December the Germans raided Philemena's house, killing her and capturing Wedderburn. Challenor was caught a few days later by the SS as he continued south towards the Allies at Cassino. 'Our meeting was brutal and very hurtful,' reflected Challenor. 'I was then hauled into a car and driven to a large

2SAS and the SBS operated together during Operation *Marigold* in Sardinia. Here a group of SBS soldiers relax. Interesting to note the different footwear worn by the soldier on the far right and his comrade in the front row. It was common for the SAS and SBS to wear whatever they felt most comfortable in the desert and Mediterranean. This picture was sent home as a postcard to a loved one in January 1945. (Courtesy of the SAS Regimental Archive)

building in Popoli where I was marched to a courtyard and shown a wall pock-marked with bullet holes and obvious blood stains on the ground … the officer told me that I was not a solider but a spy and I would be shot.'

Before the Germans could execute Challenor he had escaped – disguised as an Italian peasant woman – and for the next three months he profited once again from the courage and care of the local population. In April he finally linked up with the Allies advancing from the south, literally running slap bang into a giant Indian soldier. 'It was the greatest moment of my life,' Challenor recalled. 'In a short time I was sitting on an ammo box with my back against a tree soaking up the sunshine with a mug of tea in one hand and a mess tin of creamed rice in the other, a tin of cigarettes in my lap, and all I could say over and over again was "I've done it, you bastards".'

Challenor's comrades were not so fortunate. Though Wedderburn survived captivity, Bill Foster and James Shortall were caught and executed in the grounds of a disused pottery factory. Foster was shot first, his request for a priest refused because the officer in charge of the firing squad was in a hurry to get the job done. Shortall witnessed the death of his friend and was then similarly despatched, a Lieutenant Grether applying a coup de grâce as he lay on the ground. A few days after the killings one of the firing squad, Lance Sergeant Fritz Bost, was informed by Grether 'that the execution squad would probably have to function again. Two Englishmen, one of whom was a captain who spoke good German, had been arrested.'[5]

The captain was Pat Dudgeon who, along with Bernie Brunt, had been stopped in a German staff car as they drove over the Cisa Pass, about 30 miles west of Parma. A short while earlier the pair had hijacked the car, killing the two German signallers inside, and driving off in the hope of evading capture having earlier blown a railway line. Dudgeon and Brunt were shot within 24 hours of their arrest. 'Dudgeon, in legal terms, deserved what he got because he stopped a staff car and killed the occupants,' reflected Tony Greville-Bell, who himself had led a charmed life during his part in Operation *Speedwell*.

Group One's DZ was near Castiglione, a mountain village to the north of La Spezia. Greville-Bell landed on a tree and broke two ribs, and there was more misfortune when no trace could be found of Captain Phil Pinckney.★

The next morning the six remaining men split into two parties; one with the job of sabotaging the railway line between Bologna and Prato, and Greville-Bell taking George Daniels and Pete Tomasso to attack the Bologna to Florence stretch. Five days after landing, and still dosed up with morphine on account of his shattered ribs, Greville-Bell and his two men blew a train off the rails inside a tunnel. A week later they repeated the feat and the week after another train was destroyed. Reliant on locals for food and shelter, the trio were told that the Germans had offered 10,000 lire for information leading to their capture as well as drafting in a Division of Mountain troops to hunt them down. Greville-Bell was unimpressed by the news: 'David Stirling's idea in forming the SAS was that cunning was much more important than macho toughness and he was right,' he reflected. 'The more cunning you were the more chance you had of surviving. The Germans had tunnel-vision; they also had big boots and if you were chased by the Germans on foot they didn't have a hope of catching you. They were also inclined to charge about in trucks shouting and blowing whistles.'

★ For two years Pinckney's disappearance remained a mystery. His mother placed adverts in *The Times* appealing for information but none was forthcoming. Then shortly after the war his remains were discovered in Baigno, northern Italy. In all probability, Pinckney was badly injured on landing and fell into German hands. Whether he was executed or died of his wounds is unknown.

Pete Tomasso, Tony Greville-Bell and George Daniels demonstrated in Italy what a small unit of well-trained men could achieve with nothing more than explosives and initiative. (Author's Collection)

Despite suffering frostbite and dysentery, the men marched south through the snow-clad mountains, always keeping one step ahead of the enemy. On the evening of 4 November, day 58 of the operation, Greville-Bell led Daniels and Tomasso through a wood and then straight into a German encampment. There was nothing else to do but try and bluff it out. The three sauntered nonchalantly past the two sentries. 'When we were very close one of them caught my eye, then looked away,' remembered Greville-Bell. 'I'm sure he knew … but he would have died straight away.'

A week later the three men crossed the river Sangro and reached the British front line. Greville-Bell spent several weeks in hospital having his ribs reset and regaining the three stone he'd lost during Operation *Speedwell*. When news reached him that the other half of his stick had derailed a train before linking up with Canadian troops, Greville-Bell was able to reflect on a successful mission despite the loss of Pinckney. 'SAS operations rarely went according to plan,' he said. 'I can't remember one that ever did, but one has to make up ways to get round that. Which we did. General Alexander sent us a note later thanking us and saying we really did help slow down the German reinforcements going south. *Speedwell* was very much a strategic operation, something that affected the war, which is what David Stirling always wanted, as opposed to just a tactical operation like blowing up a few lorries for the sake of it.'

CHAPTER 6

ROY FARRAN: FROM TARANTO TO TERMOLI

O n 7 September, the day on which Operation *Speedwell* had begun, the remainder of 2SAS were bound for the southern Italian port of Taranto in support of an airborne invasion. Five under-strength squadrons of SAS soldiers were aboard an American cruiser, one vessel among a large convoy steaming towards Taranto. 'We were not long out of Africa when we heard over the ship's intercom that the Italians had packed in,' remembered Charlie Hackney, a member of Captain Roy Farran's D Squadron.[1] The news cheered the men, as did the disclosure that Taranto harbour had been swept for mines.

Charlie Hackney was on deck late in the evening when he heard a thundering explosion and saw a sheet of flame. 'It was the destroyer, *Abdiel*, hitting a mine,' he remembered. 'It seemed to split into two and go down in a couple of minutes. It was packed with British airborne and it was terrible to hear these blokes in the water screaming for help.★ Our ship sent out some small boats and they brought back some Welshman, but it didn't [do] much for our morale after being told the harbour was clear of mines.'

The five SAS squadrons eventually landed on 10 September without encountering any opposition, just wide-eyed stares from nervous Italian sailors.

OPPOSITE
Sandy Scratchley (left foreground) and Roy Farran await the inspection of General Montgomery at Termoli. Charlie Hackney is behind Scratchley's left shoulder. Note that the censor has blacked out the SAS cap badge to prevent identification. (IWM E 26182)

Charlie Hackney was a pre-war regular who joined the SAS in 1942. (Author's Collection)

Their orders were to push inland in different directions and reconnoitre the rugged countryside for signs of German opposition. 'There was an uncanny air about our silent advance up that deserted highway,' wrote Farran later. 'We had a vague idea that there might be Germans somewhere inland from the port, but we could not guess how many or where.'[2]

Roy Farran was a 22-year-old former officer in the 3rd King's Own Hussars. Having distinguished himself in action in the early days of the Desert War, he later saw action at Crete in 1941 where he was awarded the Military Cross. There was an undeniable swagger to Farran's bearing, one his men found reassuring, and his courage was similarly inspiring. The character of Farran's second-in-command was in complete contrast; Lieutenant Jim Mackie was a strong and silent Scot, a medical student from Edinburgh who had put his studies on hold while he saw action with the SAS. 'He was a good man and an excellent soldier, was Jim,' recalled Hackney. 'Never seemed to have a care in world. I think that might be why Farran always had him up front [of the patrol]. But Big Jim took it all in good heart and we had complete confidence in him to spy out the land.'

Farran and his D Squadron were heading north in the direction of Bari, approximately 180 miles distant, and it was soon dark as they motored towards the small village of Pogiano. Suddenly Jim Mackie's lead jeep stopped. The Scot dismounted and walked back down the road to his commander, explaining that there was a bridge ahead guarded by some men. Just then one of the men shouted something in Italian to which Farran replied 'Inglesi, Inglisi'. 'Farran got out of his jeep and started to walk towards them to talk,' recalled Hackney. 'Then one of the Italians fired a shot. It missed Farran but Sergeant-Major Mitchell opened up with his Bren and shot the Italian dead. The rest of the Italians quickly threw down their weapons. Once we'd established we were British everything was fine. They gave us some wine and one of them apologised for the shooting, saying the fellow had just been jumpy.'

They rested that night in Pogiano and at dawn the next morning watched the vanguard of the airborne brigade arrive on bicycle. Farran received fresh orders, to head north-west along the coast to discover the limits of the German position. A few miles beyond Pogiano, at a village called Ginosa, D Squadron surprised a large column of Germans approaching from the west. 'We were all lined up alongside the road, in ditches and behind hedges,' recalled Hackney. 'Farran gave the signal to open fire and we just cut them down. It was an absolute slaughter.' The British unleashed what Farran described as a colossal barrage of firepower. Eventually he called a halt and the ambushers emerged on to the road to inspect the result of their work. 'I walked down the road towards a tiny knot of Germans waving white flags from behind the last vehicle,' wrote Farran. 'All those in front of the trucks were dead. Still panting from the excitement of the ambush, we screamed at them to come forward with their hands up. A totally demoralised group of Germans was led up the column by an officer, bleeding profusely from a wound in his arm and still shouting for mercy. It was plain that there would be no question of further resistance from any of them.' The squadron diary noted that the ambush resulted in the destruction of ten vehicles and the death of six Germans with a further 42 taken into captivity.

Over the course of the next few days D Squadron roamed over a large area inland from Taranto Bay. Farran established his HQ in the town of Bernalda and set off for the nearby village of Pisticci. En route they encountered what for all of them was the first sinister face of fascism. 'We came across this camp with barbed wire all around,' remembered Hackney.

> Inside was a hell of a mess, stinking men and women dressed in rags. I went into one of the bunk houses and there was one old lady lying there covered in sores with only a filthy blanket to keep her warm. A lot were afraid to come out of their huts, they thought it was a ruse, but they came out eventually and Farran told them they were now free. They were all desperate to go with us but we couldn't take them so Roy reassured them they were safe, and we left them as much rations, cigarettes and water as we could.

Farran put the few remaining Italian guards of the concentration camp (that housed mainly political prisoners) under the jurisdiction of the inmates and then left. On 16 September D Squadron ran into Canadian armoured vehicles from the Eighth Army advancing up from Messina. After handshakes all round and the donation by the Canadians of 'cigarettes, gum and oxtail soup', Farran continued on his reconnoitre, sending Jim Mackie and 12 men through a mountain tunnel on foot to investigate what was on the other side. Mackie returned the following day with a sorry tale. Farran listened as the Scot described how the two soldiers he'd posted at the mouth of the tunnel had wandered off for a drink in a local village. A battalion of Germans had driven through the tunnel in their absence and Mackie almost ran straight into them on his return from the patrol. 'Farran was bloody furious with the pair,' said Hackney. 'First he bawled them out and then he RTU'd them. One of them was down on his knees, crying, literally begging not to be RTU'd but Farran wasn't having it. They left that night on an Eighth Army truck.'

With the Canadians now advancing in strength, Farran's squadron was pulled back to Taranto to await further orders. First they moved up to Bari, and from there they embarked upon a long-range patrol to Melfi, 50 miles to the west. Then it was back to Bari where 2SAS were being gathered for a new operation.

One offshoot of Italy's surrender was the huge number of British prisoners-of-war released from captivity by their Italian guards. Many were now wandering through central Italy trying to reach the advancing Allies while also avoiding recapture by the

Germans. It was decided therefore to launch Operation *Jonquil*, a joint 2SAS and airborne division venture in which soldiers would parachute into Italy, round up as many POWs as possible, and lead them to four muster points on the coast between Ancona and Pescara. From there the SAS would ferry them by boat to Termoli, about to be seized by the commandos and Paddy Mayne's Special Raiding Squadron.

D Squadron's role in the operation was to drive north to Termoli and establish a suitable base in the port from which the rescue mission could be launched. Farran arrived on the afternoon of 3 October to hear SRS describe a 'great victory'. That evening some SRS officers entertained Farran and Mackie to dinner. For most of the following day, 4 October, all was peaceful and Farran 'selected a rather slummy building near the harbour where we waited for our tiny fleet to arrive'.

Then the German counter-attack began and Farran and his men were shelled and strafed by Focke-Wolfe fighter aircraft throughout the day. 'All I did was to improve the safety of our billet,' said Farran. 'As far as we were concerned the battle was someone else's affair… I could not see where we could fit in with our twenty-odd men. It may have been a weak view but we had had a good run from Taranto and were supposed to be resting.' The D Squadron diary made mention of several dive-bombing attacks by German Focke-Wulfe fighter planes on the harbour on 5 October during the arrival of Major Sandy Scratchley, a 37-year-old former steeplechase jockey who had recruited Farran into 2SAS at the start of the year, which shook D Squadron from its slumber. 'He quite rightly reprimanded me for sitting idle like a rat in a hole,' remembered Farran, who was instructed to take his men to the Special Service Brigade HQ in the centre of Termoli. They arrived not long after the HQ had taken a direct hit from a shell that killed Staff Captain Lincoln Leese. Farran was ordered by the brigade major, Brian Franks, to reinforce the eastern flank overlooking the railway line one mile to the north. Collecting discarded Bren guns from the battlefield, D Squadron positioned themselves either side of the line with Lieutenant Mackie and ten men (and three Brens) on the left and Lieutenant Peter Jackson with a similar strength on the right.

KILLED THREE MONTHS AFTER WEDDING

ON SPECIAL MISSION

Lieutenant David B. Leigh (27), Special Air Service, a Londoner, who married Miss Ethel C. Stewart, Atholl Lodge, 34 Ayr Road, Prestwick, on June 1, has been killed in action. This news reached his wife and parents-in-law, Mr and Mrs J. A. Stewart, recently.

The wedding took place at St. Nicholas Church, Prestwick, Lieutenant Leigh's wife being a former member of the Royal Observer Corps in Ayr. He himself was the son of parents now dead, who were in business in Shanghai, and he was educated in England. He was on the staff of the Air Ministry in London, but was released for the Services and he joined the famous Green Howards. When the Special Air Service was formed of picked men, he volunteered and was accepted, and afterwards was stationed in this country for a period.

The Special Air Service, about which the public only recently learned, is sent on daring missions into enemy-occupied territory, and it is believed to be on one of these that Lieutenant Leigh lost his life. News that he had been killed was first sent by Captain Ian Millar, who was best man at the wedding.

A tragic feature is that Lieutenant Leigh's only brother, Flying Officer T. B. Leigh, was one of the 50 R.A.F. officers recently shot by the Germans at a prison camp. His name in a newspaper report was the first intimation of his death, and it was a great shock to brother.

For the next few hours they repelled several German forays down the railway line, although at 1715 hours Farran was compelled to call for reinforcements when three enemy tanks rumbled into view; the thrust was beaten back 90 minutes later after several salvos from some British six-pounders were fired. 'Termoli was hellish,' reflected Charlie Hackney. 'I was up on one side of the embankment with a Bren and my loader, a fellow called Cookhouse, was next to me. We were running low on ammo so we could only fire in intermittent bursts. They got to within 600 yards of our position before withdrawing.'

The men from 2SAS passed what the squadron diary recorded as a 'cold uncomfortable night' above the railway line and at dawn the next day – 6 October – the Germans began 'mortaring, machine gunning and shelling' their positions while there was also accurate sniper fire directed their way.[3] Only when the London Irish Rifles advanced in the afternoon did the German fire slacken and then stop, allowing 2SAS the chance to be relieved.

Despite the firepower directed against them, D Squadron suffered only three minor casualties (including Cookhouse, who was wounded in the left cheek), yet the experience at Termoli was not one Farran enjoyed. 'It was the only pure infantry battle I fought in the war and I never want to fight another,' he said.

Although the British fought off the German counter-attack at Termoli, the operation to repatriate hundreds of Allied prisoners-of-war was not a success. Only 50 were lifted from the beaches and the official report on Operation *Jonquil* described how the failure had left everyone 'disillusioned and dispirited'.[4] Bill Stirling blamed the disappointment on interference from staff officers who had planned the operation without taking much advice from him. Fortunately, other units of 2SAS were showing what could be done if they were left to operate free from top brass meddling. A small party of men under Lieutenant Alistair McGregor had dropped inland near Chieti, 50 miles north of Termoli, as part of *Jonquil*, before turning his attention to an SS unit that had moved into the area to track down escaped Allied prisoners. McGregor's men killed dozens of SS men in ambushes and they remained behind enemy lines until January, operating as guerrillas and causing considerable inconvenience to the Germans.

2SAS continued to launch attacks through the autumn of 1943 and into January 1944. Farran, Scratchley and Grant Hibbert had all led units of men to blow railway lines and mine coastal roads between Ancona and Pescara. In the New Year, under the command of Lieutenant David Worcester, Operation *Thistledown* derailed trains and attacked vehicles between Rimini and Ancona, while Operation *Pomegranate* involved six men landing by parachute near Perugia and attacking San Egidio airfield. One of the men, Lieutenant Jimmy Hughes, was subsequently captured and interrogated by the Germans at Perugia. 'May I remind you,' said the officer questioning Hughes,

'that you are not a prisoner of war. You are a political prisoner. Under the Kommando Order issued by our Führer all saboteurs, whether in uniform or not, are to be shot.'[5]

Hughes managed to escape and eventually he made his way to Britain whereupon he informed Major Bill Barkworth, 2SAS's intelligence officer, of the Kommando Order. It was the first the British had heard of the order – issued by Hitler in October 1942 – and though Barkworth believed it to be true, his superiors at HQ 1st Airborne Corps were more sceptical. 'Hughes' case was dismissed as mere interrogation technique,' commented Barkworth later. 'Reference to other men of the Regiment who had neither returned, nor had been reported as casualties, was explained away by the fact that the enemy probably wished to keep us in the dark about the success of operations.'[6]

Jim Mackie (standing, far right) was Roy Farran's right-hand man, a cool and courageous Scot respected by all his men. (Author's Collection)

CHAPTER 7

BACK TO BLIGHTY

Four days after the cessation of hostilities at Termoli, on 10 October, the SRS received a visit from General Miles Dempsey, Commander of XIII Corps under whose auspices the SRS had been operating in Italy. Dempsey addressed the men and began by praising the 'brilliant' way in which they had captured the guns at Cape Murro di Porco. He then commended their courage in repelling the Germans at Termoli, explaining how the enemy had been obliged to bring up the 16th Panzer Division from Naples, on the east coast, in a vain attempt to retake the port. In addition, said Dempsey, the SRS had 'eased the pressure on the American Fifth Army', who were now advancing.[1]

Dempsey, who had won a Military Cross during World War I, saved his most heartfelt congratulations until the end. Regretting that the alliance between his Corps and the squadron was about to end, he said:

> In all my military career – and in my time I have commanded many units – I have never yet a met a unit in which I had such confidence as I have in yours. And I mean that!
>
> Let me give you six reasons why I think you are as successful as you are. Six reasons which I think you will perhaps bear in mind when training newcomers to your ranks to your own high standards.

OPPOSITE
Jeff Du Vivier married Rea, the girl he met during his commando training, in April 1944 and gave her this photograph as a keepsake. (Author's Collection)

129

1SAS RUGBY

TOP The 1SAS rugby team before one of their matches in Darvel. Paddy Mayne, a former Ireland international, is second from left in the middle row. (Author's Collection)

BOTTOM Mayne (centre) laughs as he supervises an SAS scrum at Darvel. Mayne was the fittest man in the regiment and placed a huge emphasis on physical training, often organising games of football and rugby. (Courtesy of the SAS Regimental Archive)

First of all, you take your training seriously. That is one thing that has always impressed me about you.

Secondly, you are well disciplined. Unlike some who take on the specialised and highly dangerous job, you maintain a standard of discipline and cleanliness which is good to see.

Thirdly, you are physically fit, and I think I know you well enough to know you will always keep that up.

Fourthly, you are completely confident in your abilities – yet not to a point of overconfidence.

Fifthly, despite that confidence, you plan carefully.

Last of all, you have the right spirit, which I hope you will pass on to those who may join you in the future.

Three days after Dempsey's visit, the SRS embarked for Molfetta, a coastal town further down the east coast of Italy. It wasn't a happy stay. The squadron war diary noted that they hard trouble securing billets with 'Italians not helpful or even truthful'. The men vented their displeasure in the bars of Molfetta and on 21 October the diary stated: '9pm curfew imposed. Result of general rowdyism in town.'[2]

Paddy Mayne organised some sports events to relieve the boredom, and then on 1 November came word that the squadron would be sailing home in three weeks. The news thrilled the 200 men, nearly all of whom hadn't seen family and friends for more than three years. But shortly before they were due to sail, a message arrived from Whitehall cancelling the embarkation order. They were to remain in Italy. 'It is hard to realise the feelings of the men,' the war diary commented on 21 November. 'On the day upon which we thought we were finished with this depressing camp, after a week of being told "domania" every day, we get this blow … it's difficult to gauge the true extent of the effect upon morale, but it may cause a lack of spirit or it may cause carelessness or abandon on future ops.'

The squadron finally sailed for Britain from Algiers on Christmas Day 1943. After a festive dinner of tinned turkey, followed by pears and custard, the squadron boarded the SS *Oranto*. 'This really is the best way of spending Christmas, embarking for the UK,' wrote the diarist.

Shortly after docking at Greenock the squadron was given a month's leave. Then they reassembled at their new base, the village of Darvel in south-west Scotland, where the men were billeted in two disused lace mills. 'It was cold and miserable because they shut off all the heating in the mills,' remembered Jeff Du Vivier, who had married his sweetheart shortly after returning to Britain. Bob Tait was his best man at the small ceremony in Ayr and Du Vivier's SAS colleagues sent a congratulatory telegram: 'Trickiest "jump" a parachutist ever made. Happy landings and the very best of luck.'[3]

Upon its return to the UK the SRS reverted to 1SAS and now belonged to the SAS Brigade, an adjunct to the Army Air Corps under the command of Brigadier General Rory McLeod. The brigade also included 2SAS, two French regiments – the 3rd and 4th – and 5SAS, comprised of a squadron of Belgian paratroopers. In April 1944, F Squadron GHQ Liaison Regiment Phantom was attached to the brigade to make up for the shortfall in skilled signallers, increasing its strength to 2,500 men. One unwelcome upshot of the restructuring was the decision by McLeod that the SAS replace its sand-coloured beret with the red one worn by airborne troops. The decision didn't go down well with the desert veterans and some, led by Paddy Mayne (newly promoted to lieutenant colonel), continued to wear the old beret.

One of Mayne's first tasks was to expand the 200 men of the SRS into a full-blown regiment. 1SAS was to consist of four squadrons, each of 12 officers and 109 other ranks (in addition there was a squadron HQ and two Troops); A Squadron, commanded by Major Bill Fraser, which considered itself the elite and included original L Detachment members such as Du Vivier, Reg Seekings and Johnny Cooper; B Squadron under the command of Eric Lepine; C Squadron, led by Tony Marsh; and D Squadron, whose commanding officer was Ian Fenwick.

Fenwick, a brilliant cartoonist whose work had graced numerous publications, was one of a number of new officers recruited from the auxiliary units of the British Resistance Organisation. These units had been formed in 1940 when a German invasion seemed imminent, the aim being to launch guerrilla attacks against the enemy from underground hideouts. Altogether, Mayne recruited about 130 officers and men from the redundant Auxiliary Units, including Roy Bradford and Peter Weaver. Mike Sadler, recovered from his stomach ulcers, remembered that the officers who arrived from the Auxiliaries were all likeable 'with a good deal of self-confidence and authority'.[4]

Among the rankers was 19-year-old Bob Francis, a fluent French speaker and one of 200 men from the Parachute Regiment to volunteer for 1SAS. 'Mayne queried me about my French, asked me how good it was and he joked that he wasn't in a position to test me,' recalled Francis. 'I passed but only about 20 of the 200 [paratroopers] made it through.'[5]

Vic Long, like Mayne a native of Belfast, was another paratrooper who responded to Mayne's recruitment drive. 'We were in camp at Salisbury at the time,' he recalled. 'Paddy and a couple of officers came down to interview all those who'd volunteered. "What benefit would you be if I picked you in the regiment?" he asked. I told him I was a three-inch mortar instructor, knew how to

Sgt. J. Duvivier, M.M., S.A.S., Worcester Park, Surrey, and Miss Rachel Love, A.T.S., 54 Content Street, Ayr, who were married on Saturday in St. Margaret's R.C. Church.

read a map and had done a course at the Netherhaven small arms school. I finished by saying I thought I could be some use to the regiment. "Hmm," he said. "Very well. Next".'[6]

The training was rigorous, both for new recruits and those who had been with the regiment since the desert. Everyone had to undergo a parachute course at Ringway, Manchester, and there were lessons in explosives, firearms and unarmed combat as well as endless physical training sessions. 'One of the best aspects was the weapons training,' remembered Bob Francis. 'We were allowed to try everything and pick the weapon we liked. I was good with the Tommy Gun but most of the boys treasured the US carbines. They were good weapons and because the rounds were so much smaller you could [carry] more.'

Vic Long recalled that they spent a lot of time navigating their way round the Scottish countryside. 'We'd go up in a plane at night, fly around for an hour or so and then drop. We had no idea where we were headed, only that we had to lay [dummy] charges on a line at such and such a point. We had to find out where we had dropped, locate the target, and then lay the charges. Then a couple of officers would appear to see if we'd done a good job.'

The Du Vivier's wedding was reported in the local press. Note that while Jeff wears the sand-coloured beret, best man Bob Tait avoids a clash of colour by opting for the recently introduced maroon beret! (Author's Collection)

RIGHT
While the rest of 1SAS trained hard at Darvel, Graham Rose, Mike Sadler, Bob Tait and Major Oswald Rooney (2SAS) were sent on a tour of USA cities to help encourage Americans to buy war bonds. (Courtesy of John Robertson)

BELOW RIGHT
Mike Sadler admitted he 'took rather a fancy' to Martha Vickers, the Hollywood actress he met during the tour of the USA in 1944. Vickers gave Major Rooney a signed photo and dedicated it to 'Mickey', his regimental nickname. Ironically, she later married the real Mickey Rooney. (Courtesy of John Robertson)

It wasn't all work and no play, however, for the officers and men. There were nights in the village pub, dances in the village hall and parties in the squadron mess. One of the new officers was Ian Wellsted, who had joined 1SAS from the Royal Tank Regiment. 'Men and selected guests, from the major down to the last non-operational sanitary man, would get uproariously drunk on a dreadful concoction of red wine and rum, known as "Suki",' he recalled.[7] Wellsted was in A Squadron, as was another anonymous officer who wrote home describing a shindig held on Thursday 4 May: 'What a party it was. We made a most potent brew, 50% rum. It was passed round in pint and ½ pint glasses so you can get some idea of the resulting havoc. It had a kick like a mule and people passed out right and left. We put many men and officers to bed. We took advantage of one of the latter and cut off half his moustache. He was not awfully pleased the following morning.'[8]

When the men of A Squadron were in their cups they sang from the songs sheets they all carried. There were 20 songs in all, from 'Inverary Inn' to 'Underneath the Arches' to 'Moonlight Becomes You'. But the song they liked best was 'Lilli Marlene', which came with an 'apology to the Afrika Korps'. The SAS had appropriated the love song from Germany's desert troops and added a few verses of their own in honour of their worthy foe:

Verse 1:
Check you're in position, see your gun's all right,
Wait until a convoy comes creeping through the night.
Now you can press the trigger, son,
And blow the Hun to Kingdom Come,
And Lilli Marlene's boy friend will never see Marlene.

Chorus:
Back to the rendezvous we'll steer,
To drink more beer ('cause there's none here).
But poor Marlene's boy friend will never see Marlene.

Verse 2:
Forty dozen rounds of tracer and of ball,
Forty dozen rounds of the stuff that makes them fall.
Finish your strafing, drive away,
And live to fight another day,
And poor Marlene's boy friend will never see Marlene.

The new recruits saw increasingly less of Paddy Mayne as the spring wore on but one morning he appeared unannounced in the lace mills. 'It must have been about 9 and we were still asleep on the floor,' recalled Long. 'He called us on to parade at the games field at Darvel and tore us off a strip, particularly the officers.'

A SQUADRON SONG SHEET

"A" SQUADRON SONG SHEET - SHEET I.

Parachute Song.

Imagine a 'plane just leaving the 'drome,
Bound for the Lord knows where,
Heavily laden with parachute troops,
Don't know where they're going - don't care.
There's thousands who've baled out before,
With a grin as they started to fall,
If your 'chute doesn't open you'll get no promotion,
So cheer up my lads, bless 'em all.
Here goes "nowt", here goes "nowt",
Watch 'em as they bale out,
Long ones and short ones and fat ones as well,
Fifty per cent will all finish in hell.
So we're saying goodbye to them all,
As to our objectives we fly,
If your 'chute doesn't open you'll get no promotion,
So here's to the next man to die.
Let him die, let him die,
The staff men are too blooming fly,
If your 'chute doesn't open you'll get no promotion,
So here's to the next man to die.

Inverary Inn.

There's a grand wee inn, the Inverary Inn,
A nicer inn I've never been in before.
There's a wee Scots lassie in the Inverary Inn,
The bonny, bonny lassie I adore-ore-ore.
She's simply wonderful, wonderful,
The barmaid at the inn at Inverary,
On the twentyfirst of June
I'll be on my honeymoon
With the barmaid at the Inn at Inverary.

I parted frae my dearie at the Inverary pier,
I'd barely time to kiss her on the cheek, cheek, cheek,
I said to her "My dearie ,
You'll no hae time to weary,
I'll write you forty letters every week, week, week".
She handed me a locket and I'll cherish it with care,
Although the case is only made of tin, tin, tin,
It's a photograph of my lady,
She is a grand wee lady,
It's taken at the outside of the inn, inn, inn.

Chorus:

It's a grand wee inn etc........

Nobody's Darlin' but Mine.

Be nobody's darlin' but mine love,
Be honest, be faithful, be kind,
And promise me that you will never
Be nobody's darlin' but mine.

3. You're sweet as the flowers of Springtime,
You're fair as the roses that twine,
You're sure to be somebody's darlin',
Be nobody's darlin' but mine.

2. My mother is dead and in Heaven,
My sister has gone there as well,
And father has gone to join mother,
But where I'll go no one can tell.

Be nobody's darlin' but mine dear,
Be honest, be faithful, be kind,
And promise me that you will never
Be nobody's darlin' but mine.

!!!!! S I N G !!!!!
IF YOU CAN'T SING, HUM OR WHISTLE !!!!!

A Squadron might not have possessed the best singers in 1SAS but no other squadron sang with as much gusto following a hard day's training in Darvel. Their favourite song, reprinted here on the right, owed much to the Afrika Korps. (Author's Collection)

Lilli Marlene (With apologies to the Afrika Korps).

There was a song we always used to hear
Out in the desert, romantic, soft and clear,
Over the ether came the strain, the soft refrain, each night again,
With you Lilli Marlene, with you, Lilli Marlene.

Check you're in position, see your gun's all right,
Wait until a convoy comes creeping through the night.
Now you can press the trigger, son,
And blow the Hun to Kingdom Come,
And Lilli Marlene's boy friend will never see Marlene.

Chorus:

Back to the rendezvous we'll steer,
To drink more beer ('cause there's none here),
But poor Marlene's boy friends will never see Marlene.

Forty dozen rounds of tracer and of ball,
Forty dozen rounds of the stuff that makes them fall.
Finish your straffing, drive away,
And live to fight another day,
And poor Marlene's boy friend will never see Marlene.

Chorus:

Now back to Cairo we will come,
To make things hum with lots of rum,
But poor Marlene's boy friends will never see Marlene.

Creeping into Fuka, 30 'planes ahead,
Belching ammunition, filling them with lead,
A flower to you, a grave to Fritz,
He's like his planes - he's shot to bits,
And poor Marlene's boy friends will never see Marlene.

Chorus:

Now back to Blighty we will steer,
To drink our beer with ne'er a tear,
But Lilli Marlene's boy friends will never see Marlene.

Afrika Korps have sunk into the dust,
Gone are their Stukas, tanks have gone to rust.
No more we'll hear that soft refrain, that lilting strain, each night again -
With you Lilli Marlene,
With you Lilli Marlene.

Paper Doll.

I'm gonna buy a paper doll that I can call my own,
A doll that other fellows cannot steal,
And then that flirty, flirty guy with a flirty, flirty eye
Will have to flirt with dollies that are real.
When I come home at night she will be waiting,
She'll be the grandest doll in all the world,
For I'd rather have a paper doll to call my own
Than have a pickle-minded real live gal.

Dearly Beloved.

Dearly beloved how plainly I see,
Somewhere in Heaven you were fashioned for me.
Angel eyes knew you, angel voices led me to you.
Nothing could change me, you gave me a sign,
I know that I'll be yours come shower or shine.
Though I say dearly, dearly beloved be mine.

!!!!!! S I N G !!!!!!

IF YOU CAN'T SING - HUM OR WHISTLE !!!!

It wasn't just the 1SAS officers who angered Mayne in the spring of 1944. Since their return from the Mediterranean, the regiment had been unsure of their exact role in the forthcoming invasion of France. Mayne had greeted with caution the appointment of Roderick McLeod as SAS brigadier, unsure of how he viewed the SAS. It wasn't just another airborne unit, like the parachute regiment, dropped en masse near targets in view of the enemy; Mayne still clung to David Stirling's original ethos that they were most effective when inserted deep into enemy territory in small units to operate for long periods of time without interference from the top brass.

On 25 March 1944 McLeod wrote to Mayne informing him of the SAS's participation when the invasion of France began: 'Infiltration will be by land, sea or air according to circumstances, and training in all methods will be carried out.'[9] Four days later, 29 March, the Supreme Headquarters Allied Expeditionary Force (SHAEF) issued the SAS Brigade with its operational instructions for the invasion. Their intention was for the SAS to parachute into Normandy between the landing beaches and the German reserves (three panzer divisions) 36 hours in advance of the main invasion fleet. Once on the ground the SAS would deploy as a blocking line, preventing the German reserves from reinforcing their comrades at the landing beaches.

'There has always been divided opinions about the SAS in higher quarters… The bright officers were always for it and the stick-in-the-muds were always against it."

Anthony Greville-Bell

Bill Stirling was livid when he learned of the order and drafted a letter to SHAEF in which he made clear his opposition to the role envisaged. He demanded that the SAS operate in France as they had in the desert, adhering to the principles laid down by his brother. 'Paddy was useless with dealing with senior officers because if they did something to annoy him he threatened to punch their noses,' reflected Tony Greville-Bell on why it was Stirling and not Mayne who took SHAEF to task. 'He was tactically very clever, very bright, and he got a hell of a thrill from operating – he was the epitome of an SAS officer. But he wasn't the right man to command the regiment because he had no patience with boring people.'[10]

Before Bill Stirling could send his letter, however, Lieutenant General Frederick 'Boy' Browning intervened, writing to the Chief of Staff, 21 Army Group, to say that he considered it preferable if the SAS Brigade was dropped deeper into France to attack German lines of communication while training Maquis groups. The operation order was duly amended but Bill Stirling sent his letter nonetheless, unable to suppress his frustration with the army's perpetual misreading of the SAS. 'There has always been divided opinions about the SAS in higher quarters,' reflected Greville-Bell. 'The bright officers were always for it and the stick-in-the-muds were always against it.'

The letter caused something of a furore within SHAEF and Stirling was asked to withdraw his criticism. He refused and, after Browning had visited 2SAS's base at Monkton, in Ayrshire, Scotland, Stirling resigned. 'We were in absolute agreement with his decision because of that thick-headed idiot Boy Browning,' said Greville-Bell, by now a captain with a DSO. 'In fact the senior officers, of whom I was one then, were inclined to resign as well but Bill told us not to… Really, David's [Stirling] capture was a disaster for us. Though we did fairly well after that I think with him handling the upper levels of authority everything would have gone his way and would have been much better.'

CHAPTER 8

D-DAY FOR 1SAS

On 28 May, 21 Army Group issued the amended order for the SAS Brigade in the impending Operation *Overlord*; Bill Stirling hadn't fallen on his sword in vain. Instead of the suicidal mission laid down by SHAEF in its original order of March, the SAS Brigade would carry out 43 missions in France involving the two British regiments, two French regiments and the squadron of Belgian troopers. With the exception of one operation – *Titanic* (involving a six-man party dropping into Normandy a few hours ahead of the main invasion fleet to spread confusion with dummy parachutes) – all missions would occur deep behind enemy lines with the objective of harassing German forces heading north and attacking their lines of communication.

The honour of leading 1SAS into France went to A and B Squadrons. A Squadron's operation was codenamed *Houndsworth* and entailed dropping into the Massif du Morvan, west of Dijon, to cut railway lines between Lyon and Paris, arm and train the numerous local groups of Maquis, and generally make a nuisance of themselves. Operation *Bulbasket* involved a party of men under the command of Captain John Tonkin parachuting into the Vienne region of France, between Poitiers and Chateauroux, and attacking the Germans whenever possible. Specific orders were flexible with squadron commanders told to use their judgement in the selection of targets.

OPPOSITE
Regular resupplies were vital for the SAS in France but nonetheless they were a logistical headache with the containers having to be collected as quickly as possible before the Germans arrived at the scene of the drop. (Courtesy of the SAS Regimental Archive)

At the end of May a small trickle of SAS soldiers left their base in Darvel and travelled south to Fairford aerodrome in Gloucestershire, among them lieutenants Ian Stewart, Norman 'Puddle' Poole and Ian Wellsted. When they arrived at Fairford they were told of their mission: Poole would be leading Operation *Titanic* and Stewart and Wellsted would be the advance reconnaissance party for *Houndsworth*. 'From then our days were spent in studying maps and aerial photographs,' recalled Wellsted, '[and] in learning ways to avoid being tracked by trained police dogs and other methods of eluding the enemy.'[1]

On 3 June, Poole, Stewart and Wellsted, along with two officers from B Squadron – John Tonkin and Richard Crisp – were driven to London for a final briefing in the presence of Special Operations Executive (SOE). They provided the SAS officers with the 'griff' on the ground, information about the strength of the German presence in their operational area and the quality, reliability and political affiliations of the Maquis groups with whom they would come into contact. Escorting the SAS officers was the regiment's intelligence officer Mike Sadler. 'I accompanied a lot of officers on these briefings and it was always an interesting insight into human behaviour to see how the men reacted on the eve of the operation' he reflected.[2]

After their briefing from the SOE, Wellsted and the others were treated to lunch at an upmarket restaurant in Regent Street, and in the evening they took in a cabaret. The next day they were driven to Hassells Hall, near Sandys, Bedfordshire, only to learn shortly after their arrival that the invasion of France had been postponed from 4 June to the following day because of poor weather in the Channel. The delay was excruciating. 'We fitted our chutes, talked to the pretty Fanys [The First Aid Nursing Yeomanry], listened to the radio and heard the king's speech,' recalled Wellsted. 'How we blessed those girls whose pleasant chatter kept our minds off what was in store.' Mike Sadler remembered Puddle Poole showing off his skills as a pianist by playing the 'Warsaw Concerto', composed by Richard Addinsell for the 1941 film *Dangerous Moonlight*. The effect on his audience was 'amazing'.

On the evening of 5 June, Wellsted and Stewart, along with three SOE officers, were driven to RAF Tempsford where they boarded a Halifax bomber. Strapped to their legs were cylindrical duffle bags which contained the men's equipment; the bags were hooked to the men's leg and were released once they were floating to earth, the bag then being paid out on the end of a 15ft length of rope. Wellsted and Stewart wore the red airborne beret (though a helmet for jumping) as well as the airborne Dennison smock over standard issue battledress and rubber-soled boots.

The five men dropped into the Morvan in early hours of 6 June, just as the Allied invasion fleet crossed the Channel towards Normandy. Their task was to ensure the area was safe for a second SAS party to land two or three days later under the

No. 3/AAC/112

(If replying, please quote above No.)

Army Form B. 104—83

A.A.C., A.C.C. Record Office,
AND G.S.C.,
17 JUL 1944
RECORD OFFICE,
EDINBURGH, 7.

.........19...

SIR OR MADAM,

I regret to have to inform you that a report has been received from the War Office to the effect that (No.) 921086 (Rank) Cpl

(Name) LEADBETTER William

(Regiment) **ARMY AIR CORPS**

was posted as " missing " on the 1st June 1944,

In North West Europe.

The report that he is missing does not necessarily mean that he has been killed, as he may be a prisoner of war or temporarily separated from his regiment.

Official reports that men are prisoners of war take some time to reach this country, and if he has been captured by the enemy it is probable that unofficial news will reach you first. In that case I am to ask you to forward any postcard or letter received at once to this Office, and it will be returned to you as soon as possible.

Should any further official information be received it will be at once communicated to you.

I am,

SIR OR MADAM,

Your obedient Servant,

G. Hawkey

Officer in charge of Records.

IMPORTANT.

Any change of your address should be immediately notified to this Office.

Wt. 30051/1249 400,000 (16) 9/39 KJL/8812 Gp 698/3 Forms/B.104—83/9

Not all the jeeps dropped to A Squadron during Operation *Houndsworth* landed intact. Here Ian Wellsted (centre) poses beside a vehicle whose parachute failed to open. (Author's Collection)

command of Bill Fraser, but for the first two days they were unable to make contact with the local Maquis. When they did they radioed SAS Brigade HQ with the map coordinates of a DZ close to the hamlet of Vieux Dun.

On 11 June Fraser and 18 others parachuted into the area in two sticks as part of the main reconnaissance party of Operation *Houndsworth*. As Fraser described in his operational report it was by no means a tidy drop:

Planes unable to find Vieux Dun DZ, scatter men over wide area. Major Fraser and tpr [trooper] Kennedy land near Lormes. German troops with guns seen and they lay up in woods. Eureka [a radar beacon] destroyed by drop. Lt Moore landed a little more to the east and subsequently made his own way to the Vieux Dun area. Lt [Johnny] Cooper dropped at 0210 hours near Fetigny and had contacted all his men including [Reg] Seekings, Maclennan and Sgt Zelic by 1100 hours except for tpr Docherty who was not picked up till that evening. His w/t [wireless] was working OK and he managed to get in touch with London. He also contacted Maquis through a farmer.[3]

By 12 June Cooper had gathered up his stick and was told to sit tight for 24 hours while the Maquis organised transport. The following night the French arrived to collect the SAS men. 'This big bus appeared out of the darkness with Wellsted on board,' remembered David Danger. 'It was one of those steam buses that ran on brushwood fed into a cylinder at the back. Most of the boys piled onto the bus and went off back to the Maquis camp. Me, Johnny [Cooper] and Reg Seekings remained on the DZ to await the arrival of the rest of the squadron the following night. Not long after the bus had gone a German patrol appeared on the road but they didn't see us.'[4]

In fact the arrival of the rest of A Squadron, under Johnny Wiseman and Alex Muirhead, was postponed to 17 June. On that night Fraser, Wellsted and Seekings drove to the DZ in a Maquis car to prepare the fires that would guide in the three aircraft. At the same time back at Fairford the 64 SAS soldiers were preparing for take-off. One of them was Sergeant John Noble, a Scot who had won the Military Medal at Cape Murro di Porco. 'I admit here and now, I was afraid,' he wrote in the journal he was keeping for his girlfriend back in Edinburgh. 'My chief fear was getting shot down in the drink.'[5]

Alex Muirhead's mortar section demonstrates the weapon to some Maquisards in the forests of the Morvan during Operation *Houndsworth*. (Author's Collection)

Once they were over the Channel, Noble's aircraft came under fire from German anti-aircraft guns and the pilot was forced to take evasive action as the men crammed into the fuselage listening to the sounds of shells exploding all around. 'Eventually we were told half an hour to go and for the next fifteen minutes chaos reigned supreme,' wrote Noble. 'There were blokes in all sorts of positions, testing chutes, strapping on leg bags etc. At last all was ready and in take off positions … after circling around for 20 minutes and no sign of lights, we had to return to England. Still in our take off positions on the plane, the order gave us a bit of a shock. Personally I had a feeling of relief mixed with fear. We were crossing back over the Channel at dawn.'

Noble and a second aircraft touched down in England at 0700 hours but the third plane never returned. Lieutenant Les Cairns and his 15 men had vanished, never to be found. 'The men on that plane are all posted missing presumed dead,' wrote Noble. 'It was a great blow to the unit.'

Down on the DZ Fraser and the reception committee had looked up in dismay as the three aircraft passed overheard. Mist and heavy rain prevented them from glimpsing the aircraft and the pilots from spotting the recognition fires on the ground.

Four nights later, on 21 June, they tried again, this time with more success, though one trooper broke a leg in landing and another, L Detachment original Chalky White, injured his back. On the same day that the main party of A Squadron inserted into France, RSM Graham Rose posted the same typed letter to the families of every soldier. It read:

The following information is available regarding your [Rose added by hand the name and number of each soldier]. He was dropped by parachute into France on 21.6 and up to the time of writing was quite safe and well. You may take it for granted that he is safe unless you hear to the contrary from us.

He will not be able to write to you for some time but will be able to receive your letters, so please keep writing.

Cheerio, keep smiling, and don't worry.[6]

With his squadron all present and correct, Bill Fraser established his HQ at the Vieux Dun camp, which included the sections belonging to Johnny Wiseman and Roy Bradford. Close by was the forest hideout of Maquis Camille.

Approximately ten miles south, not far from the village of Montsauche, Alex Muirhead's Two Troop was camped in a dark forest near to Maquis Bernard. Ian Wellsted was in this camp and described the Maquis as lightly armed and poorly trained. In addition, 'although full of enthusiasm, none of the Maquisards, even the

1st S.A.S. Regiment,
A.P.O.,
England.

...?/.8./44.

Dear Sir/~~Madam~~,

We are pleased to pass on the following information regarding your *son, Tpr. A Middleton.*
He is still quite fit and well, doing very good work, and we have received some excellent reports since the battle for Germany began.
He is being well fed and clothed, and medical comforts are in good supply.

Owing to the very secret nature of his activities, we have been unable, as yet, to arrange for your sending "Duty Free" cigarettes and tobacco, but we are at present working on the matter. We keep him supplied to a certain extent, but I am sure he would be grateful if you were to send him a small parcel of comforts. I suggest something like this: cigarettes or tobacco, tooth paste, tooth brush if procurable, reading matter, and any small edibles you know he would like. Please do not make the parcel too large. Pack it securely, and the rest you can leave to us.
He is still unable to write, but you may rest assured that he is receiving your mail quite regularly.
If there is any matter over which you are worried, and in which you think we may be able to help, please write to me at the above address.

With best wishes.

Yours sincerely,

[signature]

R.S.M.

To: *Mr. A. J. Middleton*
6 Collegiate Cres.
Sheffield

149

most military of them, had any idea of true discipline and were liable easily to be discouraged. Their true worth depended entirely upon the capacity of their leader and the use of their local knowledge.'

The Maquis had other uses, too, as David Danger remembered from his time at Vieux Dun. 'We got most of our food from the Maquis and on one occasion one of them said he would kill a cow for me. He borrowed my pistol and told another chap [a Frenchman] to hold the horns of this cow while he shot it. The bullet passed through the cow's head and into the other chap's arm!'

What was undeniable was the efficiency of the Maquis' bush telegraph. Little went on in the heavily forested and hilly Morvan without it coming to their attention. On the afternoon of Saturday 24 June a Frenchman came racing into Muirhead's camp to breathlessly inform the SAS that a detachment of Germans and so-called White Russians (Soviet troops fighting for Germany) had arrived in the village of Montsauche. John Noble later described to his girlfriend the reaction of the SAS:

> It appeared that this patrol had been sent out to ambush 'Canadian' troops, reported in that vicinity. So we proceeded to ambush them. We just toddled off to a road that they would have to pass back to their camp. We waited four hours on that road until at long last they came. We were spread over two hundred yards along the road and on a pre-arranged signal we opened up. Their order of march was a truck with a 20mm [cannon] on it, a private car, another truck with a 20mm, followed by a motorcycle. I had the first truck to deal with. As I opened fire with a Bren, an ex-Russian POW (more anon) very thoughtfully chucked a grenade in the truck.

Further up the ditch from Noble were Ian Wellsted and Peter Middleton. It was Wellsted's first time in action and he was glad to have the experienced trooper for company. Middleton was a 23-year-old Yorkshireman, a former clerk with the Sheffield Coal Control Office who had joined the SAS from the Royal Artillery in the summer of 1942. Wellsted later recalled how Middleton had nursed him through his baptism of fire.

> 'Take a shot at those Germans in the ditch, sir.'
> 'Where?'
> 'There! Look, that one's popping his head up, sir.' Bang
> 'I think I got the bastard, sir. Look, just beyond him, have a go at that one, sir.'
> Bang, bang, bang.
> 'Oh, you missed, sir. Better luck next time.'

With the vehicles ablaze and the motorcyclist killed, the ambushers emerged from the ditch to mop up any survivors. Wellsted, encouraged by Middleton, emptied his revolver into the canvas side of a truck and 'heard a satisfactory yelp', and then threw a grenade at a cluster of Germans cowering behind a stack of timber on the other side of the road.

Noble suddenly dropped to his haunches and fired a burst from his Bren into a thick bush, wounding a German corporal. 'The ambush was a complete success,' wrote Noble. 'Three prisoners were taken, the rest were killed. We destroyed the trucks and the car, and kept the motorcycle.'

The German and Russian dead lay on the road until their comrades came to collect them the following day. En route the German salvage squad paused at the village of Ouroux and murdered three Frenchmen on their way to Mass in reprisal for the ambush. They continued on their way towards Montsauche only to be ambushed themselves by the Maquis; 14 of their number were killed. Now the Germans arrived in force, eight truck-loads of soldiers burning the villages of Montsauche and Planchez to the ground and killing indiscriminately.

In all probability the Germans forced some unfortunate local to talk for at 1800 hours on Monday 26 June they attacked the camp of Maquis Camille. Nearly 300 Germans and White Russians began mortaring the woods, exchanging fire with the Frenchmen within. The SOE agent with the Maquis relayed a message to Bill Fraser suggesting it might be an idea for the SAS to set up an ambush on the forest road down which the enemy had launched their assault. Fraser instructed Johnny Wiseman to cover one stretch of the road while he took care of another section. As Fraser moved his men into position, he spotted two Germans on the road about 200 yards away. 'He held his fire and decided to await developments,' ran the Operation *Houndsworth* report. 'In ones and twos more enemy arrived until about 50 men assembled in the area, and forming threes they marched back up the road. At this moment, Major Fraser ordered both his Brens to open fire, and SQMS [Squadron Quartermaster Sergeant] Maclennen had an absolute field day. It was afterwards estimated that not more than 10 men escaped injury from the fracas.'[7]

Wiseman's section, meanwhile, had used the heavy rain and gathering dusk to crawl to within a few yards of the road. Though Reg Seekings had with him Sergeant Jack Terry, a desert veteran, there were also several men who had never before seen action with the SAS. 'I said to Jack "Look across there, there's some trucks and machine gun about 800 yards away, we'll go across and deal with it",' recalled Seekings. 'As we had green men I never told them. We were going down into dead ground and I thought well, if I tell them they'll get all bloody shaky, so we'll come up and then I'll give them a brief before we attack.'[8]

Seekings led his men on their stomachs through the forest undergrowth towards the trucks. At one point he peeked his head up to check the lie of the land, and found himself face to face with the enemy. 'I misjudged it a bit and came up practically straight in front of this bastard machine gun,' reflected Seekings. 'I was just turning my head to shout to the chaps "Get round to the left" and it caught me [the bullet]. I tried to find my rifle and fire left handed but I couldn't move my arm.'

Seekings had been shot in the neck but the next bullet jammed in the chamber of the machine gun. Terry dragged Seekings under cover while Lance Corporal Gibb shot the German as he tried to clear the blockage in his weapon. 'The way my battledress was smothered in blood I thought my arm had been blown off,' said Seekings, who remained conscious throughout the drama. 'I said [to Terry] try and get a tourniquet on my arm. Then I got up and ran 50 or 60 yards to where there was a tree blown down. The funny thing is I remember dropping my pipe and running back to pick it up. But that was the last time I ran for a bit because everything seized up.' Seekings, swearing profusely, was carried back to the SAS hideout whereupon he was examined by the Maquis doctor. Also present was Fraser McLuskey, the 6ft 2in 1SAS padre who had parachuted in with the main party a few days earlier. The 29-year-old McLuskey was an extraordinary character, a man with a German wife and a strong conscience. At the outbreak of war he was chaplain to Glasgow University but in 1942 volunteered for military chaplaincy because he believed his faith would be better employed on the front line. 'For the first time in my life I assisted at a surgical examination,' he wrote later. 'We laid him [Seekings] under the tarpaulin and with the somewhat uncertain light of a torch we found that a bullet had entered the back of his neck and lodged itself deeply near the base of his skull. Probe as he might, the doctor could not get hold of it, and so he decided to leave whatever it was where it was.'[9]★

McLuskey, who was later awarded the Military Cross for his gallantry in France, was admired and respected by every man in 1SAS. David Danger remembered the role he played during Operation *Houndsworth*. 'He was a marvellous man who held these services in the fields whenever possible and we'd sing a few hymns in a very low key! If morale dipped he was always on hand to boost it.'

McLuskey remembered later that 'the favourite hymn was "Stand Up for Jesus" and each Sunday Scottish and English voices belonging to men of all denominations sent the words of this hymn ringing out over German-held fields.' A number of soldiers of A Squadron became more spiritual during their time in France and were later confirmed by McLuskey back in Britain.

★ Seekings had the bullet removed back in England when the surgeon declared him a 'miracle', not just for surviving the bullet but also the probing of the Maquis doctor!

S.A.S. men attended church in German-held fields

PADRE McLUSKEY DROPPED WITH THE PARATROOPS

Padre McLuskey conducts a service for his S.A.S. men in a pinewood in France.

Reg Seekings wasn't one of them, even though he and McLuskey had a mutual regard for one another's diverse talents. 'The Padre was a great chap,' recalled Seekings. 'When we got our first containers he was dishing out these little prayer books, the New Testament, and he said to me 'Your chaps don't seem to be interested in anything like this, what would they be interested in?' Seekings told him that the men loved to read thrillers, the bloodier the better, so McLuskey arranged for a consignment to be dropped in the next resupply. 'He wanted to know if he should carry a gun,' added Seekings, 'and I said "you ever carried a gun?" He said no and I said "well don't start now. We'll look after you"… He said what happens if we're in the jeeps and the driver and gunner get wounded do you think I'm justified in using the guns to defend my comrades? I said yes so he asked me to teach him to use the guns, so I did, but he still never carried a gun.'

The Germans slunk from the forest, carrying their dead and vowing revenge. They took out their fury on the village of Vermot that evening, shooting dead six

As this newspaper reported later, Fraser McLuskey frequently led A Squadron in prayer and song during their stay in the Morvan. (Author's Collection)

French civilians and raping a 14-year-old girl. The next morning they returned to the forest but the Maquis had abandoned their camp and, along with the SAS, moved to a new location. Lusting for vengeance, the Germans drove to Duns-les-Places and rounded up 19 men. They executed them in the village square and raped their women. Then they dragged the village priest to the top of his church, tied a rope round his neck and hurled him from the belfry. In a letter to his girlfriend John Noble described the Germans as 'a lowdown lot of snakes'.

For the rest of June and into the beginning of July heavy rain fell in the Morvan and there was little activity, either from the SAS or the Germans. Fraser described the weather as 'N.B.G' (No Bloody Good) in one of this reports, but his mood improved on 5 July when they received a resupply of food and equipment, along with three jeeps dropped by parachute. There were also letters from home, prayer books for Reverend McLuskey and a selection of cheap paperbacks to amuse the men.

The day after the resupply, Johnny Wiseman left in one jeep to set up a new base in a pine forest just west of Dijon, where more than 30,000 Germans were stationed. His mission was to observe and whenever possible call up RAF air strikes on suitable targets. 'My role was communications,' recalled David Danger, Wiseman's signaller. 'When we had a good target such as a train bringing ammo, we'd get Typhoons to come over and attack. We were also to try and rescue any pilots that had been shot down and put them on to the escape line. We got one or two in the Dijon area.'

The Germans soon realised that there were spies in the forest so they set out to track them down. One day in late July Danger was sending a message when he spotted a man in civilian clothes wandering through the forest. Danger sensed something wasn't right. 'I gave a hasty message to say I was closing down and while my companion pulled the aerial down we started to withdraw. The jeep went with some of the kit and I was running with my wireless set on my back; they weren't small things, and I'd just about had it after a few miles. The others got me by the shoulders and carried me until we found somewhere to lie up.'

The man Danger spotted was a scout for the Milice, the French paramilitary unit that served the Nazis. A couple of days later the Germans and the Milice attacked the camp, unaware that Wiseman's SAS unit was no longer there; in the confusion of the assault the two groups opened fire on each other. Wiseman gleefully reported the incident to HQ, saying: 'They must have been enjoying themselves for they didn't stop before they had succeeded in killing twenty-two of their own men!'[10]

Back in the Morvan, the dropping of jeeps had provided the SAS with the means to range far and wide in harassing the enemy. In the most brazen strike Alex Muirhead had mortared a synthetic oil factory at Autun, 25 miles from the SAS camp, in the presence of an impressed Johnny Cooper. 'I recced the plant a couple

of days prior to the attack and discovered that there was about a two hour quiet period in the early hours of the morning between the end of the night shift and the start of the morning shift,' recalled Cooper.

> We got there in good time and while Alex selected a suitable place from which to fire the mortars I helped prime the bombs. Once that had been done, and Alex had set up the base plate and set the sights, we waited for the end of the night shift. He fired a couple of smoke bombs to find his range and then we popped about 30 incendiary and HE bombs over. It was a complete success and by the time we'd dug out the base plate the factory was ablaze and the Germans' ground defences were blasting away at the planes they thought must have bombed them. They had no inkling they had been mortared from less than a mile away.[11]

John Noble led a sabotage party to cut the railway line between Luzy and Nevers, while another section of men blew the tracks that linked Nevers to Paris, both of which hampered the Germans as they tried to convey men and equipment north to where the Allies were gradually fighting their way inland. An ambush resulted in the discovery of some Gestapo mail and Fraser radioed England with 'information about position and defence of Field Marshal Rommel's HQ [and] details of flying bomb dumps and assemblies near Paris'.

One of the most dramatic incidents occurred in the middle of July when an SAS jeep containing Noble, Peter Middleton, Bob Langridge and a Maquisard ran slap bang into a German staff car in the village of Ouroux. There was an exchange of fire, then the occupants of both vehicles leapt out and began grappling hand to hand. Noble was shot through the shoulder but still managed to club one of the Germans into unconsciousness with the butt of his Colt revolver; a second German went for Noble and was shot dead by Middleton, who was also trying to extinguish a fire after a stray bullet ignited the jeep's exterior petrol tank; one of the enemy fled and was chased and killed by the Maquisard; Langridge was rolling around on the dusty road with a sergeant-major. The German was a 'big bloke and a tough man', recalled Noble, 'who wasn't going to surrender. So I said "to hell with it" and shot him.' The SAS soldiers took the sole surviving German – whose name was Hans – back to their camp and he became the squadron's unofficial dogsbody for the rest of their stay in France. (When A Squadron left France they took a grateful Hans with them, handing him over to the Military Police in England.)

But Operation *Houndsworth* wasn't without its tragedies. On 4 August Noble wrote to his girlfriend to tell her of a distressing incident that had occurred on 20 July.

CABINET MILITAIRE

EXTRAIT DE L'ORDRE GÉNÉRAL N° 229
DU 12 MARS 1945

CITATION A L'ORDRE DE LA DIVISION
:o=o=o=o=o=o=o=o=o=o=o=o:

W I S E M A N   John Martin   Capitaine

Matricule : WS/Lt (T/Capt) 25 68 09
I st. S.A.S. Régt. A.A.C.

pour le motif suivant :

"Exccellent officier parachuté à l'arrière des lignes
"ennemies en Juin 1944. A conduit avec un grand courage
"l'attaque d'importantes voies de communication. Ayant
"rejoint un maquis au début d'Août 1944, a participé avec
"ce maquis à plusieurs combats. A réussi par une habile
"manoeuvre à provoquer un combat entre deux groupes ennemis
"aprés avoir réussi à décrocher son parti submergé par le
"nombre."

Cette citation comporte l'attribution de la CROIX DE GUERRE
AVEC ETOILE D'ARGENT.

Le Général de Corps d'Armée KOENIG
Gouverneur Militaire de Paris
Ex-Commandant des F.M.I.

The citation for Johnny Wiseman's Croix de Guerre for his role in Operation *Houndsworth*. It praises his 'grand courage' and mentions the incident when the Germans and Milice ended up killing one another. (Author's Collection)

Chalky [White] has been shot up. They ran into nine truck loads of Germans. Captain Bradford, the O i/c [officer in charge] gave the order to shoot their way through. The rear gunner [Bill Devine] and Captain Bradford were killed immediately. Chalky was shot through the leg, the arm and had three fingers shot off his left hand. The jeep conked out 150 yards past the German truck. The driver, sgt Maggie Maginn [sic], Chalky and a French kid (he had one through the elbow) all got out and ran into the woods. They just went in two hundred yards and lay down but the Jerries wouldn't come in. That same night, Maggie contacted a Maquis. The Maquis took them back to Maquis 'A'; the first thing Chalky said when he got in was 'Maude will give me hell for losing her ring'. An unconfirmed report says that Chalky killed 62 Germans that day.

Bradford – an architect before the war – and the men of Three Troop had been on their way to establish a new base in the Foret de Dames, 40 miles north of Fraser's HQ, when they were attacked. While Bradford had travelled by jeep, seven men under Lieutenant Ball were heading to the RV on some collapsible bicycles. One of the seven was Jeff Du Vivier who, upon finding no sign of Bradford at the RV, persuaded Ball to let him take a couple of soldiers on a 'scheme'. Du Vivier discovered from a local fisherman the whereabouts of the local Maquis and soon he was in possession of the news that a German ammunition train was due to pass through the area the following day. 'It consisted of two large engines and about 40 wagons and 25 personnel as guard,' recalled Du Vivier. The three men set out on their bikes, accompanied by a Maquis guide, pedalling nine miles through villages and countryside. 'We hid our bikes and taking our rucksacks walked some 500 yards along the track,' he remembered. 'We found a suitable spot and set about laying the charge. I had decided that we should make three charges and join them together with cortex at 50 feet apart and all under the same rail.'[12] It took the saboteurs two hours to lay the charges, Du Vivier insisting that their handiwork had to be completely camouflaged so it wouldn't be noticeable at daybreak.

It was, remembered Du Vivier, 'a very ticklish job making camp again as every road, path and even the farms were watched by the SS' but they eventually succeeded. There he was informed by Fraser of the results of his sabotage mission: 'Both engines had been completely wrecked and turned over on their sides together with a 40' wagon loaded with Ack-Ack guns,' wrote Du Vivier later. '10 wagons behind this were derailed and lying over the track… Unfortunately the carriage containing the Germans was at the rear of the train and they were unscathed, but, according to the Maquis, very frightened and demoralised.'

A Squadron continued to demoralise the Germans in the Morvan throughout August though Peter Middleton was lucky not to join the casualty list on the penultimate day of the month. Together with Tom Rennie, Middleton had accepted an invitation from the Maquis to watch as the French fought a sporadic gun battle with the Germans at the village of Corancy. As the pair strolled towards the village in the company of the Maquis chief – who was proudly describing how his men had all but routed the Germans – a burst of heavy machine-gun fire sent them diving into a ditch.

'I'm hit!' yelled Middleton.

Rennie examined his friend and discovered a bullet had passed through both cheeks of Middleton's backside and out again without causing any serious damage, other than to his underpants. As Middleton later explained to his amused comrades it was the third time his backside had stopped a German bullet. That evening

Fraser wrote in his report: 'Middleton is wounded in an embarrassing though not dangerous place!'[13]

A week after Middleton's lucky escape A Squadron set off for England, having been replaced by Tony Marsh's C Squadron. Before they went Bill Fraser presented a regimental flag to the people of Duns-les-Places in tribute to their courage and stoicism. Despite what the French villagers had suffered as an indirect result of the SAS attacks against the Germans, not one of them bore the British any resentment. France was in the process of being liberated, that was all that mattered.

A Squadron had certainly done their bit to drive the Germans out of France. In three months they had killed or wounded 220 Germans, derailed six trains, destroyed 23 motorised vehicles and mortared a synthetic oil refinery. Their casualties – excluding the aircraft that had disappeared in June – were two dead and seven wounded, one of whom was Chalky White. 'He looks rather pale,' John Noble wrote to his girlfriend, shortly before the squadron left France, 'but otherwise he is just the same as when you met him. The man's positively inhuman. With an army of men like him we could have finished the war three years ago.'

Three months earlier, at 0137 hours on 6 June, lieutenants John Tonkin and Richard Crisp had parachuted into France, 20 miles south-west of Chateauroux. It was a perfect drop, recalled Tonkin; not only were the local Maquis there to greet them but 'it was such a gentle landing that I doubt if I'd have broken an egg if I'd landed on it'.[14]

The insertion of B Squadron into their operational zone followed a similar pattern to *Houndsworth*; once Tonkin and Crisp were satisfied with the arrangements on the ground, they radioed SAS Brigade and the main reconnaissance party dropped. On the night of 7/8 June Lieutenant Tomos Stephens and eight men landed and on 12 June the main party arrived, though its strength had been depleted by a last-minute change of orders: four small sticks of men had been dropped blind in other areas to sabotage railways lines before making their way to the main camp. Tonkin was furious that he had not been informed.

Later he made his feelings known in the post-operation report but for the time being he contented himself with informing brigade HQ that instead of 50 men under his command, he had just 23, and this in an area 'lousy with Germans'.

From its auspicious beginnings, when Tonkin had executed a perfect landing, Operation *Bulbasket* became dogged by misfortune. Just as they had intended to launch a series of sabotage attacks, the SAS party found themselves in the middle of the 2nd SS Panzerdivision, Das Reich, travelling up from the south to fight in Normandy.

Sergeant Bob Holmes (front left) and three troopers during the ill-fated Operation *Bulbasket*. Holmes was one of seven men to escape when their camp was overrun by Germans on 3 July. (Author's Collection)

Forced to act with extreme caution, Tonkin also found the local Maquis jealous and distrustful and even his Phantom signaller, a Captain Sadoine was uncooperative. A couple of resupply drops were cancelled because of bad weather and poor communication so that by the end of June morale was low in the *Bulbasket* camp. On 30 June Lieutenant Peter Weaver arrived. He was one of the leaders of the four sabotage sticks that had dropped elsewhere on 12 June. Weaver was 33, considerably older than Tonkin, and though he had seen less action than his commanding officer he was experienced enough to read the danger signs. With the Das Reich division having moved on there was a slackness to the camp; soldiers were making frequent trips to a farm to collect eggs and young women from the nearby village of Verrieres were wandering into the SAS hideout to flirt with the British soldiers. Weaver thought Tonkin 'was getting a little out of his depth with his responsibilities'.[15]

The news that two of Tonkin's most experienced soldiers, Dougie Eccles and Ken Bateman, had failed to return from a sabotage mission a day earlier left Weaver with a sense of foreboding. 'I thought the camp was becoming far too well known,' he recalled, 'and suggested to John we should split up and disperse in small parties to another area, but he was against the idea. I think he thought he would lose control.'

On 1 July, however, Tonkin did agree to Weaver's suggestion, and they moved camp, only to discover the water supply was inadequate. The 50 men – which included nine Maquisards and a shot-down American pilot – returned to their hideout near Verrieres with Tonkin intending to relocate to another camp on 3 July.

But at first light on 3 July the men of *Bulbasket* came under attack from an SS Panzer Grenadier Division. Peter Weaver was woken by the sound of an explosion. 'For the life of me I couldn't think what all the noise was about in my semi-sleepy state,' he reflected. 'Then it dawned on me: "Christ, we're being mortared!"'

The word went round the camp that they were surrounded by 500 Germans. There was panic among the Maquisards and the SAS, many of whom were young and inexperienced. Most rushed en masse down a slope towards a valley and into the arms of the Germans. The seven men who survived, one of whom was Tonkin, kept their heads and thought about which direction offered the best hope of escape. Peter Weaver 'shot off into the trees and turned south' before crawling through a field of corn. He was spotted by four Germans and chased but Weaver, a former first-class cricketer, outpaced them and evaded capture.

Thirty-one of his comrades, including the American pilot, weren't so fortunate. They were taken to Poitiers for interrogation and then, on the evening of 6 July, the prisoners were loaded into trucks and driven deep into the forest of Saint Sauvant. There they were machine-gunned.

A similar fate befell some of the men on Operation *Gain*, a 1SAS mission carried out by 58 members of D Squadron that commenced on the night of 13/14 June. *Gain's* objective was to cut the German lateral railway communications in the bottleneck area of Rambouillet – Provins – Gien – Orleans – Chartres, all towns south of Paris that took trains to Normandy. Under the command of Ian Fenwick, the SAS established camp in the Foret d'Orleans and for the first couple of weeks the operation was a great success. Several railway lines were blown, a railway locomotive and 30 wagons were destroyed in their sidings and a motorized patrol was ambushed. 'We went out in small groups, between two and four men usually,' recalled Vic Long.

A scheme [to blow a railway line] would last four or five days and when we returned to camp there wouldn't be many people around. We'd rest for a while, more would return, and then we'd go off again, and that's the way it went.

The station master at Nibelle, which was just down the hill from where we were in the forest, used to let the Maquis know which trains were leaving and when, and that made life easier. The main trouble at night was dogs, not Germans. You went through the village and just as you got on the outskirts you heard this yapping and then windows opened. You would remain still, the window closed, you go on another 100 yards and then another dog started yapping![16]

On 4 July a 12-man stick under the command of Captain Pat Garstin left England to reinforce Operation *Gain*. The DZ was near a little village called La Ferte-Alais, 30 miles south of Paris and some distance from the Foret d'Orleans, so it was arranged that a party of Maquisards would collect them and bring them to their D Squadron comrades.

'I admit here and now, I was afraid… My chief fear was getting shot down in the drink.'

John Noble

Mike Sadler decided to accompany the soldiers on the flight to France, not just because he was a good friend of Garstin's but also for a spot of excitement. 'My role at this time [as intelligence officer] was to take the chaps to the aircraft, see them off, and then get a debrief from the pilots when they returned from the drop. But I thought it was much easier and quicker to go myself, and I still liked a little bit of adrenaline.'

As the Stirling bomber approached the DZ Sadler, situated in the aircraft's bomb aimer's seat below the pilot's floor, searched for three lighted fires down below spaced 100 yards apart and the recognition letter – B for Bertie – flashed from a torch. With the recognition letter correct and the fires on the DZ well lit, the men jumped from 800 feet at 0153 hours (5 July) on a moonlit night. Garstin was first out, followed by Lance-Corporal Howard Lutton. The last three men to leave the aircraft were troopers Morrison (his first name has been lost to history, but the initial was 'R'), Leslie 'Titch' Norman and Herbert Castelow, the latter a brick maker from Stockton-on-Tees.

The moment Garstin hit the ground the firing started. Having extracted the information about the DZ from a captured Maquisard, the Germans had prepared a reception committee of their own with a combined force of around 50 security police and French Milice. Garstin was shot in the neck, Lutton was mortally wounded and a bullet hit the spinal column of Lieutenant Jean Wiehe, a French officer from Mauritius known as 'Johnny'. The last three men to jump – Morrison, Norman and Castelow –

landed in some woods just outside the DZ. 'Realising things had gone wrong, I cut off my parachute and hid as quickly as possible,' recalled Castelow who had lost sight of his comrades.[17]

Norman and Morrison had made contact, however, and advanced towards the gunfire. As they approached the edge of the woods they heard a voice call, 'Who's there?' It was Wiehe. In hushed tones he explained that he was lying on the edge of the clearing, badly wounded and unable to move. Norman said he was coming to his aid, Wiehe ordered him to remain where he was. There was no point risking their lives on his account. Norman later explained that 'Wiehe gave instructions for [us] to make off and endeavour to reach the beachhead.'[18]

Norman and Morrison did as ordered, running through the woods in a north-westerly direction. On the outskirts of the woods they encountered some Germans scouring the area for any parachutists they might have missed. The Germans fired wildly into the trees but Norman and Morrison were already on their stomachs, crawling noiselessly for 200 yards before slithering into a corn field and continuing in a north-west direction. During the next three hours the pair crossed a railway line, crept through a village, skirted the banks of a river and climbed a wooded slope before deciding to lie up for a few hours. They chanced upon a cave and settled down to sleep.

When they woke Norman and Morrison observed the countryside from their vantage point on the hillside as they shared a tin of milk and a bar of chocolate. They then discussed their next course of action. The official SAS report on the 'Garstin Stick' incident described what followed:

Norman volunteered to do a recce and Morrison would remain at the cave and keep a lookout. Off Norman went, heading into the wood. After travelling about a mile he came across a house and just as he reached it a woman came out to feed some chickens that were running around the yard. Norman beckoned the woman into the wood and explained that he was a British parachutist, had a fellow parachutist in the wood, and that both were very much in need of food. The woman looked around and after assuring herself that the coast was clear, took Norman into the house and gave him bread, milk and some very fat bacon. Norman, feeling very much happier at the thought of a reasonably good meal, returned to Morrison and soon the old Tommy cooker was going hard at it. After the meal a consultation was held us to whether or not they should move that night. They agreed that possibly patrols would be on the lookout since it was known that they had landed and therefore they decided to lie up in the same place for a second night.[19]

For the next few days the men continued cautiously in a north-west direction, relying on the munificence of locals for food and water. On the night of 11 July they bedded down in a small wood between a road and a river and at one point were woken by a great commotion on the road. At first light Norman and Morrison watched through the trees as a battalion of Germans troops broke camp and climbed into their trucks, leaving behind a mass of empty rations tins and ripped envelopes. The SAS men inspected the abandoned camp and surmised that the Germans had just come from the Normandy beachhead and were heading for a rest, happy to have received their first batch of mail from home in weeks.

Norman and Morrison trekked north-west again and that evening (12 July) climbed out of a wood and onto a road. 'Norman turned left and Morrison looked to the right,' stated the SAS report. 'Norman could not speak and Morrison seeing the expression on Norman's face looked in his direction. He too must have felt queer for there was a road block (of barricade type) and a German sentry. Fortunately for our men the sentry was looking in the opposite direction so Norman and Morrison nipped across the road and went across country.'

At 1100 hours on 14 July the pair came to an isolated farm near the village of Saint Cheron, approximately 14 miles from where they had landed. Inside the farm was a woman of about 30, cheerfully preparing a large meal for that evening. She fed the SAS men and then directed them to a nearby wood where they could rest, telling the pair she would return later. When the woman reappeared she was carrying a basket of food and some wine, and she had in tow five members of her family and four of her friends. It was Bastille Day, explained the woman to Norman and Morrison, and she thought it only fitting they should celebrate with their British allies. Over supper the soldiers were persuaded by their French hosts to remain hidden in the wood rather than strike out north-west again; the Allies would soon be here and in the meantime they would contact the local Maquis to see if they could help.

The Maquis sent a bespectacled, bookish man who turned out to be the headmaster of the local school. He gave Norman and Morrison some civilian clothes and told them he'd contacted London and plans were afoot to extricate them by air, but on the day he promised to return the headmaster never showed. A few days later, resigned to the fact the man had broken his word, the two soldiers walked out of the wood for their daily meal at the farm. 'They were just coming out of the house,' recounted the SAS report, 'when they walked bang into a German officer. Morrison just calmly walked passed him and down the garden path, and Norman turned to the right and "shooed" some ducks away from a nearby pond. Both men made their way back to the wood and fortunately all was well.'

A few days later the farmer appeared in the wood with two young women, both of whom were schoolteachers and fluent English speakers. They explained that the headmaster had been captured by the Gestapo, interrogated and then shot, though he hadn't talked before his death. There would be no airlift, said the women, but the Americans would soon arrive so it was just a question of patience. They handed a collection of English-language books to the soldiers expressing the hope that they would help pass the time of the day. Three weeks later, at 1900 hours on 15 August, the two women arrived at the farm in the back of an American jeep. 'The officer in the jeep told them [Morrison and Norman] that the Americans had just arrived and that if they had a look around they would soon find someone who would take them back… On hearing the news our two men dug up their uniforms, had them dried at the farm, and on the following morning set off in search of the Americans. Morrison went towards the village and Norman in the opposite direction. Norman met a jeep, the driver of which took him to a headquarters.'

At the time Norman and Morrison's ordeal was drawing to a satisfactory conclusion, Herbert Castelow was 18 miles to the east in the village of Vert-le-Petit. Having remained hidden in the wood for 24 hours after the initial drop, Castelow broke cover on the morning of 7 July and walked north until he came to Vert-le-Petit. There he had the good fortune to encounter Michel Leduc, the village butcher, who knew the head of the local Maquis and for six weeks – wearing the garb of a civilian – Castelow operated as a resistance fighter while living above the butcher's shop. 'We were mainly engaged in ambushing transport on the roads,' he recalled. 'I travelled about quite freely, and spent two weeks in Paris. About mid-August, however, the Gestapo got to know I was in the vicinity and it became too dangerous to remain.'

Castelow was given a bicycle and advised to head south-west, in the direction of the Allied forces now pushing east after the battle of the Falaise Pocket. Unfortunately the SAS trooper found himself in the middle of the retreating Germans. He stopped at a village for refreshment and while he was eating someone made off with his bicycle. 'On discovering this I swore in English,' recalled Castelow. 'This was overheard and I was immediately arrested by a German patrol. At first I was going to be shot out of hand as a spy but the officer present decided to send me behind the lines for questioning.'

Castelow was bundled into a lorry and driven 200 miles east to Verdun. 'I was put in a cell and given a little food once a day, and made to stand all the time during questioning, and at one period I was kicked about,' he recalled. 'I refused, however, to tell them what I had been doing or that I was a paratrooper.'

In early September Castelow was removed from his cell, put in a truck and driven east. On 9 September the vehicle crossed the river Moselle between Metz and Nancy, and a few miles further on it stopped in a village. 'I was put in a cottage with one SS guard to look after me,' recounted Castelow. 'I was not tied down, and at about 2359 hours I killed the guard and took his rifle. I then walked out of the cottage and climbed the wall into the street. I was not challenged and was able to make my way without opposition to the river. I swam the Moselle and started walking back towards the Americans.'

Castelow reached safety not long after and was taken first to Paris. Then on 21 September he was repatriated to the UK where he was reunited with Norman and Morrison, as well as two other members of the Garstin Stick – Thomas 'Ginger' Jones, a desert veteran of the SAS, and Serge Vaculik, a Frenchman. Theirs was a dreadful tale.

Having been captured on the DZ on the night of 5 July, they and the rest of the stick were taken to Gestapo headquarters in Paris and brutally interrogated for four weeks.[*] By the time they were ordered to change into civilian clothes on the evening of 8 August, Captain Garstin – in addition to his serious neck wound sustained during the exchange of fire on the DZ – had sustained a double fracture to his right arm and one to his leg.

Jones, Vaculik, Garstin and four other troopers were driven to a forest and marched into a clearing whereupon they were informed they were terrorists. 'Oh God, we are going to be shot,' moaned Garstin, at which point Vaculik, Jones and Tom Varey bolted for freedom. Caught off-guard by the spontaneous and audacious reaction of the trio, the firing squad shot Garstin and the other three men but failed to prevent their comrades disappearing into the trees.[20]

Varey was tracked down and slain but Vaculik and Jones escaped execution, finding shelter with locals who in turn handed them over to the Maquis. The testimony of the pair, once back in England, was the first definitive proof of Lieutenant Jimmy Hughes's claim in March 1944 that the Germans were executing captured SAS personnel. In late September Mike Sadler and Harry Poat visited the area where the execution had occurred and, with the assistance of the local Maquis group, the pair were led to the clearing. Villagers had laid flowers on the shallow grave that contained the corpses of Garstin and his four men. Sadler, who had been a good friend of Garstin, was horrified by what he found under the soil. The bodies were badly decomposed but it was still possible to identify Garstin 'because of his height, it was more than six feet, and by the shape of his head which was somewhat unusual'.

---

[*] Lieutenant Johnny Wiehe was taken to a Paris hospital to be treated for his wounds. Though he survived captivity, Wiehe succumbed to his injuries shortly after the war and is buried on his native Mauritius.

'*Our orders were to cause mayhem and we were told to choose our own targets… The phrase they used was "alarm and despondency"; that's what we were to spread among the Germans.*'

Albert Youngman

The bodies were disinterred and removed to Beauvais, where they were buried in the Marianne cemetery.★

———————

On 7 August, the day before the murder of Pat Garstin, Paddy Mayne had parachuted into France along with Mike Sadler and two other SAS soldiers. 'Our aircraft actually crashed on take-off because the undercarriage collapsed,' recalled Sadler. 'It was all pretty dramatic but they quickly loaded us into another aeroplane minus all our stores and minus our despatcher [who had been injured in the crash]. So we had to throw the panniers out of the plane and then jump out after them without anyone to supervise us, which was a bit nerve-wracking.'

Mayne's original intention had been to drop east of Orleans, where D Squadron was still engaged on Operation *Gain*, to inform them of their impending role in a new mission codenamed 'Transfigure'. *Transfigure* would involve D Squadron as well as Bill Fraser's A Squadron, acting as reconnaissance troops in a major Allied offensive aimed at crushing German resistance west of the Rhine. In fact, *Transfigure* was never put into operation because of the American breakout from the Cotentin Peninsula that began in late July. Mayne parachuted into France, not just to personally brief Ian Fenwick and Fraser on *Transfigure* but also to assess the strength and morale of German troops in the area before committing his men to the scheme.

Mayne was forced to reorganise his plans, however, when he learned from Fenwick early on the morning of 7 August that D Squadron's camp in the Forêt d'Orleans had been overrun by a large force of Germans. Fenwick, along with some of his men (including Vic Long and Jim Almonds, one of the SAS 'originals') had been absent during the attack, instead preparing a DZ for Mayne's imminent visit. Fenwick radioed Mayne to tell him to abort his drop and then set off in a jeep to investigate exactly what had happened at the camp. With him in the vehicle were four men, three SAS soldiers (one of whom was French) and a Maquis guide.

The jeep was spotted by a German reconnaissance plane as it drove along the narrow country roads and an ambush was set up at a T-junction just outside the village of Chambon-le-Foret. A woman flagged down the jeep as she fled from the village, warning Fenwick of the ambush and informing him that the Germans were holding a large group of men hostage inside the village church. On being informed of the Germans' presence, Fenwick told the woman: 'Thank you, madame, but I intend to attack them.'[21]

OPPOSITE
Mike Sadler behind the wheel somewhere in France. The figure in the passenger seat, partially obscured, may be Paddy Mayne, who accompanied Sadler as they visited A and D Squadrons in August 1944. (Courtesy of the SAS Regimental Archive)

———————

★ The fate of the SAS soldiers executed during Operation *Bulbasket* wasn't discovered until December 1944 when a Frenchman searching for mushrooms in the forest stumbled upon the mass grave.

Albert Youngman (right) seen here in Belgium in the autumn of 1944 was awarded a Military Medal for his bravery during Operation *Haggard*. (Author's Collection)

Fenwick sped towards the village, shooting his way past one German machine gun nest before being killed by a round from a 20mm cannon. The two Frenchmen also died and the two badly wounded SAS troopers were taken into captivity. Vic Long says the rest of the squadron were shocked when they learned of Fenwick's brave but reckless behaviour. 'We thought it was bloody stupid and Jim Almonds said he was sure if he had been with him he could have talked him out of it. The SAS had said you do not want to be caught [and] you do not fight unless you can get out of it.' Instead of dropping into *Gain*'s operational area, Mayne landed in the Morvan, where Bill Fraser met him. He didn't remain long in the company of A Squadron, however, and on 9 August motored north towards Orleans. 'It wasn't really a morale booster when Paddy arrived, just another face passing through,' recalled Long. 'He told me to go and do a listening patrol on the Orleans-Pithivers road.'

Mayne informed Jock Riding, Fenwick's successor as OC of Operation *Gain*, to increase road watching patrols ahead of the planned Operation *Transfigure* and radio back all information. This they did before they were overrun by the vanguard of the American breakout from the Cotentin Peninsula. Vic Long sold his silk map of the area (provided to all SAS troops prior to insertion into France) to a GI for $50 and American trucks transported the men of D Squadron to the coast from where they were flown back to England. In the two and a half months of Operation *Gain* they had cut 16 railway lines, derailed two trains, destroyed two engines, wiped out 46 enemy vehicles and killed at least six Germans. In addition, they had provided invaluable information on the strength and movement of German forces south of Paris.

The purpose of Operation *Haggard* was purely aggressive and to that end it was overwhelmingly successful. Comprising those men of B Squadron who hadn't been involved on the ill-fated *Bulbasket*, *Haggard* began on 15 August under the command of Major Eric Lepine. They dropped west of the Loire and established a base between the towns of Bourges and Nevers, an area described by SHAEF as 'extremely important following the destruction of the Seine bridges below Paris'.[22] One of the men who dropped with Lepine was Lance-Sergeant Albert Youngman. 'Our orders were to cause mayhem and we were told to choose our own targets,' he remembered. 'The phrase they used was "alarm and despondency"; that's what we were to spread among the Germans.'[23]

By the time Operation *Haggard* was wound up on 9 September, B Squadron had more than fulfilled its objective. They had killed or wounded an estimated 233 Germans, destroyed 37 motorised vehicles and blown up two bridges. In his assessment of *Haggard*, Brigadier Roderick McLeod, commander of the SAS Brigade, wrote: 'It is clear that one or two highly successful ambushes were arranged and that this Operation no doubt assisted in the general German collapse south of the Loire.'[24]

While B Squadron was involved in Operation *Gain*, to the north-east Tony Marsh's C Squadron was conducting Operation *Kipling*. The initial insertion had been made by Captain Derrick Harrison and five men in the early hours of 14 August. They landed in Foret de Merry-Vaux with orders to establish a suitable landing zone for the rest of the squadron, who would come in by glider, and carry out reconnaissance patrols. Four days after Harrison's arrival 13 more men of C Squadron dropped by parachute with the news that the glider operation had been scrapped and instead Major Marsh would bring the men in on Dakotas, landing at Rennes and then driving down in jeeps.

It was from around this corner in the village of Les Ormes that Derrick Harrison's SAS patrol attacked an SS execution squad in August 1944. (Author's Collection)

James McDiarmid (far left) in France during Operation *Kipling*. The 'X' marked on the house in the right of the photo is where McDiarmid machine-gunned a group of captured German soldiers. (Author's Collection)

Marsh's 40-strong detachment arrived at the Foret de Merry-Vaux on the day that the squadron suffered its first fatality of the operation. Two jeeps, one driven by Jimmy Hall and containing Harrison and the other consisting of Lieutenant Stewart Richardson and two troopers, inadvertently drove into the village of Les Ormes just as an SS unit were in the process of executing 20 civilians. Two had already been shot when the SAS vehicles appeared and in the ensuing firefight Hall was killed and Harrison wounded in the hand. Several Germans were killed and the 18 hostages had taken advantage of the confrontation to escape with their lives. 'Harrison was pretty shaken up when he came back,' recalled Sid Payne, who had just returned to their forest camp with Sergeant James McDiarmid after an all-night listening patrol.[25]

The death of the popular Hall infuriated McDiarmid, a desert veteran of the SAS who had joined from the Black Watch Regiment. McDiarmid was a curious character, the life and soul of the party when the mood took him whose celebrated 'Puddle Dance', a sort of highland fling interspersed with forward rolls, always had the men in stitches. He had a young daughter on whom he doted, and was inspiringly brave in combat. In Bagnara he had been awarded the Military Medal for his outstanding leadership when wounded but now learning of Hall's death, McDiarmid's dark side emerged.

A couple of days later while leading a two-jeep patrol McDiarmid ran into a small enemy convoy. Those Germans not killed by the fire from the jeeps' Vickers were dragged up against the wall of a nearby house by McDiarmid and machine-gunned. In a subsequent incident, McDiarmid stopped a car carrying two men in civilian clothes who were discovered to be German officers. Both were shot.

On 28 August, five days after Marsh's arrival at the Foret de Merry-Vaux, Peter Davis appeared with a second contingent of C Squadron troops. The following day Marsh led his men south to the Morvan where they took over operations from Bill Fraser's A Squadron; Davis and 34 men, meanwhile, remained to continue Operation *Kipling*, ranging far and wide, carrying out reconnaissance and engaging the enemy whenever possible. Bob Lowson, now a sergeant, destroyed three trucks full of German troops on 7 September – for which he was awarded the Military Medal – and five days later Lieutenant Mike Mycock and his patrol, working with the French First Army, accepted the surrender of 3,000 demoralised German troops at Autun. On 24 September, C Squadron were withdrawn from their operational area and ordered north towards Brussels. They were the last soldiers of 1SAS to depart France, nearly four months after Ian Wellsted and Ian Stewart had dropped into the Morvan at the start of Operation *Houndsworth*.

Lieutenant Roy Close receives an enthusiastic welcome as he passes through the village of Chatillon-en-Bazois in September 1944 during Operation *Kipling*. The villagers thought Close was the vanguard of a large liberating force but in fact the SAS patrol was returning to base having attacked a German convoy. (Author's Collection)

CHAPTER 9

2SAS EARN THEIR WINGS

The officer who succeeded Bill Stirling as OC 2SAS was Lieutenant-Colonel Brian Franks, who had been at the battle of Termoli as brigade-major of the Commando Brigade. Franks came from the same social set as the Stirlings – Ian Fenwick and the actor David Niven were close friends – and he was terribly well-connected having worked as assistant manager at London's Dorchester Hotel in the 1930s. 'We were lucky to get Brian Franks, who was a brilliant officer,' reflected Tony Greville-Bell.[1]

When Franks assumed command of 2SAS SHAEF had agreed to amend their original plan for the regiment in the impending invasion of France so his immediate concern was to continue the recruitment of new soldiers. High calibre officers were in particular demand and Franks was fortunate to unearth two in Henry Druce and Bob Walker-Brown. He encountered Druce on a train bound for Manchester, where the pair were scheduled to undergo a parachute course at Ringway. Druce was a former officer in the Middlesex Regiment whose linguistic abilities – French, Flemish and Dutch – had led to a secondment to MI6.

Walker-Brown was an ever so slightly eccentric Scot, who had distinguished himself during the war in North Africa as an officer in the Highland Light Infantry. 'I happened to be in the Caledonia Hotel in Aberdeen one day when I saw a very glamorous-looking officer covered in wings and pistols and God knows what,'

OPPOSITE
Brian Franks (left) replaced Bill Stirling as OC 2SAS and parachuted into the Vosges to take charge of Operation *Loyton*. (Courtesy of the SAS Regimental Archive)

remembered Walker-Brown. 'I asked him what unit he was in and he said the SAS. "Right," I said. "What's your CO's name and telephone number?" I phoned up Brian Franks and joined the SAS.'[2]

Experienced officers such as Druce and Walker-Brown were invaluable to Franks and 2SAS; when the regiment returned from the Mediterranean in late March, Paddy Mayne had already toured the Auxiliary Units and the Airborne depots to cream off the talent. Franks was still able to recruit some very well-trained soldiers into 2SAS but when the regiment left their Ayrshire base for Salisbury Plain in late June 1944, 140 men had yet to be blooded in battle.

The next few weeks in southern England were ones of immense frustration for Franks as he tried to obtain a role for his regiment similar to that of 1SAS. Operation *Rupert* to be launched near Nancy, eastern France, in mid July, was cancelled at short notice because of objections from Special Forces Headquarters (SFHQ). Franks was furious at what he perceived as outside interference and said so in a letter to Brigadier McLeod, writing:

> I have been trying to mount the initial operations of this regiment, which in each case entailed the dropping of a reconnaissance party into areas which you have ordered me to go. Although the personnel of these parties are perfectly prepared to drop blind, it is obviously preferable that in every case they should be received by a S.F.H.Q. reception committee. The difficulties and time wasted in endeavouring to arrange [these] reception committees satisfactorily has been appalling to say the least of it.[3]

Finally, 2SAS were given a mission – Operation *Defoe* – though Franks sensed it was designed to keep him quiet rather than achieve any worthwhile aims. Nonetheless on 19 July 22 men dropped into southern Normandy and spent the next few weeks on listening patrols, radioing back information to disinterested British and American regiments. A fortnight after *Defoe*, Tony Greville-Bell led 59 men into France on a scheme codenamed *Dunhill*. 'I didn't know what the operation was called,' he recalled. 'But I know it was a complete waste of bloody time.' Having landed east of Rennes, the SAS party was quickly overrun by the American Third Army pushing towards Paris and 16 days later they were back in England.

Operation *Rupert* finally got the go ahead in late July, their orders being to sabotage the railway lines in eastern France between Nancy and Chalons-sur-Marne. The advance party left Fairford on board a Stirling bomber on the night of 23 July only for their aircraft to smash into a hillside as it approached the DZ.

It was a further fortnight before a replacement advance party was dropped and by the time the bulk of men on Operation *Rupert* jumped in late August, the

American Third Army was sweeping through the countryside. For a brief while the Americans encouraged the SAS to act as their eyes and ears, but then General Patton arrived. 'We hoped to move east and link up with those 2SAS boys on Operation *Loyton*,' recalled Cyril Radford, one of the soldiers on *Rupert*. 'But when Patton came along he put a stop to that. He didn't like the British so he gave orders for us to be escorted out of the Third Army area by US MPs [military policemen].'[4]

Unbeknown to Radford, the '2SAS boys' on Operation *Loyton* were in sore need of the support of their comrades from Operation *Rupert*. From the start there had been ominous signs for Operation *Loyton*; the officer initially scheduled to lead the mission backed out at the eleventh hour and so Brian Franks turned to Captain Henry Druce, as it transpired an inspired decision. 'With the men standing by the aircraft I was telephoned in Scotland and told to rush down to Fairford,' remembered Druce.[5]

Druce arrived at Fairford on 12 August and was briefed on the operation: now that the Allies had broken out of the Normandy beachhead the German Army was making a rapid retreat through France towards their homeland. Before they reached the German border, however, they had to negotiate the Vosges, a wooded range of hills that run north to south on the French side of the river Rhine: *Loyton*'s role was to drop into the Vosges and attack the retreating Germans. Druce was familiar with the terrain having passed through the Vosges before the war; he knew therefore that it was a landscape ripe for guerrilla warfare with its thick forests, deep ravines and flowing rivers. Druce knew too that the Vosges was a region of divided loyalty, an area long fought over by the French and the Germans with a minority of its inhabitants harbouring affection for the Nazi cause.

Druce led the advance party of *Loyton* into the Vosges in the early hours of 13 August. Packed into the plane were several canisters containing over 200 weapons with which to arm the local Maquis in the hope they would provide additional firepower during the operation. There were 14 men in total, none more experienced than Ronald Crossfield, better known as 'Dusty', an 'Old Sweat' who had joined the army in 1934 and whose seven brothers were all in uniform. He wrote an account of their insertion:

Brian Franks's first problem when he took charge of 2SAS was to turn hundreds of recruits into special forces soldiers in a short space of time. These three members of 3 Squadron look the part but some others were sent into France without adequate training and suffered as a consequence. (Courtesy of John Robertson)

All lights were doused as we approached the coast and I remember that as we flew over my home town, Brighton, thinking about my wife and three year old son down there and wondering whether this was going to be a one way trip. We were to be dropped in the forests of Vosges, roughly fifty miles from Strasbourg near the village of Petit Renou [in fact it was the village of La Petite Raon]. A tot of rum each warmed us up just before we got the order to 'Hook up' – I followed Captain Druce and Hislop [captain John Hislop was the leader of a three-man Phantom signalling team] out and breathed the usual sigh of relief as my parachute opened with a welcome crack.

Not the best landing for me as I could see that I was drifting towards the trees and pulling hard on my rigging lines didn't help. Both helmet and kitbag were wrenched off as I crashed through the branches and came to rest swinging gently with no idea of the distance between me and the ground. I punched my quick release and dropped heavily to the deck – it must have been about fifteen feet. Someone was running towards me and I reckon I had my [colt] 45 out faster than John Wayne, but the cry of 'Tres Bien, Angleterre' saved the lad from being shot. I fared better than some: Captain Druce had concussion and Ginger had damaged his knee so it was a slow march to cover the nine miles to the first camp.[6]

Druce recalled that it had taken him a couple of hours for his senses to unscramble, by which time the Maquis had made off with several of the SAS containers. 'I think straight away we got to realise the Maquis weren't playing the game,' said Druce.

Nor did it take much time for Druce to appreciate the strength of the German forces in the area into which they had been dropped. On 15 August he radioed SAS Brigade to report that 'between one thousand and five thousand' enemy soldiers were moving east through a neighbouring valley.

Deciding that they needed a more secure base, Druce divided his party in two and set off on a scouting patrol. With him went the Phantom signallers and a Jedbergh team★ while a French captain called Robert Goodfellow was given command of four SAS men comprising Crossfield, Hay, Ginger Hall and 36-year-old Robert Lodge. Lodge was actually Rudolf Friedlaender, a German Jew who had fled his country with his family in the 1930s and settled in Twickenham. Lodge had won the Distinguished Conduct Medal earlier in the war and despite being significantly older than the average SAS trooper, he was considered one of the finest men in the regiment. In addition a shot-down Canadian pilot, Lou Fiddick, who had been

---

★ Nearly 100 Jedbergh teams dropped into France in the summer of 1944. Each team comprised three men from either the SOE or the American Office of Strategic Service (OSS) and their job was to coordinate attacks on the Germans with the aid of the Maquis.

brought to Druce by the Maquis, was attached to the second party.

Lodge was leading the patrol through the forest when he froze and signalled for the men following to do likewise. 'Suddenly all hell broke loose and everyone dived flat,' remembered Crossfield. 'Schmeissers, Lugers and rifles were all firing at us. We retaliated with our Brens and carbines. I know I used up three magazines very quickly. The Germans, firing through thick scrub, were not more than thirty yards away. They could not see us but we heard a scream or two.'

Members of 3 Squadron 2SAS on a training exercise during the summer of 1944 as they waited impatiently to drop into France. (Courtesy of John Robertson)

Goodfellow, in fact a Frenchman called Robert de Lesseps, a grandson of the man who constructed the Suez Canal, ordered the men to withdraw but as Crossfield began to crawl back through the trees he spotted Ginger Hall lying wounded. 'I went to drag him away but he moaned "leave me, I've had it. Get away." He had been hit twice in the chest and we no choice to leave him. It was a fiercely fought withdrawal and at some point Lodge disappeared through the bushes never to be seen again.' The body of Lodge, bearing a bullet wound to the head and bayonet wounds to the stomach was later buried by locals in a nearby cemetery.

Druce, meanwhile, had also run into some Germans and some of the party became separated in the flight across the hills. Sergeant Seymour, a member of the Jedbergh team, was captured, and signaller Gerald Davis sought sanctuary in a village church. The priest departed promising to return with the Maquis but it was the Germans he brought and Davis was shot.

Druce and Goodfellow were finally reunited on 23 August. The two groups exchanged stories but were interrupted by the arrival of some Maquisards, dragging by the hair two young women whom they accused of betraying their presence to the Germans. Crossfield said the Maquis were all for shooting them but Druce, unconvinced as to their guilt, argued for leniency. 'A compromise was reached,' recalled Crossfield, 'and their hair was shaved off and they were set to work on camp duties.'

On 26 August Druce should have welcomed in a ten-strong reinforcement party under Major Peter le Power but a breakdown in communication resulted in their landing 25 miles west of the DZ. With Druce increasingly concerned by the competence of the local Maquisards, as well as Captain Goodfellow, and with Germans swarming through the Vosges, Operation *Loyton* teetered on the edge of

Operation *Rupert* achieved little but at least Cyril Radford (centre) picked up a cute French girlfriend! Alongside Radford are Bill Robinson (far left) and Bill Rigden (far right). (Author's Collection)

calamity. 'We were really boxed in trying to save our skins,' recalled Druce. 'The Germans had sent a division from Strasbourg to find us and we were pretty oppressed.'

As a result Lieutenant-Colonel Brian Franks decided to take personal charge of the operation, leaving Sandy Scratchley in charge of 2SAS as he and 23 men dropped into the Vosges on the night of 30 August. It was a daring decision by Franks, and not one his predecessor Bill Stirling would have taken. Even Paddy Mayne – who had parachuted into the Morvan three weeks earlier to gather specific strategic information – might have thought twice about parachuting into such a volatile region without transport and surrounded by Germans.

Franks landed just after 0300 hours, to be met on the DZ by Dusty Crossfield. '"Hello Dusty", I said, "where are the porters?" I remember thinking "Christ, this isn't Victoria Station", when a tremendous racket started: one of the canisters had exploded and it was like bloody Guy Fawkes night. Things had just quietened down when suddenly there was a burst of gunfire right in the middle of us. A German collaborator had infiltrated the Resistance group, seized a Sten gun and fired at random and then bolted.' The man was caught and shot but then more screams erupted. One of the Maquisards, on pilfering the contents of a canister, had taken a bite out of what he thought were army rations. 'He had eaten great chunks of plastic explosive,' recalled Druce, 'and the explosive had arsenic in it so he died really quite an uncomfortable death.'

'Suddenly all hell broke loose and everyone dived flat… Schmeissers, Lugers and rifles were all firing at us. We retaliated with our Brens and carbines.'

Ron Crossfield

Franks arrived in the Vosges at the moment the Allied advance lost momentum. So rapid had their drive east been that the Americans overstretched their supply chain and the battlefield became temporarily static. The Germans needed the respite and used it to strengthen their new defensive positions along the banks of the Moselle, 15 miles west of where the men of *Loyton* were trapped. On 5 September the US Third Army relaunched their advance east, liberating the city of Nancy ten days later; but the Germans had been bolstered by the arrival of the Fifth Panzer Division from Brussels and the Allied advance became painstakingly slow.

More men and supplies were dropped to *Loyton* in early September but on the 9th of that month the SAS camp was attacked and they were forced to withdraw leaving behind much of their equipment. Throughout September the Germans captured a steady trickle of SAS soldiers, some through misfortune others through betrayal. Often the locals were forced to reveal information at the point of a gun though many refused to talk in spite of the inevitable consequences. One of the Maquis couriers was a middle-aged spinster called Madame Bergeron, who lived with an elderly aunt in a remote cottage. 'There were few things they [the Germans] wanted to know which she could have told but she never gave in,' remembered the 2SAS intelligence officer Christopher Sykes. 'They heaped every humiliation on her to break her spirit and they failed absolutely. They made her house into a brothel, they beat her, they tortured her, with no avail. This quiet, prim, very ordinary-looking, well-dressed woman had the strength of a tiger. Their final revenge is too disgusting to describe: in the same house there lived her invalid aunt, about 80 years old … they dragged this wretched old woman out of her bed and made her dance for them in her nightgown. She died. They smashed up the house, and left.'[7]

This photograph is believed to show members of Operation *Loyton* with a village priest somewhere in the Vosges. (Courtesy of the SAS Regimental Archive)

On 19 September three jeeps were dropped to Franks and he could barely contain his fury at their state: faulty brakes, dirty guns and no spare fuel. He ordered three more vehicles and they arrived two days later, along with a further 20 men. Finally the SAS were able to go on the offensive and patrols were sent out to harass the Germans; three staff cars and a lorry were shot up on the Celles–Raon L'Etape road and Druce attacked a unit of SS troops as they formed up in the village square of Moussey. The Germans retaliated by transporting the male population of Moussey to concentration camps; only 70 of the 210 men returned.

Even with six jeeps, Franks recognised by the start of October that Operation *Loyton* had run its course, particularly now that the American advance was held up west of the river Meurthe. It had been a botched operation all in all, chiefly the fault of SHAEF who had instructed 2SAS to operate in the wrong area at the wrong time. Added to that fundamental problem was the unreliable Maquis, the shoddy resupplies and the poor quality of some of the latter reinforcements. 'They arrived very nervous,' Franks said in his operational report, 'and were either so scared as to be useless or so confident that they were extremely careless. Most of these men were new recruits who were clearly not of the right type and had not had sufficient training.'[8]

Druce had already been sent through the lines on 29 September to hand to the Americans important enemy documents they had captured, and on 6 October the exfiltration began of Operation *Loyton*. Franks split his men into five parties, all of whom would withdraw independently, departing their camp at staggered intervals. Dusty Crossfield set off in the company of four men, including Jock Robb.

> The colonel saw us all off and scrounged a packet of fags from me as he wished us goodbye and good luck. All went well for us over the next couple of days despite some very close calls with the enemy. We then came up against a fairly wide river [the Meurthe] and as we undressed to swim across I became aware that Jock Robb was doing nothing. He then told me that he was staying where he was because he couldn't swim. He'd lied during training and got through somehow without being found out. It was too difficult a crossing for me to ferry him over and I was damned if I was going to leave a good pal so I got dressed again and we decided to find our own way by a different route back to safety.

Splitting from their three comrades, Crossfield and Robb headed cross-country, spending the night in a barn before scrounging some eggs and bread from a farm at first light. The farmer put them in contact with the Maquis, who provided them with civilian clothes and informed them that some of the SAS comrades had been caught by the Germans earlier in the day. In the company of a Maquis guide, Crossfield and Robb crossed the river Meurthe by bridge, continuing into the town of Baccarat which was teeming with Germans. 'They sat on doorsteps, leaned against walls chatting away and taking no notice of us at all,' recalled Crossfield. 'I had a bit of tension when a German approached me but he was obviously asking for a light. After I had done this from my box of matches I realised that I had displayed a box of "Blue Cross" [a brand of British safety match].'

The pair eventually made it through the Germans lines where they were reunited with Franks and the others who had returned safely. Others weren't so fortunate, however, including the six men who were the last to leave the SAS base near Moussey. They were caught and executed. In total, 31 soldiers on Operation *Loyton* who were murdered by the Germans.

In direct contrast to the misery endured by the men on Operation *Loyton*, Roy Farran's C Squadron enjoyed a rich harvest throughout the six weeks of operations *Hardy* and *Wallace*. The advance party codenamed 'Hardy', under Captain Grant Hibbert, dropped 40 miles east of Auxerre at the end of July and established a base in the Foret de Chatillon from where they carried out reconnaissance and built up a supply dump. Farran landed at Rennes in Dakotas on 19 August before

LEFT The village of Moussey paid a heavy price for the help it gave the 2SAS with 210 of its male inhabitants sent to a concentration camp. Later the SAS returned to honour their sacrifice in a ceremony conducted by the local priest. (Courtesy of the SAS Regimental Archive)

motoring east across France in a convoy of 20 jeeps and 60 men to link up with Operation *Hardy*.

From the moment Farran landed on French soil to launch Operation *Wallace* he attacked the enemy with singular ferocity, aided in his work by the fluidity of the Allied advance and the confusion of the enemy retreat. Unlike the Vosges, where the Germans were determined to dig in and defend, the countryside between Auxerre and Dijon was perfect for Farran to launch hit-and-run raids against an already demoralised opponent.

On 8 September a section of approximately 20 men under Lieutenant Bob Walker-Brown, acting on a tip-off from the Maquis, ambushed five German petrol bowsers en route from Langres to Dijon. 'We took the advice of the French and chose the position at a point where the country road crossed the main road,' remembered Walker-Brown. 'We took up positions on a bank overlooking the road, probably 20 feet above the road. It was a good field of fire but in retrospect it was a thoroughly bad position and I should have recced it myself but time was short and of course we didn't want to appear to the French that we were chickening out.'

Charlie Hackney was behind a Bren gun waiting for the word from Walker-Brown to launch the attack. The first vehicle in the convoy was a motorcycle sidecar, followed by a truck. Hackney let them pass and then fired on

RIGHT AND CENTRE Though the men involved in *Loyton* had little chance to liberate French villages, many of their 2SAS comrades were able to celebrate with locals as the Germans fled east towards their homeland. (Courtesy of the SAS Regimental Archive)

the first of the five bowsers. 'I was first to open up as the bowsers came round the bend and that was the signal for the ambush to start,' he said. 'We murdered that convoy. My opening burst hit the driver of the leading vehicle and he slumped over the wheel. Then I got the passenger next to him as he tried to jump clear. I remember seeing bits of his tunic flying off as he was struck by the bullets. We killed them all and you could see this thick black smoke for miles.'[9]

Despite the success of the initial onslaught the Germans didn't react as the 2SAS had expected. 'We allowed the German leading escort vehicles to run through the killing area, thinking they would continue south towards Dijon,' said Walker-Brown. 'As we opened up on the fuel bowsers, which went up in quite a cloud of smoke, we were suddenly fired on from the rear and we found that the German escort had turned right and then right round us and we had a very unpleasant job extricating ourselves.'

On 16 September, Farran made contact with the US Seventh Army, bringing to an end operations *Hardy* and *Wallace*. In his report Farran estimated that he and his men had killed or wounded 500 Germans, destroyed 59 motorised vehicles, plus a train, and blown up 100,000 gallons of enemy fuel. The casualites of 2SAS were seven dead and seven wounded. *Wallace* had succeeded, wrote Farran in an operational report, for exactly the same reasons that *Loyton* failed, namely: 'This operation proves that with correct timing and in suitable country, with or without the active help of the local population, a small specially trained force can achieve results out of all proportion to its numbers. This operation must surely rank as one of the most successful operations carried out by a small harassing force behind enemy lines.'[10]

Overall, the SAS Brigade including the two French regiments and the Belgian squadron achieved considerable success in France though it could have been greater. Instead of reverting to the small units that caused so much damage in the desert – and which had been for David Stirling the guiding principle of the SAS – the regiment was inserted into France in units so large they became vulnerable to enemy attack. They were instructed to train and arm disparate Maquis groups, some of which were effective and some of which were not, containing men who were politicians more than soldiers and who hated rival Maquis groups more than the Germans.

In addition, some of the SAS units – particularly in 2SAS – contained soldiers who had neither the training nor the temperament for guerrilla warfare. This was not the fault of the senior officers such as Paddy Mayne and Brian Franks but the upper echelons of the British military who had sacrificed quality for quantity by expanding the SAS into a brigade too quickly.

Yet despite these handicaps the SAS Brigade were estimated to have killed 7,733 German soldiers during operations in France. Some 740 motorised vehicles were destroyed, as were seven trains, 89 wagons and 29 locomotives. Thirty-three trains were derailed and railway lines were cut on 164 occasions. SAS troops also called in 400 air strikes on German targets and carried out countless valuable reconnaissance patrols for the advancing Allied forces.

General Dwight Eisenhower, Supreme Allied Commander in Europe, expressed his gratitude in a letter to Brigadier Roderick McLeod: 'I wish to send my congratulations to all ranks of the Special Air Service Brigade on the contribution which they have made to the success of the Allied Expeditionary Force,' wrote Eisenhower. 'The ruthlessness with which the enemy have attacked Special Air Service troops has been an indication of the injury which you were able to cause to the German armed forces both by your own efforts and by the information which you gave of German disposition and movements.'[11]

As for the SAS Brigade's casualties, they were 330 killed, wounded or missing. But what that figure didn't take into account was the mental toll of operations in Occupied France.

It had proved an oppressive and claustrophobic environment, utterly different to the desert. There the sun shone on a never-ending vista; in France the rain was

relentless, the summer of 1944 was exceptionally wet, and the dark forests felt at times like a prison. There was also the constant fear of betrayal, another factor absent from the desert. 'It was so much more open in the desert that you felt freer and able to escape,' reflected David Danger, who was highly commended for his signalling work during Operation *Houndsworth*. 'In France you were on your toes the whole time, and the first few weeks we were there we had the most terrible weather. Morale went down very quickly. I had to [send and receive by radio] the messages and bring them to Fraser and the men would always ask me if a resupply was coming.'[12]

In his report on 1SAS operations in France the regimental padre, Fraser McLusky, stressed the importance of regular resupplies from home in lifting the spirits, particularly those that contained letters and reading matter. He went on to say:

> The morale shown in A Squadron was on the whole very high, but in quite a number of cases the cumulative effect of the strain imposed by this and previous campaigns

With a Union Jack flag attached to the front of the jeep, these two French children hitch a ride while their playmate salutes the SAS liberators. (Courtesy of the SAS Regimental Archive)

August 27, 1944.

'Ghost' Army Paved Way For The Allies

SUTTON TIMES AND CHEAM MAIL

PARATROOPER'S NINE LIVES

His Long Hike Through Enemy Lines

THRILLS IN NORTH AFRICA

IN a dramatic letter to his mother, Mrs. A. A. Du Vivier, St. Philips-avenue, Worcester Park, Paratrooper Lance-Sergt. Jeffery Du Vivier, who has been awarded the Military Medal, tells of his experiences when, with 60 other men, he was dropped far behind the enemies lines in North Africa.

"Everything went O.K. until Jerry spotted us as we were ready to 'hop it,'" writes Sergt. Du Vivier. "For several hours we were bombed, strafed, and God knows what. It was absolute hell, but the worst part of it was that our transports were destroyed, so we had a 170 mile 'hike' through enemy lines back to our own lines.

TRYING TREK

"The prospects didn't seem so good at the time, but somehow we made it and, after eight days of walking, contacted our own troops. During those eight days I learnt what it meant to be thirsty, what it meant to be desperately hungry and whacked to the wide world. It would fill a book to tell all our adventures on that journey

"Upon reaching our own camp we were told that we had been given up for dead. Out of a party of 60 men, only five, including myself, remained alive. The only ill effects I felt after the ordeal was a very painful swelling of the throat made worse by an ulcer.

"Although I am temporarily out of the Special Air Service, due to health reasons, I would go on another raid tomorrow if they would let me."

SECOND RAID

Apparently his wish was granted, for in another letter, Lance-Sergt. Du Vivier described how once again his party was given up for lost after being missing for 13 days.

"Jerry nearly got us this time," he writes. "If it had not been for the desert Nomads we should have starved or been taken prisoners.

"We came across one of our bombers that had crashed in the

LANCE-SERGT. J. DU VIVIER

desert after bombing Benghazi. The plane was in a bad state, yet the crew escaped without a scratch.

"I must have more lives than a cat," he writes. "Although I have seen quite a bit of action I always seem to get away with it, and something tells me I always will."

Born at Bexley Heath during a Zeppelin raid in 1914, Jeffery was educated at Mayfield College, near Brighton. He has three brothers in the Services. Arnold, the eldest, aged 35, is in North Africa. Bob, aged 29, is in the R.A.F., and Walter, the youngest, aged 21, is also in the Army.

A SECRET force of daredevil British parachutists, who created panic and chaos behind the enemy's lines, paved the way for General Patton's epoch-making advance into Central France.

This behind-the-scenes drama, revealed officially for the first time to-day, was the work of the Special Air Service, created by two young officers, Lieut. David Stirling, Scots Guards and Commandos, and Lieut. Jock Lewis, Welsh Guards and Commandos.

100 Miles Marching With Heavy Pack

It began in the Desert, and under the Eighth Army "Stirling's Rest Camp" opened its first "school" of 73 volunteers. The pupils, all parachutists, had to be expert in small arms and in close combat, and tough enough to jump off a truck at 30 miles an hour and march 100 miles with a heavy pack.

S.A.S. undertook its first operation, and it ended in disaster. Stirling Lewis knew their second venture had to succeed, or their great idea would flop for ever.

Great Success

But it succeeded—beyond their wildest imagination. In December, 1941, they set out to destroy a force of the Luftwaffe—planes, personnel and anything else. They flew to Galio, 90 miles from Benghazi.

One of the officers, Lieut. Mayne, now Lieut.-Colonel Mayne, alone destroyed 47 planes. In all about 100 aircraft were smashed.

S.A.S. next started the invasion of Sicily with an assault landing to eliminate the coastal batteries. They destroyed four batteries and took 500 prisoners.

Four days later they stormed Fort Augusta.

Took Sentry's Name

There is comedy in the exploit of one S.A.S. sergeant-major strolling along a jetty in Benghazi, his pack filled with bombs for the destruction of enemy M.T.B.s.

A sentry suddenly appeared, but failed to challenge him. So he stopped and took him to task in Italian for failing in his duty.

One day their exploits in France will be told, but for the moment they must remain secret.

In August 1944, when the media was finally able to report on the SAS, a raft of sensational articles were published, such as this one in the *Sunday Graphic*. Even the regional press got in on the act with Jeff Du Vivier's local paper, *The Sutton Times*, describing with pride his exploits in the desert. (Author's Collection)

of a similar nature was clearly observed. It would be unwise to keep men working behind the enemy lines for longer than three months, and probably a much shorter period would pay much higher dividends … the men can never relax and the resultant state of constant tension leaves its mark. After a certain period, varying with the men concerned, but ascertainable in the case of each, this tension reaches a danger point. Thereafter, men should be withdrawn for good from operations of this character.[13]

Johnny Wiseman later admitted that by end of *Houndsworth* he had reached the end of his tether. 'I preferred operating in Italy I think because we were so well trained and we could take the initiative the whole time,' he said. 'In France, being supplied from the air, it's always difficult to control the situation. They [the containers] had to be accurately dropped to be within reach of you and secondly someone's got to carry the drop. It's quite a tough game and of course by morning there had to be no sign of any drop. So physically it was quite an exhausting business.'[14]

Wiseman wasn't the only officer to suffer. Derrick Harrison, Harry Poat and Bill Fraser were also feeling the strain of operations with the latter increasingly turning to alcohol to stave off thoughts of his mortality. By the end of 1944 no other officer, Paddy Mayne included, had seen as much action with the SAS as Bill Fraser but there was a heavy price to pay for his combat experience. 'Fraser was brave, a kind man who understood people and he could sum up a man very quickly … but he deteriorated,' recalled David Danger.

None of this, of course, was of interest to the newspapers when they ran a series of sensationalist articles about the SAS in August 1944. After years of secrecy and media blackouts concerning the regiment, General Eisenhower issued a directive in the summer of 1944 authorising his commanding officers to talk to war correspondents (provided they didn't compromise ongoing or future operations) 'in order to visualise and transmit to the public'.[15] British newspapers couldn't believe their luck having been forbidden by their government from mentioning the SAS since its inception. The headline in the *Evening News* was 'Hush-hush Men at Rommel's Back' with a accompanying photograph of Paddy Mayne. The *Sunday Graphic* described the SAS as a 'Ghost Army' and explained how 'a secret force of daredevil British parachutists created panic and chaos behind the enemy's lines'. But no paper rivalled the *Sunday Express* for entertainment (if not exactitude). Calling the SAS 'Britain's most romantic, most daring, and most secret army', the paper described how the regiment had triumphed by 'introducing a kind of Robin Hood system of operations against the German and Italian fascists'.

It was nonsense, but welcome nonsense that put a smile on the faces of the SAS soldiers returning from France after weeks of demanding operations.

CHAPTER 10

2SAS RETURN TO ITALY

Christmas 1944 was a time of uncertainty for the SAS Brigade. Though A and D Squadrons 1SAS and all but 3 Squadron 2SAS were back in Britain, they were on standby to parachute into the Ardennes to counter any large-scale German airborne drop.

Already in the Ardennes were the French 4SAS and the Belgian SAS Squadron, the latter carrying out reconnaissance patrols for the 29th Armoured Division as the Allies strove to stem the German offensive launched on 16 December. On Christmas Eve, as the thermometer dropped to minus 20 degrees Celsius, 4SAS were brought in to bolster the left flank of the US VIII Corps. With the Americans increasingly jumpy at rumours of German soldiers operating in the area disguised in Allied uniform, each French soldier carried a slip of headed stamped VIII Corps paper on which was written: 'This person whose signature appears below is a Frenchman operating under control of the headquarters and in the VIII's Corp's sector only.'

On 26 December the 25 German divisions that had launched the offensive ten days earlier were halted on the eastern banks of the river Meuse. On the western side of the river was B Squadron 1SAS. 'We were instructed to infiltrate and report on German positions,' recalled Albert Youngman.

OPPOSITE
A patrol of 2SAS during Operation *Tombola* in the spring of 1945. This was a successful mission, led by Roy Farran, that caused much inconvenience to the Germans in northern Italy. (Courtesy of the SAS Regimental Archive)

A detachment of French soldiers from 4SAS in the Ardennes in December 1944. Temperatures dropped to minus 20 degrees Celsius during the fierce German counter-offensive that was eventually halted on the banks of the river Meuse. (Author's Collection)

On one patrol, led by Paddy Mayne, we came across a bridge where a bunch of Americans told us that the Germans were just down the road, and they were about to blow it. Paddy told them that we were going to cross the bridge. When they insisted that they were going to blow it, Paddy left one jeep with orders that if the American officer tried to blow it before our return they were to shoot him. We went over the bridge, found that the Germans were three miles away, and returned to find the bridge intact with our jeep keeping guard.[1]

As the Allies confronted the Germans over the river Meuse on 26 December, hundreds of miles south Captain Bob Walker-Brown prepared to lead 31 men of 3 Squadron 2SAS into northern Italy on Operation *Galia*. Once again the cause of the mission was unexpected German pugnacity, this time a reconnaissance-in-strength by the 16th Panzer Division against the 92nd US Negro Division holding the Allied positions left of the Gothic Line. The Americans had retreated in haste, necessitating the rapid deployment of the British 8th Indian Division from the Eighth Army to plug the gap in anticipation of a full-scale German offensive.

Walker-Brown's mission was to drop into the region and fool the Germans into believing that the 2nd Parachute Brigade, which had just left Italy for Greece, had returned. This was to be achieved by parachuting behind the advancing 16th Panzer Division and attacking their main supply routes so they would be tricked into thinking a large-scale airborne offensive was being mounted in their rear.

The men of Operation *Galia* landed near the mountain village of Rossano, 14 miles north of La Spezia, having jumped from four Douglas C-49 aircraft in appalling weather conditions. As Walker-Brown landed on a terraced vineyard he looked up 'as the leading aircraft made a farewell pass over the DZ and in 9/10th cloud flew straight into a mountainside … our first task was to locate the aircraft and bury the brave American crew.'[2] This was accomplished with the aid of Major Gordon Lett, the SOE officer waiting to receive Operation *Galia*, who later gave Walker-Brown a thorough briefing:

> The enemy was in the deep valleys some four hours march away.
>
> The mountain passes were covered in thick snow and ice.
>
> There were no motorable roads.
>
> Some partisan bands were well disposed; others, the Communist Red Brigades, were unreliable.

Captain Bob Walker-Brown (far right) and his men shortly before they embarked upon Operation *Galia*. (Author's Collection)

News of the SAS arrival would reach the enemy rapidly via informers, suitably greatly exaggerated.

Having absorbed the brief, Walker-Brown divided his unit into three sticks of three and issued their instructions. They weren't detailed, other than stressing the importance of maintaining a high level of aggressive activity to make the Germans believe there were hundreds of airborne troops in their rear. Walker-Brown trusted his soldiers to carry out their mission without too much interference on his part. 'In the SAS it was a totally different atmosphere to the infantry,' he reflected. 'Most of the fellows were individualists who got rather bored with serving in infantry battalions or other regiments and looked for a change. The standard of intelligence and individual initiative was very high though of course it was so much easier to show initiative in the SAS than it was in an infantry battalion.'

In the days that followed the men of Operation *Galia* carried out their instructions with such single-minded determination that they learned later the Germans believed there to be 400 British airborne troops operating in the mountains. Walker-Brown carried out his first attack on 30 December, shooting up three enemy vehicles on the road from La Spezia to Genoa. He then ushered in the New Year by mortaring the German-held town of Borghetto di Vara with 34 bombs from a distance of 1,000 yards. 'Two German lorries drove down the road towards Borghetto and stopped on hearing the mortar fire,' Walker-Brown wrote in his operational report. 'Bren gunners moved forward a few hundred yards and destroyed both vehicles … the number of casualties is not known [but] the entire enemy garrison withdrew from Borghetto and did not return for 24 hours.'[3]

The attacks continued into January; on the 4th the SAS destroyed a truck near Valeriano, killing 12 and wounding eight; on the 6th an enemy staff car was ambushed and a high-ranking Italian official shot dead. The 125 million lire found in the vehicle was left by the SAS to the Italian partisans. On 11 January they attacked a column making its way towards Borghetto di Vara, destroying three vehicles and killing 23 Germans. Italian fascists retaliated the next day by burning houses in the village of Brugnato, the inhabitants of which were believed to be pro-Allies. As Walker-Brown was in the vicinity he began mortaring the fascists and as luck would have it, a patrol of American Thunderbolt aircraft spotted the commotion and joined in the attack, further evidence thought the Germans that they were under concerted assault.

By early February Walker-Brown judged it too hazardous to continue the operation. Sickness and fatigue, as well as one of the coldest winters in living memory, had taken its toll on his men and in addition German reinforcements were arriving to seek out the '400' British airborne troops operating with such impunity in the mountains. The

OPERATION *COLD COMFORT*

TOP LEFT 3 Squadron prepare to drop into Northern Italy as part of Operation *Cold Comfort*. At the feet of the soldier in the centre is his kit bag, which was strapped to his leg and released on a rope during his descent by parachute.

BOTTOM LEFT Some of the men near the Brenner Pass in the spring of 1945. The operation achieved little after the under-strength party was dropped miles from the intended target.

TOP RIGHT When the war in Europe ended the 11 men of *Cold Comfort* made their way to Rome for a spot of sightseeing. Here Bob Sharpe takes in the Colosseum.

BOTTOM RIGHT Bob Sharpe (foreground) and Bernard Ayling (right) relax with two pals in Rome after the frustration of the operation. (Author's Collection)

SAS began their withdrawal towards the Allied lines on 10 February and five days later they reached the village of Vinea. Here, remembered Walker-Brown, 'Bren guns had to be left with the partisans as, owing to the physical condition of the men, it was not possible for them to carry much on the last stage of the march across [the 5,587ft] Monte Altissimo.'★

On 18 February, three days after Walker-Brown's weary men reached safety, a 20-year-old Rhodesian called Ken Harvey joined 3 Squadron, 2SAS, at their Italian headquarters in Cecina. Ten days earlier he had been interviewed by Major Roy Farran with a view to serving as an officer in future SAS operations and the veteran had been impressed by the innate confidence of the 6ft African. Harvey, for his part, hadn't been much in awe of the regular British Army soldier since enlisting the previous year. 'One thing I quickly noticed when I went overseas with the army was the lack of strength among many British soldiers – we had the sunshine, the food, the outdoor life and so Rhodesians were better equipped.'

Harvey had little time to prepare for what lay ahead. 'On the 26th February I went to the nearby parachute school for a rushed course,' he recalled. 'Four days later it was completed and with great pride and joy I spent the evening laboriously sewing my newly acquired SAS parachute wings on my right sleeve.'[4]

Although three other small 2SAS operations were inserted into northern Italy in early 1945 (codenamed 'Cold Comfort', 'Blimey' and 'Canuck'), the focus of 3 Squadron was Operation *Tombola*, commanded by Farran. The mission was his brainchild and its objective was to harry the Germans by exploiting the enthusiasm of the large number of partisans based in the Reggio valley. 'I had long toyed with the idea of a really large operation behind the centre of the front,' wrote Farran, 'close enough to be able to bring a direct effect to bear on the main tactical battle. In my dreams I visualised myself as a G. A. Henty figure [a Victorian author of historical adventure stories] at the head of a whole army of partisans.'[5]

Farran was at the head of the advance party that landed south of Reggio on 6 March, approximately 12 miles from the nearest point of the Allied front line. He was supposed to have been on the aircraft as a despatcher but Farran had no intention of remaining at HQ when he could be leading his men into action. He later claimed to have 'fallen out of the aeroplane by mistake'. Safely down on the DZ, Farran could see Mount Cusna in the distance and three miles away was the village of Febbio, 'separated from us by many gullies and folds in the ground. The tracks were mere footpaths down steep slopes and up and over hundreds of ice-covered boulders.'

★ Walker-Brown was subsequently awarded the DSO for his courage, initiative and leadership during Operation *Galia*.

Three days later 24 more SAS soldiers arrived by parachute, among them Lieutenant Ken Harvey. The squadron's immediate concern was to transport their equipment containers from the DZ to a secure base, and with that done (and having taken delivery of another supply drop) the British established friendly relations with the various bands of partisans and began to train them in guerrilla warfare. Farran, meanwhile, having apologised to 15th Army Group HQ for inadvertently falling out of the aircraft, was instructed not to operate against the Germans until he received explicit orders.

Gradually the Anglo-Italian brigade began to take shape. As well as the 40 soldiers of 2SAS it included 15 young women who cooked, sewed, nursed and gathered intelligence on German troop movements. They wore battledress blouses and grey skirts fashioned from army blankets into the waistbands of which they concealed their pistols. 'Italy being a matriarchal society I found the women far superior to the men,' recalled Harvey. 'The women looked after the wounded – they were all quite big as they were peasants – and they all lived a hard life. The women also got information for us and we were never compromised by women in the villages even though they were persecuted and some had their children taken and their fathers shot, but they never gave us away.'

Operation *Galia* was a daring and successful mission despite the challenging terrain. Here a section of 2SAS soldiers put on a brave face for the camera despite the freezing conditions. (Author's Collection)

Donkeys were often used as a mode of transport during Operation *Galia*. (Courtesy of the SAS Regimental Archive)

On 20 March Farran radioed 15th Army Group HQ to suggest an attack on the German 51 Corps HQ at Albinea, where the foothills merged into the Po Valley. The raid was first authorised by 15th Army Group HQ then rescinded but it was too late: Farran was already on his way to the target.

The 100-strong raiding force departed their camp at intervals on 24 March, Ken Harvey leading one of three columns towards the rendezvous three miles from the German HQ. 'Seven hours of continuous marching brought us to Casa-de-Lupo,' he wrote later.

Our journey had taken us over extremely rugged country, up mountains of considerable height and across rivers, the largest of which was the Secchia, which was quite flooded from the thawing snows. The fact that not one man had failed to make the journey spoke well for the general standard of physical fitness. The only mishap reported was the breaking of my braces during the crossing of the river. This small occurrence caused me considerable discomfort which I had to endure for some 24 hours before I could make some makeshift arrangements to see me through.

The three parties rendezvoused as arranged at a cow shed at 0200 hours on Monday 26 March and remained concealed throughout the daylight hours that followed. At 2300 hours that evening Farran briefed his men: Harvey would lead nine SAS soldiers and 20 partisans in an attack on Villa Calvi, one of the two buildings that comprised the German 51 Corps HQ. Inside was the operational hub of the corps. To coincide with Harvey's assault, Lieutenant Jim Riccomini would lead a similar-sized force against the other villa, Rossi, which was further back and slightly to the right and reportedly housed the corps commander.

The guerrillas moved towards the target shortly after the briefing, negotiating the hillside in a swirling mountain mist. By 0200 hours they were in position and Riccomini led his men off first, followed three minutes later by Harvey's party. Farran, whose section would provide covering fire if necessary, told the two officers he would fire a flare in 20 minutes to signal the withdrawal. Harvey remembered the 'intense excitement' as he approached the villa and readied himself for his first experience of combat.

We arrived on the large expanse of lawn in front of the villa. I had dropped off my Bren gunners with orders to shoot anyone who appeared at any of the windows or came out of any of the doors except the front door which I arranged we would use. I set up the bazooka in front of the door having tried it and found it securely bolted. We made the necessary contact – no result, damn, now bad luck was with us. Again I tried, no result. We gathered around us to try and determine the cause of the failure. Then I heard the unmistakeable crunching of boots on the gravel road between the two villas and the deep guttural voices – Germans. Well, we mustn't be caught red-handed from behind like this, messing about with a defective weapon. I got everyone to lay flat in the shadows on the lawn and ran the ten yards to the gate on the road. I hid behind the masonry pier. I could see the sentries now only a few feet away – four of them marching up the road. I stepped into the road and shot them. It was essential that this was all done at point blank range to ensure they were killed immediately for those shots would set off the whole area and we would have to act quickly to attain our desired results.

Harvey sprinted across the lawn to find his men were already shooting their way into the villa through the heavy front door. Lights went on on the upper floor and as windows were opened the Bren gunners below picked off the Germans. Harvey was first through the door, hurling in a grenade and storming the villa with his Tommy gun firing into the darkness. 'There were scuffling noises and bullets started to fly,' he recalled. 'The din was deafening in the enclosed space. I must see the lie of the room so holding my torch at arm's length so as not to attract fire to myself, switched it on and had a quick look around. The firing increased, they could see me, so I dived under the table, torch still on, and my sergeant opened up as I went to ground and killed the chief offender.'

Harvey led his men in a charge up the staircase towards the Germans firing over the balustrade, one of whom tossed a grenade down the stairs. Harvey heard its thudding progress down the steps and just had time to shout a warning when it exploded, wounding one of his men. The raiders withdrew to the ground floor and went from room to room, killing the occupants and gathering furniture into a pile. Harvey added some plastic explosive and then put a match to the bonfire before withdrawing. 'Despite our accurate and determined Bren gun fire, grenades from above were being thrown on the lawn and we had to run the gauntlet,' he remembered. 'Germans were now on the road where I had killed the sentries and were firing towards the house. Our exit fully silhouetted against the fire was not easy and how we managed to get out without further casualties I do not know. We kept up our fire from outside as more and more of the trapped enemy in the house tried to get out. I got the men together, assessed the position and looked at the time.'

To Harvey's alarm he saw that the attack had taken 35 minutes instead of the allotted 20. He pulled back his men and they headed north into the mountains. After a few miles they wheeled round and returned to the rendezvous at the cow shed. There they found Farran and the survivors of the party that had attacked Villa Rossi. Though Riccomini and another SAS soldier had been killed in the assault, the daring raid on the German Corps HQ had been a stunning success. Sixty Germans were later reported to have been killed, including a Colonel Lemelson, the chief of staff.

For the next 22 hours Farran led his men non-stop on a torturous trek across the mountains. They swallowed Benzedrine tablets to boost their energy and made several detours to evade the German search parties. Finally they arrived back at camp, recalled Farran, to a tumultuous welcome from the locals. 'Fried eggs, bread and vino by the gallon was produced all over the village but I think most were too tired for merry making. I was soon fast asleep … and did not wake up for fourteen hours.'

Ken Harvey was awarded the DSO for his part in the raid on the German Corps HQ,★ and the men of Operation *Tombola*, in alliance with the partisans, continued to cause the Germans considerable discomfort throughout the spring of 1945. By the second half of April, with the Eighth Army having broken through the Argentan Gap in the east and the US IV Corps pushing up through central Italy, the Germans were a defeated force and Farran's men withdrew to Florence. Their part in defeating Germany was over but for the rest of the SAS there was still much fighting to be done.

Ken Harvey (back row far right) and some of the other members of Operation *Tombola*, photographed along with one of the female Italian partisans who proved such able allies. (Courtesy of the SAS Regimental Archive)

★ Brian Franks, in radioing a report of the attack on the German HQ to Christopher Skyes, said: 'Farran seriously criticised by 15 Army Group … for premature attack disregarding orders. Rocket being sent from Brigade.'

CHAPTER 11

OPERATION *ARCHWAY*: THE DRIVE INTO GERMANY

The men of B and C Squadrons 1SAS spent the first two months of 1945 in Antwerp. They had been sent to the Belgian city after the Ardennes quietened down but they found life in Antwerp far more disturbing than in the forests to their east. 'We were getting three to four V2s hitting us each day,' recalled Albert Youngman.[1] The German rockets dropped on the city with indiscriminate brutality and the SAS troopers helped in digging out the dead and wounded.

When they finally returned to England, B and C Squadrons arrived at 1SAS's base at Hylands House in Essex to discover A and D Squadrons were preparing to leave for Ostend on a joint operation with 2SAS codenamed 'Archway'.★ Shortly before the force departed they were issued with a new fleet of jeeps. 'Each one,' recalled Peter Weaver, 'had two circular armour plated glass windscreens. Two inches thick, protecting the driver and front gunner. Armour was also protecting the front of the jeep.'[2] The jeeps still carried the twin and single Vickers but each third vehicle was mounted with a .50-calibre Browning which was fitted with a searchlight to aid the gunner. A dozen spare drums of ammunition were studded to the bonnet and sides of the jeep and in the rear was a bazooka and a Bren gun.

OPPOSITE
Peter Middleton and Ian Wellsted are among the SAS men undergoing some ski instruction from the *Chasseurs Alpins* (the French elite mountain infantry) in the French Alps in early 1945. (Author's Collection)

★ Although the operation was codenamed *Archway*, the men of 1SAS and 2SAS were known collectively as 'Frankforce' after Brian Franks, CO of the 2SAS contingent.

A jeep from 1SAS somewhere in Germany with the treasure chest secured to the front of the vehicle and the driver protected by the armour plated glass windscreen. This soldier is wearing his SAS beret in defiance of the order to don the headgear of the Tank Corps. (Author's Collection)

The men were issued with flak jackets (most of which were quickly discarded) and ordered to replace their SAS or airborne berets with the black beret of the Tank Corps. After confirmation of the fate that awaited captured SAS personnel the brigade was determined to do all it could to prevent any more executions. The men were instructed to remove all reference to the SAS from their pay books and they were ordered to refer to themselves over the radio as 'the little ones'.

Shortly before their departure the men received a visit from Field Marshal Bernard Montgomery. The last time the SAS had seen Monty was after the battle for Termoli, when his flippant words of praise hadn't gone down well with men still on edge after three days of ferocious fighting. 'I disliked Montgomery, he was a funny bugger,' reflected Seekings.

When we were going across to Germany he came round to visit our unit ... so we lined the men up and he said: 'You are some of the original members of the glorious army, the Eighth Army, we've come a long way, we won the desert – brilliantly planned, brilliantly carried out. We went to Sicily – brilliantly planned,

brilliantly carried out. We went into Italy and we had a good fight. Now we are going to hit him where it hurts the most, in the Fatherland'. Then he said there's only one good German, and that's a dead German. So we'll make them all good – men, women, cats and dogs, the lot. That finished me with him. I didn't need that sort of bullshit.[3]

The SAS left Hylands House on Sunday 18 March, escorted to Tilbury Docks along the A12 by the Metropolitan Police. There were 284 soldiers in total, 129 of 2SAS and 155 men of 1SAS under the command of Harry Poat. Among the 1SAS men there were still a sprinkling of desert veterans, including Jeff Du Vivier, Johnny Cooper and Reg Seekings. Also present in A Squadron were Jim Blakeney and Roy Davies, both L Detachment originals who had been captured on the first disastrous raid three and a half years earlier. Following the surrender of Italy, the pair escaped from their POW camps and found their way back to the regiment.

Meanwhile, Ian Wellsted and Peter Middleton were among the force having only recently returned from an enjoyable few weeks in the French Alps. The pair,

James McDiarmid (rear) helps carry Bob Melot's coffin into a church in Brussels after the popular intelligence officer was killed in a car accident in October 1944. (Author's Collection)

205

along with five other SAS personnel (all officers except Middleton), had flown out of England on 27 January to Grenoble where they were attached to the *Chasseurs Alpins*, an elite unit of French mountain troops. Throughout February the British soldiers learned to ski like experts in preparation for a mission into German-occupied Norway but, for reasons never revealed to the men, the operation was cancelled and they were posted back to England in early March.

The crossing of the Rhine itself commenced on the evening of 23 March when commandos of 21 Army Group boarded amphibious landing craft called 'Buffaloes' and set out for the east bank 500ft distant. At 1000 hours the next day the last great airborne operation of the war, codenamed *Varsity*, began as 1,590 troop-carrying aircraft dropped the British 6th Airborne Division in Hamminkeln and the US 17th Airborne just a few miles east of the Rhine. It was a successful drop, but a costly one, with 440 aircraft destroyed or badly damaged in the operation.

The SAS crossed the Rhine at 1130 hours on 25 March, landing at Bislich, and they soon saw for themselves the tenacity with which the Germans had tried to repel the

Johnny Cooper (centre) and Jeff Du Vivier (right) in front of Brussels' Arch of the Cinquantenaire shortly before a composite force of 1SAS and 2SAS crossed the Rhine into Germany. (Author's Collection)

'The regiment had been used to operating behind the lines ... but now we were in a country that wasn't occupied, except by Germans, and they were going to fight to defend their country.'

Denis Wainman

airborne invasion of their homeland. 'The crossing of the Rhine was quite easy but when we got over into the wood there were a large number of dead Germans and Americans,' recalled Sergeant Harry Vickers, who had won the DCM while serving under Roy Farran in France. 'After we had got to the other side of the Rhine the front had moved on and we were waiting for orders to move on with them. But we had to go round this forest to make certain there was nobody left. We came across an US captain dead on the ground with several dead Germans around him. I often wondered if he had been surrounded and shot these Germans before being killed.'[4]

The day after crossing the Rhine, 26 March, 1SAS and 2SAS parted company with the former embarking on a series of reconnaissance patrols for the 6th Airborne north-east from Hamminkeln.

The SAS encountered little resistance when they crossed the Rhine but saw plenty of evidence of the heavy fighting that had preceded their arrival on the east bank. The two German soldiers in this photo – one injured and the other dead – were typical of the extreme youth of the enemy. (IWM BU 2344)

2SAS were attached to the 6th Independent Guards Armoured Brigade near Schermberck and ordered to head east. 'The journey from the Rhine towards Wessel and Munster was bloody awful,' remembered Charlie Hackney. 'We kept encountering these pockets of SS soldiers concealed by the roadside who were quite happy to fight and die. One time we were driving along and suddenly we came under fire from this farmhouse. Nothing much, just small-arms fire. So we roared up to farmhouse, raked it with Vickers fire, and then dived in and shot them all up. We never took prisoners on those occasions.'[5]

On 29 March 2SAS were approaching the town of Dulmen, protecting the left flank of the Guards Armoured Brigade. They were negotiating a muddy, rutted track when one of the jeeps became stuck. As they attempted to free the vehicle, the British soldiers spotted some German troops two fields away. Lieutenant Lord John Manners, son of the Dowager Duchess of Rutland, told Sergeant Harry Vickers to find Captain Jim Mackie and report the sighting. As Vickers reversed down the track he encountered Mackie coming in the other direction 'He asked me what I was doing,' recalled Vickers. 'I said there were Jerries up at the top of the field. "So why aren't you fighting them?" he said. He took a dim view of things like that. I went back with him and he sent me and my two men from my jeep to attack them on a flank while he attacked them frontally. There was an open field between us and them and they just blazed away and I got one in the left arm.'

The view from one of the Buffalo amphibious landing craft as 2SAS cross the Rhine on 25 March. (Author's Collection)

Johnny Cooper at the wheel of his jeep, 'Constance', christened in honour of his girlfriend. (Courtesy of the SAS Regimental Archive)

Vickers was taken to an American casualty clearing station, where it was discovered the bullet had shattered his bone and taken a two inch chunk out of his arm. As Vickers was flown to England, his comrades continued pushing into Germany. On 1 April, Easter Sunday, as the Allies entered Munster, 2SAS were 15 miles north-west in Osterwick attached to VIII Corps Reserve. On the same day their sister regiment, 1SAS, was 25 miles north-west in Elte, gathered for Easter Communion in the presence of Fraser McLuskey, although Bill Fraser was a noticeable absence.

On 27 March, the day after they were attached to the 6th Airborne, 1SAS had their first contact with the enemy.★ The Operation *Archway* report described what happened:

> Major Fraser's 1st SAS Troop passed up through the forward troops and met a battalion of Canadian paratroops who reported having attempted to take a wood … they had been driven back by heavy Spandau, bazooka and infantry fire, with

---

★ The force had been divided as follows: Squadron HQ under Harry Poat, HQ Troop under Lieutenant McNaught, M Troop under Captain Alex Muirhead, T Troop under Major John Tonkin, C Troop under Major Bill Fraser and B Ecehelon under Captain G. White.

Showing an admirable contempt for German authority, this SAS jeep proudly displays a sign that says 'Zutritt Verboten', or 'No trespassing' in English. (Author's Collection)

the loss of eight men. The Canadians were preparing to re-engage the enemy with mortar and artillery fire before attacking again.

Major Fraser decided to attempt to take the enemy unawares by attacking from some dead ground on the left flank. The troop approached unseen to within 30 yards of the enemy positions when a well camouflaged machine-gun opened up at Major Fraser's jeep which ran into a ditch. Major Fraser was wounded in the hand. The troop fanned out in front of the wood and Lieut. [Pat] Riley's section destroyed the infantry gun together with its crew. Lieut. Johnson's section on the left engaged Bazooka and Spandau positions and silenced them one by one, Lieut. McLellan engaged the enemy in a group of houses on the right flank and Sgt White's jeep was detailed to tow out Major Fraser's jeep under covering fire. The troop then dismounted and, covered by the jeeps, cleared the wood and eliminated enemy sniper positions. 10 Germans were killed and 32 POWS taken in this action.[6]

Lieutenant Denis Wainman, a recent arrival in 1SAS, was in Fraser's C Troop and saw his commanding officer shortly before he was driven to the casualty clearing station. 'He had a hand wound, I think it was a spent bullet,' he recalled. 'He didn't seem to be relieved to get such a wound, I think he wanted to see it through.'[7]

Captain Ian Wellsted took over C Troop and 1SAS pushed on towards Peddenburg, watching every ditch, hedgerow and farmhouse for signs of a possible trap. Nine months earlier in France they had been the ones launching hit-and-run raids from the woods, now it was the Germans with the element of surprise on their side. 'The regiment had been used to operating behind the lines,' said Wainman, 'but now we were in a country that wasn't occupied, except by Germans, and they were going to fight to defend their country. At times it was like hitting a brick wall you could never penetrate, and of course it was ideal country for ambushes.'

On the morning of 28 March Wellsted's C Troop was tasked with supporting the 6th Airborne Division as they advanced the seven miles east from Erle through Ostrich and on to Rhade. At a crossroads the convoy of 12 jeeps met three British tanks and a Dingo armoured scout car and together they began to move down the road. 'The scout car had not gone 50 yards down the road when it was knocked out by an anti-tank weapon,' ran the operational report. 'This was the signal for a burst of small-arms fire from the woods on both sides of the road.'

As the jeeps' Vickers began to thump their reply towards the trees, Reg Seekings heard the signaller in his vehicle shout a warning. 'I turned round and there were about a dozen of these old German soldiers, like our Home Guard [the Volkssturm], creeping up this ditch which I had backed in to,' he recalled.

> God only knows why they hadn't opened fire. I whipped round and snatched up the Bren gun I always carried and riddled the bloody lot. The next thing I knew Mac [Trooper Mackenzie, his front gunner] said 'I'm hit, Sgt-Major.' I looked him over and couldn't find anything wrong with him. I said 'are you sure you're hit?' and he said 'of course I'm bloody sure. Can't you see I'm bleeding like hell.' And there was this pool of blood, and then I saw it was his armpit. A bullet had exploded into his armpit and ripped a bloody big hole.

As the SAS laid down suppressing fire, the infantry was brought up to clear the woods and by the end of the engagement 70 Germans were dead and 80 captured.

Fate dealt a cruel hand to Duncan Ferguson (far right), a desert veteran who was killed a few weeks before VE Day. The other men in this photo, taken in 1943, are (L–R) David Goldie, Alan Thurston and Bill McNinch. McNinch was killed at Termoli. (Courtesy of John Robertson)

'1SAS casualties, two slightly and two seriously wounded, were surprisingly light in the circumstances,' stated the operational report, 'as the column of jeeps must have been plainly visible to the enemy as it advanced along the road and it was probably the presence of the tanks which deterred them from opening fire sooner … the advance continued but no more resistance [was] met. Prisoners, however, continued to give themselves up all the way to Rhade.'

Once Rhade – a town approximately 20 miles north-east of Bremen – was secure 1SAS pulled back to Raesfeld and rested, imposing themselves on the locals. 'If we came to a village or farms we spelt out that we wanted to take over a place and that was it,' recalled Wainman, who was surprised at the reaction of the villagers. 'They weren't really antagonistic. I thought they would be more so. I got the impression they realised they'd been beaten and were just shattered by the war.'

With the VIII Corps having advanced to the Weser, a new role was devised for 1SAS on 4 April. Instead of reconnoitring for the 6th Airborne, they were attached

A 2SAS mortar section rain bombs on a stubborn pocket of resistance as 'Frankforce' pushed ever deeper into Germany. (Author's Collection)

to the 11th Armoured Division in the belief they would advance faster through the better country after the Weser. On 7 April 1SAS forded the Weser at Petershagen and laagered for the night in the village of Windheim. The next morning Tonkin's T Troop headed north-east towards Neustadt as the advance guard for the Inns of Court, the reconnaissance regiment of the 11th Armoured Division. Alex Muirhead's M Troop was detailed to protect the left flank of the advance and the nine jeeps of Ian Wellsted's C Troop received instructions to support an Inns of Court unit on the Nienburg to Neustadt road.

There were reports of fanatical German resistance in the area and C Troop was on heightened alert as it departed Windheim. 'We were having problems with these youngsters hiding in hedgerows with a Panzerfaust [anti-tank weapon] which could only fire one shot,' recalled Wainman. 'They were nothing more than suicide troops.'

C Troop passed through the village of Scheernen, bumped along a sandy track, and finally emerged on to the Nienburg to Neustadt road where they rendezvoused with three Dingo armoured scout cars. Just as the column had turned left at a crossroads an ambush was sprung. A German hidden in the hedgerow fired a Panzerfaust at the lead Dingo. A salvo of small-arms fire erupted from some trees and suddenly more Panzerfausts were being launched at the British from point-blank range. One rocket destroyed Corporal Jack Corbett's jeep, killing John Glyde, the Welsh gunner, and another just missed the vehicle containing Tom Rennie, Charlie Backhouse and Roy Davies, the L Detachment veteran recently returned from three years' captivity.

A youth leapt up a roadside ditch and aimed his Panzerfaust at the sixth jeep in the convoy, the one with Jeff Du Vivier manning the Vickers in the front passenger seat. Du Vivier opened fire and the German, remembered Ian Wellsted, 'was blown to bits'.[8]

Johnny Cooper manoeuvred his jeep from the back to the front of the column to warn Wellsted they were in danger of being encircled by Germans moving up from the rear. As Wellsted ordered the SAS to pull back to the crossroads Du Vivier dragged two young Germans from the ditch. 'They were very arrogant,' he recalled, 'so we made them sit on the bonnet of the jeep so the Germans wouldn't fire as we moved to a safer location.'[9]

Back at the crossroads two more jeeps roared into view. It was Harry Poat and Lieutenant McNaught. Wellsted gave his squadron commander a situation report but it was largely unnecessary: Poat could see for himself their parlous situation. The Germans were now less than 200 yards away, and closing. The SAS opened up with a two-inch mortar and all their Vickers. The Germans went to ground and then came a report that three British armoured vehicles were approaching through the forest from the village of Scheernen. Jeff Du Vivier and Denis Wainman were in the jeeps at the rear of the SAS column, and as they turned to look at the approaching armoured cars they suddenly realised they weren't British but German. Wainman sent his corporal to inform Wellsted 100 yards away at the crossroads. 'He wasn't having it,' remembered Wainman. 'He insisted that intelligence had reported there were no German troops in that area. I was told later we had hit the Hitler Youth Panzer Division, we ran into their rear guard as they were retreating.'

One of the German prisoners on Du Vivier's jeep tried to make off across the fields but he was shot. Meanwhile Wainman sent a second message to Wellsted, who still couldn't conceive that the Germans had armoured vehicles in the area. He looked through his field glasses and saw two armoured cars and a troop carrier full of German soldiers 'coming up the sandy track towards Denis's jeep. They appeared to be firing at it. Denis and the two nearest jeeps, Du Viver's and Rennie's were gallantly firing back.'

Wainman's jeep took a direct hit from the armoured car's 20mm cannon and the vehicle exploded in a ball of flame. Wainman and his crew – Jim Blakeney and Alec Hay – staggered away from the flames but another shell from the armoured car killed Blakeney. The other armoured car turned its fire on Du Vivier. 'I was hammering away at this armoured car and the whole time it was bearing down on me,' recalled Du Vivier. 'I could see the fire coming from its cannon and then I felt a pain in my leg.'

Back at the crossroads the SAS and Inns of Court armoured cars were repelling a large assault from the east. Neil McMillan, who had replaced the wounded Mackenzie as Reg Seekings's front gunner, recalled that Seekings didn't seem perturbed by their predicament. '"Blimey, there are a lot of the buggers, aren't there?" he said. I was glad I was with Reg at a time like that.'[10]

Harry Poat was similarly unruffled by the appearance of the German armour. Having absorbed Wainman's report, he walked over to the two British Dingos and explained the situation. 'He just stood in front of the armoured car and directed fire [on to the Germans],' recalled Wainman. 'Typical Harry, very quiet and calm.'

Two shells from the British armoured cars knocked out their German opponents. The assault appeared to be faltering. Wellsted took off down the road to help his wounded men. Du Vivier was already being assisted back up the road by Sam Weller. Under Tom Rennie's smouldering jeep Wellsted discovered Roy Davies, wounded and in great pain. He gave him a shot of morphine and told him he would soon be safe. Suddenly Wellsted saw the Germans from the troop carrier streaming towards him. He told Davies he'd be back and ran in the direction of the crossroads. He was dropped by a bullet to his left leg, rose, staggered a further 20 yards, and was hit in the right leg. Dixie Deane and Tony Trower appeared at his side and carried him to safety. Wellsted screamed that Davies needed rescuing. Dougie Ferguson, Poat's Glaswegian batman and an L Detachment veteran, ran down the track towards Davies and the enemy. With the Germans threatening to overrun their position,

THE SAS IN GERMANY

TOP LRFT
Men of C Troop adorn their jeep with a looted Nazi flag on the road to Lubeck while Lieutenant Peter Weaver stands in the back of the vehicle. (Author's Collection)

TOP RIGHT
Lieutenant Denis Wainman (left) looks on as some captured Germans push a carriage through a rural village. (Author's Collection)

MIDDLE RIGHT
The more the SAS penetrated into Germany the more they saw evidence of the collapse of the Third Reich. These abandoned half-tracked rocket launchers were in a forest near Celle. (IWM BU 3431)

BOTTOM RIGHT
Men from Henry Druce's 2SAS section look on as guards captured at Neuengamme concentration camp are made to dig their own graves. A mock execution followed which the guards took well, only one flinching as bullets cracked over their heads. (Author's Collection)

A patrol of 1SAS were the first Allied troops into Belsen and Duncan Ridler acted as translator for Josef Kramer, the camp commandant, seen here in irons awaiting removal to a prison. (IWM BU 3749)

Poat ordered C Troop to withdraw towards Neustadt. 'I sent Johnny Cooper off first with the wounded at top speed,' Poat wrote later in a letter to Johnny Wiseman. 'Then [I] made a dash with the rest later. The Jerry was about 30 yards away when we left, and believe me, I never thought the old jeeps were so slow; 50 mph seemed a snail's pace. The first vehicle we met at our lines was the ambulance and so we got the wounded straight aboard. I then went and asked for tanks to clear the woods in an attempt to reach Ferguson.'[11]

The corpse of Davies was retrieved two days later in a hospital morgue when 2SAS entered Nienburg; no trace of the 27-year-old Ferguson was ever found and he is commemorated on the Groesbeek Memorial in Holland. From Nienburg 2SAS drove east, reaching the town of Celle at dawn on 12 April. The unit's medical officer, Captain Joe Patterson, was approached by a local man. He told Patterson of 'some bad casualties in a concentration camp in the town without any medical attention. The words "Konzentration Lager" didn't have any particular significance to me then.'

A few hours later Patterson and some men of 2SAS arrived outside the gates of Celle. A high screen of matting around the wire fence prevented them from seeing inside, but the stench was already overpowering. Once inside Patterson all but gagged. 'Some straw had been spread over the thick manure and there half buried in the manure were ten creatures with life in them, not much, but a little,' he remembered. 'The staring eyes gleaming out of the slaty skeletons faces in the filth made an impression it is impossible to describe.'[12]

Patterson was horrified to learn that Celle was just a subsidiary camp; the main Konzentration Lager was a few miles north, at a place called Belsen, the direction in which 1SAS was headed.

Three days later, on the morning of 15 April, a 1SAS jeep patrol was driving through a pine forest. In one of the jeeps was Sergeant Duncan Ridler of the regiment's intelligence unit. He had read Stefan Lorant's *I was Hitler's Prisoner*, an account of the six months he spent in a German jail in the 1930s, but he was still utterly unprepared for what the patrol encountered at the Belson camp. Ridler described later what he found:

[We] imagined that a concentration camp was similar to a barracks, a relatively small area of huts. The jeeps were left guarded at the entrance. There seemed to be no one else much about in the small entrance compound, enclosed by several low buildings. Wide dirt tracks with shallow concrete drains led off in several directions. All very quiet and somehow ominous. Machine gun posts were manned in watchtowers. We split into several parties… Bodies of prisoners were lying here and there in the drains and against huddled bundles of nondescript clothing [it was estimated that there were approximately 10,000 unburied corpses at Belsen]. Other prisoners were moving slowly and silently in the compounds behind 10 foot wire fences. Gates were padlocked. A crowd was clustered around one. We had never seen people looking like this, they were all trying to say something – not shouting – their faces dull, exhausted, emotionless, not capable of expressing joy or excitement as had everyone else in Europe. I told them in English, French and German that we were British, that they were about to be freed, that the main forces were arriving. A Frenchman showed me the number tattooed on his wrist. We filled our smocks and blouses with rations, mostly biscuits, and passed some through the wire. The crowd started to struggle and push, some fell … towards us came a file, perhaps 50 or 60, of young girls carrying buckets and wearing the Star of David, marched by an SS woman. They seemed better clothed and less gaunt, perhaps being part of the original 'hostage' population of the camp. We stopped them, piled our remaining rations into a bucket, sent them back, told the guard the camp was taken over and ordered her back to her quarters.[13]

Soon the SAS patrol was joined at Belsen by the 63rd Anti-Tank Regiment of the 11th Armoured Division, commanded by Lieutenant-Colonel Taylor. As his comrades

Harry Poat and his men didn't stay long in Kiel dockyards before heading south for a rendezvous with Paddy Mayne in Poperinghe. (Courtesy of the SAS Regimental Archive)

ventured further inside the camp, Duncan Ridler remained at the entrance with Taylor, translating his instructions to the camp commandant, Josef Kramer. 'The colonel wanted Kramer's identity and his formal surrender,' recalled Ridler. 'We must have checked with him that there were no [British] POWs in the camp. Incredibly, a delousing unit had already been set up in one of the huts, and we filed through to have a white powder puffed inside our collars. Then we departed. In one minute we were back in the woods and there was no sound behind us in that horrible place. It might not have existed.'

There was little time to dwell on the bestiality that they'd witnessed; 1SAS and 2SAS continued probing deeper into Germany in the days that followed but by now they had broken the back of the enemy resistance. All that were remained were the 'Werewolves', members of the Hitler Youth whose allegiance to the Nazi cause soon evaporated when faced with the Twin Vickers. 'One burst from our guns and they came tumbling out of their trenches as fast as they could with their hands up,' said Peter Weaver.

On 19 April 1SAS, still operating with the 11th Armoured Division, entered Lubeck in search of several high-ranking SS officers. With that task completed they were stood down for several days. One of Denis Wainman's men, who had taken photographs of Belsen's unburied dead, went to have the film developed. 'A couple of days later the MPs [military policemen] came to see me and said the chemist who had done the photographs was quite concerned about what the photos showed,' recalled Wainman. Informed that his compatriots were responsible, the chemist refused to believe it. No German could be guilty of such barbarity.

CHAPTER 12

OPERATION *HOWARD*: PADDY MAYNE'S LAST HURRAH

On 6 April B and C Squadrons of 1SAS prepared to depart Hylands House for Tilbury Docks on their final operation of the war in Europe. Rumours were already circulating that the SAS Brigade would soon be on its way to the Far East so there was little sense that peace was only weeks away. 'In the morning we all lined up outside Hylands and helped ourselves to this big breakfast all laid out on tables,' recalled Bob Lowson.[1]

Three days later the force was laagered just south of the German town of Meppen, listening to their commanding officer, Paddy Mayne. They were about to embark on Operation *Howard*, the objective of which was to act as the eyes and ears of the 4th Canadian Armoured Division as they penetrated into northern Germany in the direction of the medieval city of Oldenburg. Nobody liked the idea of the mission, not Mayne nor his men. 'It was awkward operation, a little bit foolish really,' said Sid Payne. 'We were supposed to be accompanying the Canadian armoured brigade but we couldn't see them as there was some distance between us. We were also too lightly armed for the task.'[2]

On 10 April the two squadrons set off on the road to Oldenburg. Tony Marsh led C Squadron while B Squadron was commanded by Major Dick Bond, recruited from the Auxiliary Units in 1944. Having crossed the river Hase they drove north towards the village of Borger. Mayne was travelling with C Squadron with David Danger

OPPOSITE
Oh! What a Lovely War. Beer, fags and food on offer as a group of 1SAS celebrate the end of the war. (Courtesy of the SAS Regimental Archive)

Paddy Mayne won a third bar to his DSO in Germany but those who witnessed his gallantry in rescuing his men were convinced he deserved a Victoria Cross. (Courtesy of the SAS Regimental Archive)

sitting in the back of the jeep with his radio. Also in the jeep was a gramophone and loudspeaker. 'Paddy had the idea that he was going to harangue the German forces through this loudspeaker and call on them to surrender,' remembered Danger. 'I was to operate this thing and play some of Paddy's Irish records that he'd also brought along.'[3]

Before Mayne had had time to rig up his gramophone, Danger received a message over his radio reporting that B Squadron had been ambushed and Major Bond was dead. 'Paddy asked what was happening,' recalled Danger, 'and when I told him he threw me off the jeep and set off down the road.'

Mayne arrived at the scene of the ambush to discover that Bond was dead, as was his driver, and several men were trapped in a ditch with the Germans taking pot shots at them from their concealed positions. One of the trapped SAS men was Albert Youngman: 'We'd been patrolling up a road when we came under heavy gunfire,' he said. 'We baled out into a ditch to make our way back to the column but as we crawled along the ditch we found we were trapped by a drainage pipe.'[4]

Though thousands of Germans surrendered others fought to the death, inflicting casualties on the SAS right up to the end of the war. (IWM BU 2944)

From their concealed position back down the road, Mayne was briefed on what had happened; the three jeeps had come under fire from the woods to their right and the L-shaped farm buildings in front. Major Bond had tried to reach his stranded men by crawling up the ditch to the left of the road, but a sniper shot him dead as he climbed over the drainage pipe. His driver, a Czech Jew called Mikhael Levinsohn, had met a similar fate in attempting to squeeze through the pipe. 'He was small and I thought he would be able to climb through the drainage pipe,' Lieutenant John Scott told Mayne. Mayne's reaction was to mutter 'Poor Dick, poor Dick.'[5]

Bond was one of the cartel of privileged officers who had arrived at the SAS from the Auxiliary Units and it was felt by some of the more experienced NCOs that they lacked the requisite temperament for SAS operations. 'I did some patrols with Bond and [Captain Tim] Iredale when we were in France and Iredale kept on saying "Ossy, we're off to see the wizard"', recalled Bob Lowson. 'They didn't know what they were talking about... Bond ran into trouble because he didn't realise if you hit the bloody ditch and stay there you're done for. You've got to get your weapons into action. You had to seize the initiative, get in first.'

Mayne assessed the situation in a matter of seconds and then swung into action. Sprinting across the field to the nearest of the three farm buildings (which had been strafed by Scott's Vickers a short while earlier), Mayne checked to make sure it was free of Germans and surmised the sniper had withdrawn to one of the other buildings. He returned to his jeep, removed a Bren gun and several spare magazines, and signalled for Billy Hull to follow. The pair doubled back to the first of the farm buildings and Mayne instructed Hull to slip upstairs and open fire from a top floor window with his Tommy gun. Mayne, meanwhile, crept round the side of the building and readied himself for Hull's salvo.

Hull fired a long burst into the second building and drew the fire of the German sniper, just as Mayne anticipated. As the German prepared to take aim Mayne stepped out from the building and killed him with his Bren gun. The Germans hidden in the wood opened up with Panzerfausts and small arms but Mayne and Hull withdrew without further incident.

Mayne now asked for a volunteer, and John Scott stepped forward. A year earlier Scott had been commissioned in the field having already won the Military Medal, and now he wished to make amends for the guilt he felt at ordering Levinsohn into the ditch.

With Mayne at the wheel, the jeep roared down the road towards the stranded men. Lieutenant Scott stood in the back, pummelling the woods with the twin Vickers oblivious to the German fire coming his way. Mayne slowed briefly as he passed Youngman and the others, yelled 'I'll pick you up on the way back' and continued down the road. Mayne swung the jeep round when they reached the crossroads and came tearing back with Scott still pouring fire into the woods. Twice more the jeep drove up and down the road until finally the enemy fire subsided. Satisfied that the woods no longer posed a threat, Mayne braked by the ditch and hauled on board his wounded and bewildered men. He was later recommended for a Victoria Cross but this was downgraded to a Distinguished Service Order, his fourth of the war.

The SAS pressed on the following day, having buried Bond and Levinsohn three miles from where they had died. C Squadron passed through the village of Esterwegen and picked their way across some flooded woodland. That afternoon they reached the outskirts of Friesoythe, 35 miles west of Bremen, and ran into another ambush on another narrow country road. Mortar bombs began dropping on the lead vehicles; some were able to swing round and get out of harm's way, one or two were hit sending their occupants diving into the flooded ditches. The jeeps at the rear of the column

A patrol of 1SAS somewhere in Germany. Note that the soldier on the far right is wearing the SAS badge on his beret but the soldier next to him appears to have on that of the Tank Corps. (Courtesy of the SAS Regimental Archive)

raced to assist their comrades. 'I began laying down fire with my Browning,' recalled Bob Lowson, 'and as I did so I could see all these soaking wet figures emerging from the ditch. Tony Marsh being one of them.'

Alerted by the mortar attack, B Squadron, to the rear of C Squadron, decided it was too risky to drive to their aid. Alighting from their jeeps, the SAS men began moving through the flooded fields on foot. Lieutenant Gordon Davidson led his eight-man section (including his section sergeant Albert Youngman) towards the ambush unaware that their assailants weren't old men or callow youths, but the 7th German Parachute Division, deployed with the specific aim of repelling the Allied advance. 'We reached the ditch and prepared to cross the road when a German motorised column of at least ten vehicles appeared a hundred yards away,' recalled Davidson. 'The Germans dismounted rapidly from their transport and in a few minutes we were surrounded. In the ditch I could only see a Schmeisser before and behind me. No point in arguing.'[6]

Youngman said he and his seven comrades were made to sit on top of an ammunition wagon as they were driven into captivity. 'The idea was to deter our own troops from

attacking the convoy but as we drove along I saw a jeep come out of a wood, turn and I thought, "That's Paddy and we're in the shit".' Mayne opened fire but to his men's relief missed the ammunition wagon.

It had been a costly attack for the SAS; as well as the men taken prisoner, the enemy had also captured four jeeps and destroyed a further two. That evening they laagered in a forest as they waited for the approach of the 4th Armoured Division, kept alert by the occasional German sniper hidden somewhere in the trees. The next morning the Canadians appeared and Mayne withdrew his men south to a village quiet enough in which to brew up and scrounge food. Bob Lowson was just making himself comfortable when he was ordered by Bob Lilley to take his jeep back into the forest to hunt for a missing SAS trooper.

Lowson set off with his driver, Andy Coutts, and Sergeant Major Nobby Clarke and Sam Cooper of B Squadron who had decided to offer their support. Clarke's jeep led them down the forest track and into the dense mass of conifers. 'I was in the front passenger seat listening to "Dufflebag", the GI request show, on the radio when we came under fire,' recalled Lowson.

The dense forests encountered by the men on Operation *Howard* made life hazardous for the SAS. Bob Lowson and Peter Davis were both wounded by snipers in such terrain. (Courtesy of the SAS Regimental Archive)

227

A group of 1SAS soldiers in Germany share a cigarette while one appears to have his wallet out ready to barter for some war booty. (Courtesy of the SAS Regimental Archive)

The sniper's first bullet missed but his second hit Cooper in the head. Clarke was shot in the leg as he tried to pull his dead driver into cover. Coutts scrambled out of the driver's seat and threw himself down the embankment. Lowson followed but was shot in the thigh as he leapt clear of the jeep. 'I slid down this bank and pulled my trousers down,' recalled Lowson. 'There was this bloody great hole in my leg and another one on the other side where the bullet had exited.' He plugged the hole with his field dressing and Coutts offered him his to stem the blood. Coutts then helped Clarke back along the embankment, promising Lowson he'd be back with reinforcements. Lowson remained hidden from the sniper but fearful nonetheless that the Germans might come to finish the job. 'I knew what the Germans did to captured SAS men and I didn't fancy that much,' reflected Lowson.

Lowson was rescued a short while later and left in the hands of a Canadian field hospital, whose first act was to give him a pint pot full of rum and a cigarette.

———

Meanwhile, Gordon Davidson and his men were handed over to the SS not long after their capture, and removed to a farmhouse for questioning. 'The interrogator was not so much a Nazi bully boy as a mini-Himmler,' remembered Davidson.

The SAS helped themselves to what they wanted from German farms but sometimes they had to fall back on army rations, as seen here. (Courtesy of the SAS Regimental Archive)

Corporal Sid Payne (right) had a couple of close shaves in Germany but emerged unscathed and with a reputation as one of C Squadron's coolest operators. (Courtesy of the SAS Regimental Archive)

'Behind the starkly, simple interrogation table sat a small uniformed figure, sallow faced with sharp malevolent eyes lurking behind rimless steel-framed glasses. He exuded menace.'

Youngman was beaten by some of SS soldiers, and then thrown in a pigsty with the rest of the SAS soldiers. The 'mini-Himmler' reappeared again to inform his prisoners that he'd decided to have them shot in the morning. That night, however, the Allies advanced from the west and the SS were ordered up to the front line. In their place was a unit of the Volkssturm, the German Home Guard, who marched the SAS men east while they kept pace on their bicycles. For the next week they headed further into Germany, subsisting on dry bread and brackish water, and being subjected to the occasional beating from vengeful inhabitants of villages they passed through. On 16 April they were herded into Stalag XB near Sandbostel (approximately 60 miles north-east of where they had been captured), a POW camp containing mostly Frenchmen and Eastern European soldiers. 'After a couple of days the Gestapo turned up,' recalled Youngman. 'They were threatening us again so me and Davidson decided if we're going to be killed we might as well be killed trying to escape.'

ABOVE

Unlike some of his men hugging the ground, Paddy Mayne (far right) seems unfazed by the sniper fire directed his way in April 1945. (Courtesy of the SAS Regimental Archive)

LEFT

The SAS were ill-equipped to operate as reconnaissance patrols in 1945 and the strain of operations is etched into the faces of these men. (Courtesy of the SAS Regimental Archive)

Mike Calvert (seen here consoling the widow of a French SAS officer) replaced Roderick McLeod as brigadier of the SAS Brigade in March 1945 and discussed with Stirling the possibility of the SAS operating in the Far East. (Courtesy of the SAS Regimental Archive)

Leaving behind the rest of their section who preferred to remain as POWs, Davidson and Youngman were smuggled out of the camp by some French prisoners engaged on a working party at a nearby farm. The pair split from the French and headed west in the direction of the advancing Allies. 'A mile or two from the camp, the heady sensation of freedom soon gave way to fear,' recalled Davidson. 'We were in enemy territory, in incomplete disguise, not armed and vulnerable to any gang of thugs roaming the countryside at that time. The best plan was to get off the autobahn, make for the shelter of woods and move under cover of night towards the sound of heavy gunfire.'

For three days and nights Davidson and Youngman edged cautiously towards the gathering sound of battle. Then, just after dawn on 25 April, as they walked down a winding forest road, Youngman heard the crisp tones of the 'Home Service on the radio'. They rounded the bend and there was the Guards Armoured Brigade having breakfast.

The rest of B and C Squadron, meanwhile, were on their way towards Westerscheps, a few miles west of Oldenburg. 'Just before we got into Oldenburg we ran into this village and there wasn't a bloody soul around,' recalled Bob McDougall, a Liverpudlian in C Squadron. 'It was just after first light when we pulled up and the next thing this little kid came out, and all he had on was a little jersey, no shoes, nothing else. And one of the section, a fellow called Finch, picked this kid up and brought him over. He put a blanket over him and pulled out a bar of chocolate and gave it to the kid. You never saw a face light up, and within a few minutes Finch had this kid laughing and there was chocolate all over his face. So Finch went round collecting chocolate for the kid.'[7]

That was one of the few bright moments in an otherwise grim few days. On 29 April Trooper Tom Kent stood on a mine and, after he had died slowly from wounds, Paddy Mayne sent a signal to Harry Poat waiting to lead A and D Squadrons across the river Elbe and up towards the Baltic Sea port of Lubeck. 'Squadron now plodding along through bog and rain on their feet. Tpr. Kent killed by mine. Nobody very happy.'[8]

Mayne's disquiet was exacerbated by the uncertainty surrounding not just the regiment's future but his own. News of David Stirling's release from captivity had been radioed to 1 and 2SAS on 20 April, and the following day came a second despatch from England: 'David Stirling in great heart sends many messages and congratulations to all, and hopes to come out and visit you soon.'[9]

Mayne had led 1SAS for two-and-a-half years and now faced the prospect of handing over command to Stirling. But the more immediate problem confronting Mayne was what to do with the SAS Brigade once they had finished mopping up the last vestiges of German resistance. On 27 April Mike Calvert – who had taken over command of the SAS Brigade from Roderick McLeod in March – sent a message to Mayne and Franks in which he raised the possibility of a deployment to Denmark: 'Resistance and ground reception very well organised and country suitable for concealment and jeeping between woods.'[10]

Some of the boys of 2SAS warm themselves round a campfire prior to crossing the Elbe on the night of 29 April. Charlie Hackney is fifth from right. (Author's Collection)

Evidently Mayne had earlier voiced his concerns to Calvert about the possibility that the SAS might be misused by SHAEF for the Brigadier appended a second message specifically to the Irishman. 'Understand your worries. You are quite right to raise them… Hope can put you on good wicket soon as possible.' The crossing of the river Elbe began, as far as the SAS was concerned, at 1500 hours on Sunday 29 April. In the preceding week 2SAS had been bolstered by the arrival of 118 men of the regiment under the command of Major Grant Hibbert. They had driven up from Arnhem after their initial operation – *Keystone* – had been cancelled by the Brigade. The aim of *Keystone*, planned in conjunction with a French SAS mission, had been to capture seven bridges over the Apeldoorn Canal in Holland but bad weather prevented the French from dropping and so instead Hibbert and his men motored north to link up with the rest of 2SAS.

Hibbert led the regiment across the Elbe in the face of what Field Marshal Bernard Montgomery later described as 'generally light' opposition. The biggest shock was the sight – and sound – of the German jet fighters overhead. These were Me 262s which

An SAS jeep sits inside a Buffalo amphibious landing craft before the crossing of the Elbe on 29 April. (Courtesy of the SAS Regimental Archive)

Festooned with the spoils of war, 1SAS prepare to embark at Ostend for Tilbury where they raced away from the Customs men before their booty could be confiscated. (Author's Collection)

could reach maximum speed of 500mph. 'We got over the river more or less unscathed,' remembered Charlie Hackney, 'but as we were making for the woods on the other side we got caught by some airburst shells, which were nasty things that sent out a shower of red hot shrapnel. I was going hell for leather for the trees when suddenly the jeep in front stopped. As I came level I saw Bobby Boxall slumped dead over the wheel.'[11]

Operation *Archway*'s report had little to say after the Elbe had been crossed. Hitler was dead, Berlin had fallen and everyone just wanted to go home. On 3 May the report stated:

> Force HQ moved to Luttjensee and subsequently to Gross Handsdorf.
> Major Poat's 1st SAS Squadron reached Lubeck and moved on to Kiel with
> 30th Assault Unit.
> Frankforce embarked for UK on 10th May.[12]

Paddy Mayne's men were north of Oldenburg shortly before the armistice was signed. After the death of Tom Kent the regiment was being extra vigilant with a ceasefire so tantalisingly near. 'I'd been sitting in a ditch watching a farmhouse where Germans soldiers were walking around,' recalled Bob Francis. 'We could have done them quite easily but it all seemed too late in the day; I didn't want to hurt anybody and I certainly didn't want to get hurt. The war all sort of fizzled out.'[13]

SPECIAL
AIR SERVICE REGIMENT

EGYPT	ITALY
LIBYA	FRANCE
TRIPOLI	BELGIUM
TUNISIA	HOLLAND
CRETE	GERMANY
SICILY	NORWAY

WHO DARES WINS

1941   1945

NO. 1435568. DESMOND PETER MIDDLETON.

CHAPTER 13

DELIGHTED THEN DEMOBBED

1 SAS celebrated Victory in Europe (VE) Day, 8 May, in Belgium. Paddy Mayne and B and C Squadrons were in Brussels, en route to a rendezvous with A and D squadrons at Poperinghe, 70 miles west. The next day the regiment was reunited, celebrating in drink and song. Ian Wellsted and Bill Fraser were present, recovering from their wounds, and Wellsted recalled that: 'Belgians drifted up and grouped themselves around us. Soon they began to sing and we sang back, singing together the old songs of the last Great War.'[1]

Within 24 hours 1SAS and 2SAS were in England, but not for long. On 15 May the two regiments began embarking by aircraft for Norway and by the end of the month 760 men and 33 tons of stores had been transported north to Bergen. There they spent the summer, ostensibly overseeing the disarmament of 300,000 Germans but in reality enjoying the warmth of the weather and of the locals. Back in Britain, meanwhile, plans were afoot to send the SAS Brigade to the Far East. David Stirling, released from captivity in April 1945, formulated an idea with Brigadier Mike Calvert. The pair then lunched with Winston Churchill to discuss the possibility of the SAS operating in China to sever the Japanese supply line to Malaya. On 16 July Calvert informed the War Office of the operational strength of 1SAS (490 officers and other ranks) and 2SAS (587 officers and other ranks), and suggested they ask for 'volunteers' to fight the Japanese. The scheme appeared to be gathering momentum when, on 5 August, Field Marshal

OPPOSITE
Less than four years after formation, the SAS boasted an impressive list of battle honours, all of which were emblazoned on the certificates given to members at the war's conclusion. (Author's Collection)

The SAS parading through the streets of Bergen during their summer stay in Norway when they helped disarm 300,000 German soldiers. (Author's Collection)

William Slim, commander of the 14th Army, wrote to Calvert from London's Savoy Hotel where he was staying on a visit to the capital. 'I shall go into the question of the employment of the SAS regiments in that area [Far East] soon,' he promised. The next day the United States dropped the first of two atomic bombs on Japan and within a fortnight Emperor Hirohito ordered his country to surrender.

On 25 August the two SAS regiments sailed from Norway for Britain and soon the Brigade was being broken up. First to go were the Belgians, returned to their own army on 21 September, followed by the two regiments of French SAS on 1 October. There was no reprieve for 1 and 2SAS, even though in a letter to Calvert General Miles Dempsey, commander of the Second Army, wrote: 'I always enjoyed having detachments of the SAS in Second Army, and their work was always up to the standard one expects of them. I wish I had been able to see more of them.'

The brutal truth was what need did the British military have for such a force now that the world was at peace? The era of special forces' units was at an end, at least it was in the eyes of many staff officers, those 'fossilised shits' that David Stirling so despised.

The two British regiments received confirmation of their disbandment on 4 October, four days after 2SAS had held a service of Thanksgiving at St Peter's Church in Colchester. The Reverend Kent, the regiment's padre, read out the names of their dead before telling the congregation: 'The Lord bless you and keep you.

The Lord make his face to shine upon you and bless you. The Lord lift up the light of his countenance upon you, and give you his peace, now and evermore.'

On 1 October 1SAS paraded for the final time at Hylands House in front of Brigadier Mike Calvert. Despite their imminent demise the men were immaculate with polished boots and maroon berets. Only Paddy Mayne stood out. The man who above all others epitomised the ethos of the SAS insisted on wearing his sand-coloured beret to the very end. Six years after the end of the war Fraser McLusky published his wartime memoirs entitled *Parachute Padre*. In the epilogue he recalled the misery of the night of 26 June 1944 when A Squadron was on the run from the Germans having been forced to flee their forest camp. It was cold and wet and they were carrying a badly wounded Reg Seekings. 'I wondered why,' wrote McLusky in his book, 'in the peace and security of home, I had never realised how lucky I was. If the privileges of the normal were ever mine again, would I learn to remember their value? Fourteen days as a guerrilla had sorted out my scale of values. What would happen if I ever returned to the settled life of peace?'[2]

Fraser McLuskey died in 2005 aged 90, after a life rich in achievement. In the years immediately after the war, he was a Church of Scotland minister in Glasgow; then in 1960 he was called to St Columba's, London, one of two Church of Scotland congregations in the capital. In 1984 he was appointed Moderator of the General

Brigadier Mike Calvert, Commandant SAS Brigade, at the ceremony marking the passing of 3 and 4SAS from the British to the French Army at Tarbes in southern France. (IWM B 15783)

SAS gentlemen prefer blondes. A Bergen bombshell puts a smile on the face of these boys during the regiment's enjoyable sojourn in Norway. (Courtesy of the SAS Regimental Archive)

Assembly and in 2003, two years before his death, he addressed the wartime SAS veterans for the final time in a service at St Columba's. As for his 'parishioners', as McLusky called his former SAS comrades, they experienced both triumph and tragedy in their post-war lives:

Herbert Castelow: Having escaped the fate of Captain Pat Garstin and the others, Castelow rejoined the SAS and was awarded the Military Medal during Operation *Archway*. Returned to the north-east of England and died of a heart-attack in 1973 aged 57.

Harry Challenor: Joined the Metropolitan Police and later worked for the Flying Squad in Soho. In the 1960s he was convicted of planting evidence on a suspect and was plagued by mental health problems in later years. He died in 2008.

Johnny Cooper: Was awarded an MBE while serving with the SAS in Malaya in the 1950s, Cooper also operated in the Yemen before retiring to Portugal. He died in 2002 aged 80.

David Danger: Joined a firm of printers after the war but missed army life and reenlisted, retiring in the 1970s as a lieutenant-colonel. He died in 2009.

Gordon Davidson: Left the army and entered the world of business, while maintaining contact with the SAS. He died in 1990.

Peter Davis: Emigrated to South Africa and became a successful businessman. He was murdered during a robbery at his Durban home in 1994.

Henry Druce: Resumed his career with MI6 after the war and later emigrated to Canada where he worked in the shipping industry. He died in 2007 aged 85.

Jeff Du Vivier: Resumed his career in the catering industry and was restaurant manager of the Prestwick Airport Hotel for many years. He died in 2010 aged 94.

Roy Farran: Remained in the army and was accused of murdering a Jewish youth in Palestine in 1947, a charge on which he was acquitted. He emigrated to Canada in the 1950s, where he became a journalist and cabinet minister in Alberta. He died in 2006.

Brian Franks: Returned to the hospitality industry after the war, serving as general manager of the Hyde Park Hotel from 1959 to 1972. Franks was also Honourary Colonel of 21SAS for many years, and later Colonel Commandant of the SAS Regiment. He died in 1982 aged 70.

Bill Fraser: Court-martialled and reduced in rank for drunkenness while in command of a company of Gordon Highlanders in 1946, Fraser left the army shortly after. In 1954 Paddy Mayne wrote to tell a former comrade that 'poor old Bill Fraser has collected a three year prison sentence for breaking into some thirty odd houses'.[3] Upon his release from prison Fraser worked in a bakery and then as a costing clerk for a Midlands' engineering firm. He died in 1975.

The life of Bill Fraser, seen here in 1943, spiralled out of control after the war culminating in a three-year prison sentence for burglary in the 1950s. (Author's Collection)

Tony Greville-Bell: Served with the SAS in Malaya before embarking on a successful career as a sculptor and then script writer in Los Angeles. He wrote the cult film *Theatre of Blood* and died in 2008 aged 87.

Alex Griffiths: Spent his working life painting miniature soldiers that he sold from a Mayfair shop. He died in 2004 aged 83.

Charlie Hackney: After demob, Charlie Hackney worked for Rolls Royce and for the Yarrow Admiralty Research Department. A Chelsea Pensioner in later life, he died in 2008 aged 90.

Ken Harvey: Returned to Rhodesia and became an architect, designing many of Bulawayo's finest buildings. He continued to hunt big game into his 60s and died in 2005 aged 81.

Vic Long: Married his wartime sweetheart and for 30 years worked as a driver on the London Underground. He died in 2007 aged 83.

Des: Peter,

Des Peter Middleton frolics with a former guard dog of the German Army in Norway. (Author's Collection)

Bob Lowson: After a two-year recuperation from the wounds sustained in April 1945, Lowson married and spent his working life with Shell. He lives in the north-west of England.

James McDiarmid: Emigrated to Australia after the war, and the last contact any of his old comrades had was in the 1960s when he was a cadet instructor in a New South Wales public school.

Tony Marsh: Remained in the army until the late 1950s when he took up a position in Bermuda with the Trade Development Board. He was a leading figure in the Royal Bermuda Yacht club and died on the island in 1984 aged 64.

Paddy Mayne: Left the army and returned to Belfast where he was appointed Secretary of the Law Society of Northern Ireland. Despite the role, Mayne struggled to adjust to a life without war and his bouts of heavy drinking were legendary. In 1954 he wrote to Des Middleton to tell him that 'I have very little information about any of the chaps'.[4] A year later Mayne died at the wheel of his treasured red sports car while returning from a night out. He was 40.

Des Peter Middleton: Married and went into teaching after the war, first in Africa and then in England. He taught at the Rowena School for Girls in Kent for a number of years and died of a cerebral haemorrhage in 1980, a year before he was due to retire.

John Noble: Initially joined the Metropolitan Police after demob but emigrated to British Colombia in the 1950s and spent 18 years in the Canadian Army. He died in 2009 aged 87.

Sid Payne: Rejoined the engineering firm that he'd worked for before the war and remained with them until retirement. He lives in the Midlands.

Harry Poat: Returned to his native Guernsey and the family tomato-growing business. He died of lung disease in 1982 aged 67.

Cyril Radford: Transferred to the Parachute Regiment after the war before joining the Customs and Excise, for whom he worked for 30 years in Cyprus. He died in 2008 aged 84.

Duncan Ridler: Enrolled in the London School of Economics after the war and then worked as an economist for the United Nations. He died in 2005 aged 85.

Mike Sadler: Indulged his love of sailing after the war, while also working for the Foreign Service. He lives in the south of England.

Reg Seekings: Emigrated with his wife to Rhodesia and became a tobacco farmer, while also lending his expertise to police anti-terrorist units. Returned to England and died in 1999 aged 78.

Bill Stirling: A successful businessman after the war, Stirling later retired to run the family estate as the laird of Kerr. He died in 1983 aged 71.

David Stirling: Settled in Rhodesia post-war and founded the Capricorn African Society, an organisation devoted to establishing a community without political and racial barriers. That failed so he returned to the UK in 1961 and became involved in providing security services to foreign heads of state. He was knighted in 1989 and died the following year aged 74.

Jimmy Storie: Spent nearly three years as a POW and returned to Scotland where he worked in the tiling business. As of 2011 he is the last of 'the originals', those 66 soldiers recruited by David Stirling in the summer of 1941. He lives in Scotland.

Arthur Thomson: Returned to his native London and built up a successful second-hand car business. Later entered local politics and died in 2009 aged 89.

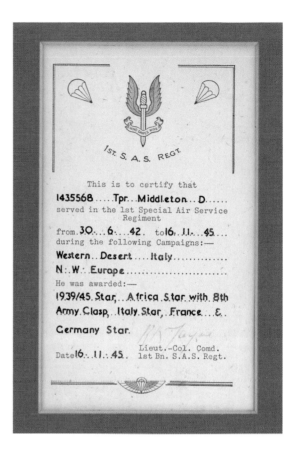

Certificates like this one belonging to Des Peter Middleton were awarded to all members of the SAS at the regiment's disbandment. (Author's Collection)

Harry Vickers: After recovering from his wounds, Vickers became an estate surveyor in the Old Ministry of Works. He died in 2007 aged 86.

Denis Wainman: Joined the Metropolitan Police but resigned and spent the majority of his working life as a teacher of art in a secondary school. He lives in the south of England.

Bob Walker-Brown: Remained in the army after the war and commanded 23SAS from 1961 to 1963. Later he worked for the Defence Intelligence Staff of the Ministry of Defence and he died in 2009 aged 90.

Peter Weaver: Ran a chicken farm in Essex for many years, played club cricket into his 50s, and died in 1991 aged 79.

Ian Wellsted: Remained in the army until 1967 before emigrating to New Zealand where he ran a holiday camp with his wife. He died in 2002 aged 83.

Johnny Wiseman: Returned to the family business of manufacturing spectacles and finished up as company director. He died in 2005 aged 87.

Albert Youngman: Unable to settle down after the war, Youngman left Britain and worked overseas, first in Nigeria and then running a thriving import-export business in Hong Kong. He returned to the UK in the late 1990s and lives in the east of England.

GLOSSARY

AA	anti-aircraft
CO	Commanding Officer
DCM	Distinguished Conduct Medal
DSO	Distinguished Service Order
DZ	drop zone
GHQ	General Headquarters
LCA	Landing Craft Assault
LRDG	Long Range Desert Group
MC	Military Cross
MEHQ	Middle East Headquarters
MP	Military Police
OC	Officer Commanding
OCTU	Officer Cadet Training Units
OSS	Office of Strategic Service
Pct	Parachutist
POW	prisoner of war
PT	physical training
Pte	Private
RAF	Royal Air Force
RSM	Regimental Sergeant Major
RTU'd	returned to unit
RV	rendezvous point
SAS	Special Air Service
SBS	Special Boat Section, later named the Special Boat Squadron
SFHQ	Special Forces Headquarters
SHAEF	Supreme Headquarters Allied Expeditionary Force
SOE	Special Operations Executive
SQMS	Squadron Quartermaster Sergeant
SRS	Special Raiding Squadron
Tpr	Trooper
TSMG	Thompson sub-machine gun
VE	Victory in Europe

ENDNOTES

Introduction

1. David Stirling, *Origins of the Special Air Service*, SAS Archives
2. Ibid.
3. Letter from Laycock to Major General Smith, May 1941, National Archives
4. Stirling, *Origins of the Special Air Service*

Chapter One

1. Alan Hoe, *David Stirling* (Warner, 1994)
2. Author interview, 2003
3. Author interview with John Kane, 1998
4. Author interview, 2001
5. David Stirling, *Origins of the Special Air Service*, SAS Archives
6. Author interview, 2003
7. Memo entitled *The First Parachute Jump in the Middle East*, National Archives
8. David Stirling, *Origins of the Special Air Service*
9. Ibid.
10. Graham Lappin, *11 Scottish Commando* (unpublished but available to view at www.combinedops.com)
11. Mike Blackman (ed.), *The Paddy Mayne Diary* (unpublished, 1945)
12. Gavin Mortimer, *Stirling's Men* (Weidenfeld, 2004)
13. SAS report on the repatriation of Blakeney, 1944, National Archives, AIR50/205
14. Hoe, *David Stirling*

Chapter Two

1. David List, *The Birth of the SAS*, BBC radio documentary 2006
2. Virginia Cowles, *The Phantom Major* (Collins, 1958)
3. Mike Blackman (ed.), *The Paddy Mayne Diary* (unpublished, 1945)
4. Ibid.
5. Author interview with John Kane, 1998
6. Blackman, *The Paddy Mayne Diary*

7. Author interview

8. John Byrne, *The General Salutes a Soldier* (Hale, 1986)

9. Jeff Du Vivier diary (privately held)

10. Operation report, National Archives, Special Service War Diaries, WO218/166-172

11. Ibid.

12. Captured Italian report on enemy sabotage, Ibid.

13. Ibid.

14. Cowles, *The Phantom Major*

15. Author interview

16. Operation report, National Archives, Special Service War Diaries, WO218/166-172

17. Du Vivier letter, privately held

18. Author interview, 2003

19. Letter from Les Ward to Jeff Du Vivier's nephew

20. Author interview, 2002

21. Author interview, 2003

22. David Stirling, *Origins of the Special Air Service*, SAS Archives

23. Quoted in Hamish Ross, *Paddy Mayne* (Sutton, 2003)

24. John Strawson, *A History of the SAS Regiment* (Guild, 1984)

25. Operation report, National Archives, Special Service War Diaries, WO218/166-172

26. Ross, *Paddy Mayne*

27. Author interview

Chapter Three

1. Author interview with John Kane, 1998

2. David Stirling, *Origins of the Special Air Service*, SAS Archives

3. George Jellico report, National Archives, Special Service War Diaries, WO218/166-172

4. Ibid.

5. Virginia Cowles, *The Phantom Major* (Collins, 1958)

6. Johnny Cooper, *One of the Originals* (Pan, 1991)

7. Stephen Hastings, *The Drums of Memory* (Pen and Sword, 1994)

8. Author interview

9. Operation Instruction No.99, republished in *Special Forces in the Desert War 1940–1943*, Public Record Office War Histories, 2001

10. Ibid.
11. George Jellico report, National Archives, Special Service War Diaries, WO218/166-172
12. Author interview
13. Author interview, 1998
14. Stirling, *Origins of the Special Air Service*
15. Author interview, 2002
16. Hamish Ross, *Paddy Mayne* (Sutton, 2003)

Chapter Four

1. Pleydell, IWM Documents 337, letter dated 15 February 1943
2. Author interview, 2002
3. Davis, unpublished memoirs, SAS Archives
4. Author interview, 2003
5. Johnny Wiseman, IWM Sound 20337
6. Author interview with John Kane, 1998
7. Author interview, 2002
8. Operation report of HMS *Tetcott*, www.hmstetcott.com
9. Author interview
10. Author interview
11. Martin Gilbert, *Churchill: A Life* (Holt, 1992)
12. Author interview, 2010
13. Letter from RSM Rose, reproducd in an issue of *Mars and Minerva*
14. Von Pohl, National Archives, CAB45/288
15. Quoted in Davis's memoirs
16. DSO Citation for Tony Marsh, National Archives, WO373/4
17. SRS war diary, reproduced in various issues of *Mars and Minerva*
18. German despatch on the fall of Termoli
19. Ibid.

Chapter Five

1. Johnny Cooper, *One of the Originals* (Pan, 1991)
2. John Strawson, *A History of the SAS Regiment* (Guild, 1984)
3. Account of Operation *Marigold*, *Mars and Minerva*
4. Author interview, 2002
5. SAS report into the deaths of Foster and Shortall, National Archives, WO309/99

Chapter Six

1. Author interview, 2002
2. Roy Farran, *Winged Dagger* (Collins, 1948)
3. 2SAS Squadron report on Termoli, National Archives, WO218/176
4. Operation report on *Jonquil*, National Archives, WO218/181
5. Quoted in Jimmy Hughes, *Who Cares Who Wins* (Charico Press, 1998)
6. SAS report by Barkworth into the execution of SAS personnel, National Archives, FO371/178763, WO311/627-629

Chapter Seven

1. Mike Blackman (ed.), *The Paddy Mayne Diary* (unpublished, 1945)
2. SRS War Diary, SAS Regimental Archive
3. Du Vivier family collection
4. Author interview
5. Author interview
6. Author interview
7. Ian Wellsted, *The SAS with the Marquis* (Greenhill, 1997)
8. Reproduced in *Mars and Minerva*
9. Hamish Ross, *Paddy Mayne* (Sutton, 2003)
10. Author interview

Chapter Eight

1. Ian Wellsted, *The SAS with the Marquis* (Greenhill, 1997)
2. Author interview
3. Operation *Houndsworth* report, National Archives, WO218/192
4. Author interview
5. John Noble journal, reproduced in *Mars and Minerva*
6. Letter from RSM Rose, reproducd in an issue of *Mars and Minerva*
7. Operation *Houndsworth* report, National Archives, WO218/192
8. Author interview with John Kane, 1998
9. Rev Fraser McLuskey, *Parachute Padre* (Strong Oak, 1997)
10. Operation *Houndsworth* report, National Archives, WO218/192
11. Johnny Cooper, *One of the Originals* (Pan, 1991)
12. Operation *Houndsworth* report, National Archives, WO218/192
13. Ibid.
14. Paul McCue, *Operation Bulbasket* (Pen and Sword, 1996)
15. Peter Weaver, unpublished memoir, privately held
16. Author interview

17. Escape report by Herbert Castelow, National Archives, WO218/192

18. Report of the fate of the Garston Stick, National Archives, WO218/192

19. Ibid.

20. Ibid.

21. Operation *Gain* report, National Archives, WO218/192

22. Operation *Haggard* report, National Archives, WO218/192

23. Author interview

24. Operation *Haggard* report, National Archives, WO218/192

25. Author interview

Chapter Nine

1. Author interview

2. Author interview

3. Letter from Brian Franks, National Archives, WO218/195

4. Author interview

5. Author interview

6. Ronald Crossfield, 'A Walk with the SAS', published in *Mars and Minerva*

7. Christopher Sykes, *Four Studies in Loyalty* (David and Charles, 1986)

8. Operation *Loyton* report, National Archives, WO219/2402B

9. Author interview

10. Operation *Wallace* report, National Archives, WO219/2401

11. General Eisenhower letter to Brigadier McLeod, reproduced at www.belgiansas.us

12. Author interview

13. Report by Fraser McLusky, reproduced in *Mars and Minerva*

14. Author interview

15. Hamish Ross, *Paddy Mayne* (Sutton, 2003)

Chapter Ten

1. Author interview

2. Walker-Brown's unpublished account of Operation *Galia*

3. Operation *Galia* report, National Archives, WO219/2403

4. Ken Harvey's account of Operation *Tombola*, published in *Mars and Minerva*

5. Roy Farran, *Winged Dagger* (Collins, 1948)

Chapter Eleven

1. Author interview

2. Peter Weaver, unpublished memoir, privately held

3. Author interview with John Kane, 1998
4. Author interview
5. Author interview
6. Operation *Archway* report, National Archives, WO218/199
7. Author interview
8. Operation *Archway* report, National Archives, WO218/199
9. Author interview
10. Author interview
11. Johnny Wiseman, IWM Sound 20337
12. J. H. Patterson papers, IWM Documents 13225
13. Duncan Ridler, 'On a Spring Evening in 1945', published in *Mars and Minerva*

Chapter Twelve

1. Author interview
2. Author interview
3. Author interview
4. Author interview
5. Michael Asher, *The Regiment* (Penguin, 2007)
6. Gordon Davidson, 'The Escape', published in *Mars and Minerva*
7. Author interview
8. Transcript of radio signals sent and received during Operation *Howard*, SAS Archives
9. Ibid.
10. Mike Calvert, IWM Sound 99245/21
11. Author interview
12. Operation *Archway* report, National Archives, WO218/199
13. Author interview

Chapter Thirteen

1. Ian Wellsted, *The SAS with the Marquis* (Greenhill, 1997)
2. Rev Fraser McLuskey, *Parachute Padre* (Strong Oak, 1997)
3. Letter from Paddy Mayne to Des Middleton, Middleton family collection
4. Ibid.

INDEX

Bold page numbers refer to illustrations

Abdiel, HMS, destroyer 121
Agedabia, Libya 34, 38–42
Agheila, Libya 34
airfields
    raids on 34–5, 37–44, **39**, 61–2, 63
    tactics 66–7, 68
Alexander, General Harold 70, 95
Almonds, Private Jim 20, 44, 169, 170
Alston, Gordon 52
Antwerp 203
Arae Philaenorum aerodrome, attack on
    42–5
Ardennes, French 4SAS in 191–2, **192**
Armistice (1945) 235
Army Air Corps 134
Arnold, parachutist 26
Athlit 81
Auchinleck, General Claude 10, 11, 33,
    45, 51
    pressure on 52–3, 70
Augusta, Sicily 89–95, **93**
9th Australian Division 63
Autun, France 154, 156, 173
Auxiliary Units 134, 176
Azzib, Palestine, SRS in 81–3

Backhouse, Charlie 213
Badger, Ted **64–5**
Bagnara, Italy 95–102, **98, 99**
Bagoush airfield 63, 66, 68
Ball, Lieutenant 158
Barce, attack on 52
Barkworth, Major Bill 127
Barnby, Captain David 82
Bateman, Ken 160
battle honours **236**
Belot, Bob, interpreter and guide 51
Belsen concentration camp **216**,
    217–8, 219

Benghazi, Libya 45–6, 51–2, 55–9, 71–3
Benina 54, 55
Bennett, Bob 52
beret and cap badge 47, 50, 134
    Tank Corps 204, **204**
Bergeron, Madame 181
Berges, Captain George 46
Berka satellite airfield 52, 54
Bir el Quseir **55**, 66
Bir Zelten 75
Blakeney, Jim 31, 205
Bolland, Stanley **28**
Bond, Major Dick 221, 222, 223–4
Bonington, Lieutenant Charles 13, 24,
    26, 31
Bonington, Sir Christian 13
Bost, Lance Sergeant Fritz 118
Bouerat, raid on 45–6
Boutinot, Roger **34**, 47
Boxall, Bobby 235
Bradford, Captain Roy 134, 148, 157–8
British Army
    1st Parachute Division 103
    6th Airborne Division 206, 207,
        209, 212
    11th Armoured Division 213,
        217–8
    11th Infantry Brigade 104, 105
    21 Army Group 143
    38th Irish Brigade 108
    78th Infantry Division 102, 103,
        106
    Fifth Army 102
    First Army 75, 112
    in Italy 102
    Royal Welsh regiment 121
    see also Eighth Army
Brough, Sergeant Jimmy 35
Browning, Lieutenant General
    Frederick 'Boy' 140
Brunt, Bernie 115, 118

Brussels, Manneken Pis **11**
Bryan, Lieutenant Gerald 24
Byrne, Private Jock 22, **23**, 38, 44, 52

Cairns, Lieutenant Les 148
Calvert, Mike **232**, 233, 237–8, **239**
Canadian Army
    4th Canadian Armoured Division
        221
    with Eighth Army 124
Cannizzaro, Sicily 95
Cape Murro di Porco, Sicily 84–9, **87**,
    88, 129
Castelow, Herbert 162–3, 166–7, 240
Caton, Geoff **77**, 88, 89
Cattell, Charlie **23**, **76**
Celle, Germany, concentration camp
    216–7
Challenor, Harry 112–3, 240
    Operation *Speedwell* 114–9
Chambers, Jim **62**
Chasseurs Alpins **202**, 206
Cheyne, Sergeant John 29
China 237
Churchill, Winston 237
    and Auchinleck 52–3, 70
Clarke, Sergeant Major Nobby 227
Clifford, Alexander 30
Close, Lieutenant Roy 173
Cookhouse, Private 126
Cooper, Johnny 16, 24, **64–5**, 82, **206**,
    209, 240
    in A Sqn 1SAS 134
    capture 78
    and first operation 28, 29
    France 146–7, 154, 156
    North Africa 44, 50–1, 53–6, 66,
        68–9
    Operation *Archway* 205, 213
Cooper, Sam 227–8
Corbett, Corporal Jack 213

Coutts, Andy 227, 228
Crisp, Richard 144, 159
Crossfield, Ronald 'Dusty' 177–8, 179, 180–1, 183
Cumper, Captain Bill 47
Cunningham, General Alan 33

Danger, David 91, 107, 187, 189, 240
    France 147, 150, 152, 154
    Operation *Howard* 221–2
Daniels, George 118, **119**
D'Arcy, Mick 20
Davidson, Lieutenant Gordon 226, 229–30, 232, 240
Davies, Roy 31
    Operation *Archway* 205, 213, 214, 216
Davis, Gerald 179
Davis, Peter 82, **82**, 83–4, **227**, 240
    France 173
    Italy 96, 97–9, 101
    Sicily 84, 85, 87, 88–9, 92, 93
    Termoli 103–4, 105–6, 109
Deakins, Sergeant Bill 85, 87
Deane, Dixie 214
Dempsey, General Miles 129, 131, **131**, 238
Denmark 233
Devine, Bill 157
Docherty, Trooper 146
Dodd, Lieutenant Roy 52
Druce, Henry 175, 176, 177–9, 180–1, **215**, 240
Du Vivier, Jeff **78**, 82, **84**, **128**, **135**, **206**, 241
    in A Sqn 1SAS 134
    early volunteer 15, **25**, **28**, **30**
    on first operation 22, 24, 26, 28–9, 31
    France 158
    on Lewes bomb 18–9
    log book **36**
    Military Medal 45
    North Africa 38, 40, 44, 45
    Operation *Archway* 205, 213–4
    parachute training 20–1
    in Scotland 134
    and training 46–7

Dudgeon, Captain Pat 115, 118
Duffy, Joe 21

Eccles, Dougie 92, 160
Eighth Army 70–1, 124
    8th Indian Division 192
    Argentan Gap 201
    El Alamein 61, 74–7, **75**
    North Africa 22, 33, 34, 51
    Sicily 124
Eisenhower, General Dwight 186, 189
El Alamein 61, 63, 74–7, **75**
El Daba, Axis fighter base 63
Elbe, River **233**, 234–5, **234**
Eliseo, Domenica 116
Eskimo, HMS 90
Evening News 189

Farran, Captain Roy 50, **114**, **120**, 121–7, 241
    C Sqn, 2SAS 183–4, 185–6
    D Sqn, 2SAS 111, 121–7
    Operation *Tombola* **190**, 196–201
Fenwick, Ian 134, 161–2, 169–70, 175
Ferguson, Duncan **211**, 214, 216
Fiddick, Lou 178–9
Finch, Private 232
Foret de Merry-Vaux 171–3
Foret d'Orleans 161–2
Foster, Sergeant Bill 115, 117–8
France 140, 143–73
    sabotage 156, 158, 159, 161–2, 170–1
    SAS and civilians **184–5**, **187**
    supplies by parachute **142**
    see also Maquis resistance
Francis, Bob 134–5, 235
Franks, Lieutenant Colonel Brian 125, **175**, 201, 241
    OC 2SAS 175–83, **177**
Fraser, Major Bill 81, 85, 189, 241, **241**
    A Sqn 1SAS 134, 159
    and attack on Arae Philaenorum aerodrome 42–3, 44
    France 146, 147, 148, 151, 156, 159
    in Italy 96
    MC 45
    North Africa 13, 22, 34, 52, **62**, 63, 73

Operation *Archway* 209–10
    raid on Agedabia 38–9, 40–2
    and VE Day 237
Free French
    as C Squadron 73, 77
    with SAS **34**, **35**, 46, 47, 54, **132–3**
    see also 3SAS; 4SAS
Fuka airfield 63, 66

Gafsa, fall of 77
Galloway, Sandy 26
Garstin, Captain Pat 162–3, 167
Gazala airfield 22, 29, 31, 51
Genoa-La Spezia railway 115–6
German Army 118
    2nd SS Panzer Division 159–61
    16th Panzer Division 192–3
    Afrika Korps 22, 70, 71, **75**
    Ardennes offensive 191–2, **192**
    Battle Group Stempel 104, 108
    France 153–4
    Hermann Goering Division 91
    in Italy 96, 98, 102, 104, 198–9, 201
    surrenders **223**
    White Russians with 150, 151
Germany
    Operation *Archway* 203–19
    Operation *Howard* 221–35, **226**, **227**
Glaze, Sergeant Major Gus 47
Glyde, John 213
Goldie, David **211**
Goldsmith, Joe **93**
Goodfellow, Robert (Robert de Lesseps) 178–9
Grether, Lieutenant 118
Greville-Bell, Lieutenant Anthony 114–5, 118–9, **119**, 140–1, 175, 241
Griffiths, Private Alex 82, 85, 96, 101, 102, 241
Guards Armoured Brigade, 6th Independent 208

Hackney, Charlie 124, 126, 184–5, 241
    crossing of Elbe **233**, 235
    Italy **120**, 121, **122**, 123
Hall, Ginger 178, 179

Hall, Jimmy 172
Harrison, Captain Derrick 93, **95**, 96, 104, 171, 172, 189
Harvey, Lieutenant Ken 196, 197, 198, 199–201, **201**, 241
Hastings, Lieutenant Steven 66, 68
Hay 178
Hibbert, Major Grant 126, 183, 234–5
Hicks, Brig Philip 85
Hildreth, Sidney 31
Hislop, John 178
Hitler Youth, 'Werewolves' 219, **225**
Holmes, Sergeant Bob **160**
Howell, William 96
HQ Raiding Forces 81
Hughes, Lieutenant Jimmy 126–7, 167
Hughes, Private 113
Hull, Billy 224
Hylands House, Essex 203–5

Iredale, Captain Tim 223
Italian forces 35, 57–8
    Sicily 88–9, **88**
    at Siwa 70
Italy 95–109
    northern 114–7, 192–4, **193**, 196–201, **197**

Jackson, Lieutenant Peter 125
Jaghbub Oasis 31, 33
Jalo Oasis 34, 42, 44
Japan 238
Jedbergh teams 178
jeeps
    acquisition 63
    new 203, **204**, **210**
    use of **46**, **48–9**, **51**, **56–7**, 62
Jeffs, Trooper **76**
Jellicoe, Lord George **46**, 62, 63, 70
    and SBS 81, 112
Johnson, Lieutenant 210
Jones, John 50
Jones, Thomas 'Ginger' 167
Jordan, Augustin 63, 77

Kabrit, training camp 16, **17**, 18, 47
Kahane, Karl 55, 57
Kairouan airfield, Tunisia 114

Kauffman, Private 18
Keith, Private Doug 20, 31
Kendall, Parachutist 26
Kennedy, Trooper Kit 146, **155**
Kent, Reverand 238
Kent, Trooper Tom 232
Kershaw, Dave **64–5**
Kesselring, Field Marshal 108–9
Keyes, Geoffrey 14
Kiel dockyards, Germany **218–19**
Kirk, 'Snowy' 92
Kitchener, William 101–2
Kramer, Josef, Belsen commandant **216**, 218

Lampedusa 114
Landing Craft Assault, Sicily 84
Langridge, Bob 156
Laycock, Colonel Robert 9, 11
Layforce, commando unit 9–10, 15
le Power, Major Peter 179
Lea, Major Richard 94
Leadbetter, Bill **145**
Leduc, Michel 166
Leese, Captain Lincoln 105, 125
Leigh, Lieutenant David **125**
Lemelson, Colonel 200
Lepine, Major Eric 134, 170
Lepine, Captain Ted 82, 92
Les Ormes, France **171**, 172
Lete, village 58–9
Lett, Major Gordon 193
Levinsohn, Mikhael 223, 224
Lewes bomb 18–9, **30**, 42–3
Lewes, Jock 9, 13, 42, 50
    death 44
    and first operation 22, 27–9
    training programme 18–21
Liaison Regiment Phantom, F Squadron GHQ 134
Libya, Cyrenaica 22
Lilley, Bob 44, 54, 55, 59, 73, **76**
    Operation Howard 227
Lodge, Robert (Rudolf Friedlaender) 178–9
London Irish Rifles 126
Long Range Desert Group (LRDG) 44, 61

and attacks on Axis airfields 34, 38
and first SAS operation 27, 29, 31
Long, Vic 135, 161–2, 169, 170, 241
Lowson, Bob **100**, 101, 173, 223–4, 226, 227–9, **227**, 242
Lubeck, Germany 219
Lunt, Ronnie 95
Lutton, Lance-Corporal Howard 162

MacDermot, Lieutenant Bill 76
McDiarmid, Sergeant James **77**, 172–3, **172**, **205**, 242
McDonald, Sergeant Edward 27
McDougall, Bob 232
McGonigal, Lieutenant Eoin 13, 26, 31
McGregor, Lieutenant Alistair 126
McLellan, Lieutenant 210
McLeod, Brigadier Roderick 134, 140, 171, 186, **232**
McLuskey, Fraser, padre 152–3, **153**, 154, 187, 189, 209, 239–40
McNaught, Lieutenant 209, 213
McNinch, Lance Sergeant Bill 99, **211**
Mackenzie, Trooper 211
Mackie, Captain Jim 123, 124, 125, **127**, 208
Maclennan, Squadron Quarter Master Sergeant 146, 151
Maginn, Sergeant Maggie 157
Malta 22, 53
Manners, Lieutenant Lord John 208
Maquis resistance 143, 146–7, 148, 150, 151, 160, 164, 181
    problems with 178, 179, 181
Mareth Line 77
Marriott, Brigadier John 33–4
Marsh, Tony 74, 96, 104, 105, 106–7, **106**, 242
    C Sqn 1SAS 134, 159, 171
    Operation Howard 221, 226
Mauritius, HMS 89–90
Mayne, Blair 'Paddy' 42–3, **45**, **90**, **130**, **168**, **222**, 242
    and 1SAS in Scotland 134–5
    on 2SAS 111, **114**
    at Augusta 89, 90, 93–5
    at Bagnara 96
    at Bagoush 63, 66

attack on Berka airfield 52, 54
attack on Tamet aerodrome 35, 37–8
and Cape Murro di Porco 87, 88, **90**
character and reputation 22–4, 39, 73–4, 82
command of A Squadron 73–4, 75–6
as commander of SAS **79**, 81–3
and drive to Benghazi 57–9
early recruit 13–4, **16**
and first operation 26–31
in France 169, 170
and invasion of France 140
and maroon beret 134
and Montgomery 83
and Operation *Howard* 221–35, **231**
promotion and DSO 45
and release of Stirling 233–4
rivalry with Stirling 43, 54–5, 75
Termoli 104, 105, 106
training 18, 46
and use of jeeps 62
and VE Day 237
media, reports of SAS in **188**, 189
Melot, Bob **205**
Middleton, Des Peter **67**, **69**, **202**, 242, **242**, **243**
France **149**, 150–1, 156, 158–9
Operation *Archway* 205–6
Mitchell, Sergeant-Major Bill 97, 101, 123
Molfetta 131
Montgomery, General Bernard 70, 234
inspection of SRS 83–4, **86**
visit to 1SAS 204–5
Moore, Lieutenant 146
Morris, Bill 21
Morrison, R. 162–4, 166–7, 169
Morvan, Massif du 143, 144, 148–54, 156–9
motto 50
Moussey, Vosges 182, **184**
Muirhead, Alex, mortar section **82**, **84**
France 147, **147**, 148, 150, 154
Operation *Archway* 209, 213
Sicily 85, 88, 90, 93
Termoli 107

Mussolini, Benito 42
Mycock, Lieutenant Mike 173

Neuengamme concentration camp **215**
Niven, David 175
Noble, Sergeant John 147–8, 242
France 150, 151, 154, **155**, 156–7, 159
Norman, Leslie 162–4, 166–7, 169
Normandy Landings 140
Norway 237, **238**, **240**

O'Dowd, Chris **41**, 73
Oldenburg, Germany 221–2
Oldfield, Major Peter **71**
Operation *Archway* 203–19, **212**, **215**, 235
Operation *Bigamy* 71–2
Operation *Blimey* 196
Operation *Bulbasket* 143, 159–69
Operation *Canuck* 196
Operation *Chestnut* 114
Operation *Cold Comfort* **195**, 196
Operation *Crusader* 22, 33, 45
Operation *Defoe* 176
Operation *Devon* 102, **103**
Operation *Dunhill* 176
Operation *Gain* 161–7, 169–70
Operation *Galia* 192–4, **193**, 196, **197**, **198**
Operation *Haggard* 170–1
Operation *Hardy* 183–4, 185
Operation *Houndsworth* 143, 144, **146**, **147**, 151, 156–7, 187
Operation *Howard* 221–35
Operation *Jonquil* 125
Operation *Keystone* 234
Operation *Kipling* 171–3, **172**, **173**
Operation *Loyton* 177–83, **182**
Operation *Marigold* 112–3, **117**
Operation *Overlord* 143–73
Operation *Pomegranate* 126
Operation *Rupert* 176–7, **180**
Operation *Snapdragon* 113
Operation *Speedwell* 114–9
Operation *Thistledown* 126
Operation *Titanic* 144
Operation *Tombola* **190**, 196–201

Operation *Transfigure* 169–70
Operation *Varsity* 206
Operation *Wallace* 183, 184–6

Pacey, Ted 21
Pantellaria 113
parachute training **12**, **14**, **15**, **17**, **19**, 20–1, 50
Parris, Thomas 96
partisans, Italy 196–9, 200, **201**
Patterson, Captain Joe 216
Payne, Corporal Sid 83, 85, 94, **95**, 96, 172, **230**, 242
Phillips, Arthur **23**, 38, 44, 50
Pinckney, Captain Philip 115, 118
Pleydell, Malcolm **55**, 66, 72–3, **76**, 81
Poat, Harry 74, **95**, **106**, 189, 242
at Augusta 93, 94
in Italy 96–7, 106
Operation *Archway* 205, 209, 213, 214, 216, **218–9**
as troop commander 81–2
Pogiano 123–4
Poole, Norman 'Puddle' 144
Prendergast, Lieutenant-Colonel Guy 34
prisoners, Italian 74

Qaret Tartura 63, 66

Radford, Cyril **180**, 242
Reggio, Italy 196–7
landings at 95
Reid, Brigadier Denys 33–4, 41–2
Rennie, Tom 158, 213, 214
Rhine, River, crossing (1945) 206–7, **208**
Riccomini, Lieutenant Jim 199, 200
Richards, Charlie 96
Richardson, Lieutenant Stewart 172
Riding, Jock 170
Ridler, Sergeant Duncan **216**, 217, 218, 242
Rigden, Bill **180**
Riley, Sergeant-Major Pat 24, 29, **39**, **64–5**, 210
in Italy 96
and Mayne 23
as training officer 46

Ringway, parachute training school 21
Ritchie, General Neil 10, 33–4
Robb, Jock 183
Robinson, Bill **180**
Robson, John 70
Rommel, General Erwin 22, 33, 45–6,
    51, 53, 61, 77
    and capture of Stirling 79
Rooney, Major Oswald 66, **136**
Rose, Graham 52, **58**, **66**, 83, **136**
    letters 101–2, 148, **149**
Royal Marines
    3 Commando 102
    40 Commando 102
Royal Navy 61, 89–90
rugby **130**
Rycroft, Lieutenant-Commander
    Richard 91

Sadler, Mike **66**, 82, 134, **136**, 242
    capture 77–8
    France 144, 162–3, 167, **168**
    North Africa 67–8, 69, 70, 73
Sadoine, Captain 160
Sardinia, Operation *Marigold* 112–3
SAS Brigade 134, **188**, 189
    in France 186–7, 189
    and Normandy Landings 143
SAS (L Detachment) 11, 13–6, 73
    attacks on German Army 75–9
    early training 18–21
    first operation 22–31
    raids on Axis airfields 34–5, 37–44,
        39, 61–2, 63, 66–7
    reorganisation after capture of
        Stirling 81–2
    tank workshop raids 64
1SAS 134, 203, **221**, 237, 239
    and D-Day 143–73
    Operation *Archway* 209–19
2SAS 134, 237
    disbanded 238–9
    in Germany 207–9, **233**
    in Italy **111**, **112**, **190**, 191–201
    under Bill Stirling 111–9
    under Brian Franks 175–83
    see also Termoli
3SAS (French) 134, 238, **239**

4SAS (French) 134, 191–2, **192**,
    238, **239**
5SAS (Belgian) 134, 191, 238
SBS (Special Boat Section) 61, 71, 112
    as D Squadron 73
Schott, Captain R. P. **62**
Scotland, SRS in 134–5
Scott, Lieutenant John 223, 224
Scratchley, Major Sandy 70, **120**, 125,
    180
Seekings, Reg 23, **64–5**, 134, 243
    early volunteer 15–16, 18, **20**
    France 146–7, 151–3
    North Africa 37, 50, 53, 54–5,
        59, **99**
    Operation *Archway* 205, 211
    Sicily 88
    Termoli 105, 109
Senior, Fred **28**, **74**
Senussi tribesmen 52, 54
Seymour, Sergeant 179
SHAEF (Supreme Headquarters Allied
    Expeditionary Force) 140–1, 182,
    234
Sharpe, Bob **195**
Shaw, George 92
Shortall, Corporal James 115, 118
Sicily 84–95, 114
Sidi Haneish airfield 68–70
Sirte, Libya 34, 35, 38
Siwa Oasis 34, 51, 61, 70
Slim, Field Marshal William 237–8
Smith, Major General Arthur 10–11
SOE (Special Operations Executive)
    144
songs, A Sqn 137, **138–9**
1st South African Division 63
SRS (Special Raiding Squadron)
    81–109
    at Molfetta 131
    return to Great Britain 131, 134–7,
        140–1
    reversion to 1SAS 134
    Sicily 84–9
    Termoli 102–9
Stalker, Billy 92
Stephens, Lieutenant Tomos 159
Stewart, Lieutenant Ian 144, 173

Stirling, Bill 111–9, 140–1, 243
Stirling, David **8**, 9, **43**, **45**, 63–4,
    141, 243
    at Bagoush 63, 66
    in Cairo 61–2, 67–8
    capture 79, 81
    command of B Squadron 73, 75–6
    compared with Mayne 73–4
    drive to Benghazi 55–9
    and first operation 22, 24, 26, 29,
        30–1
    memo on special service troops
        10–11
    news of release 233
    and Operation *Bigamy* 71–3
    planning 47, 53
    promotion and DSO 45, 73
    rivalry with Mayne 43, 54–5, 75
Stirling, Peter 47, 53
Storey, Sergeant Andy 99
Storie, Jimmy 21, 22, **23**, 24, **58**, 243
    capture 76
    North Africa 44, 50, 54, 59,
        69, 73
Sunday Express 189
Sunday Graphic 189
Sykes, Christopher 181

Tait, Sergeant Bob 29, 30, 38, 42, 44–5,
    64–5, **66**, **135**, **136**
    cap badge design 47
    Military Medal 45
Taranto 121–4
Taxis, Freddie 78
Taylor, Lieutenant Colonel 217–18
Taylor, Trooper **72**
Termoli 125–7, 129
    SRS operation 102–9, **107**, **108**,
        109, **112**
Terry, Sergeant Jack 151–2
Tetcott, HMS 89, 91, **91**
Thesiger, Wilfred **71**
Thomas, Lieutenant Peter 13
Thomson, Arthur 46, 47, 92, 243
Thurston, Alan **211**
Timimi airfield 22, 24
Tobin, Private Charlie 99, **100**, 101
Tobruk 45, 61, 71, 73